Adam Ruck is a British travel journalist whose knowledge of France goes back more than 40 years. He has written guidebooks to France for Consumers' Association and the AA (Automobile Association), and contributes regularly to the travel pages of *The Daily Telegraph*.

FRANCE ON TWO WHEELS

WHEELS

Six long bike rides for the
bon vivant cyclist

ADAM RUCK

First published in 2012 by
Short Books
3A Exmouth House
Pine Street
EC1R 0JH

10 9 8 7 6 5 4 3 2 1

A CIP catalogue record for this book
is available from the British Library.
ISBN 978-1-907595-72-1

Printed and bound by CPI Group (UK) Ltd, Croydon, CR0 4YY

CONTENTS

INTRODUCTION

"Of what shall a man be proud,
if he is not proud of his friends?"
Robert Louis Stevenson, *Travels with a Donkey in the Cevennes*

Long after I gave up eating and sightseeing my way around France, burning more petrol than calories while researching guide books for Which? and the AA, it took a chance invitation to cycle home from Switzerland with a friend to reintroduce me to the pleasures of exploring the back roads of France; and to introduce me to the bicycle as the best tool for the job. France is perfect for cycling, and cycling is perfect for France. It is hardly an original insight, but I had not woken up to it.

I had a bicycle already, but did not consider myself a cyclist. I had never done a long ride and had no idea if I would enjoy one or be able to do it. I found I did, and could. I wrote an article about the trip and positive feedback plus the desire to do more rides gave me the idea for this book.

Cycling for pleasure is the idea. A bike ride does not require extreme fitness, special clothing or any gadgetry more technical than a bicycle. It does not have to be a race, an endurance test, a self-improvement campaign or a charity fund-raiser. Rolling along at ten miles an hour is no more and no less than a great way to enjoy rural France. Potter through the orchards and vineyards, stopping to taste wine, look at a church or picnic on the river bank. No need to hold back at lunch time: after a 30-mile afternoon your appetite will not fail. French food never tasted so good, and after a week on the road you will have lost weight.

Many holiday cyclists explore a small area of the country. My team prefers the greater variety of a crossing, which makes the bike ride seem like a journey. The logistics are more complicated but not insuperable, with the aid of the train. The rides described here are 400–550 miles (or, as we are in France, 640-880 kilometres) long, and the longer ones took us a long week – two weekends and a week, typically, including a day's travel at each end of the ride. Many cyclists would cover a much greater distance in that time. Others would prefer to take it more slowly and do the ride in a fortnight. That sounds an extremely sensible approach, and I hope I have included enough information to make it possible. If you want to consult a more detailed map of each route, you can do so on the website:

www.france2wheels.com

ROUTE 1

SWISS ROLL

Lake Geneva to Caen (about 800km)
September 2007

You can find a more detailed map of this route
on www.france2wheels.com

Vézelay

Châteauneuf-en-Auxois

Beaune

Aloxe-Corton

Saône River

Arc-et-Senans

Doubs River

malbuisson

Pierre de Bresse

arbois

Vallorbe

Morges

Lausanne

START

There comes a stage, and I seem to have reached it, when friends with better-ordered lives keep ringing up with schemes to fill the leisure time that stretches ahead so problematically for them.

How would I like to climb Mont Blanc this summer? Not much. Sail the Atlantic? Not at all. Cycle to Switzerland?

I was halfway through my standard "thanks for thinking of me, but…" answer, when I realised that cycling to Switzerland meant cycling through France, and that was something I would very much like to do. "If we can do it in a week, I'm in," I said.

My friend sounded doubtful. "It's about 500 miles, you know," he said, "and I'd rather not be in a hurry." We agreed to stretch the week to eight days and reduce our daily penance to one hundred kilometres, give or take. How hard could it be, to cycle through green and pleasant France for a few hours in the morning and a few more after lunch? What kind of average speed would we manage? Would we be bored? Neither of us had a clue.

Three decades will soon have passed since I spent a long summer researching The Holiday Which? Guide to France, a fattening assignment whose waking hours were divided equally between eating, driving and visiting. Since then I have done far too much travelling through France on the motorway or in a cramped aeroplane seat.

When did I last potter through France, pausing to admire nesting storks in Alsace, transvestite Brazilians in the Bois de Boulogne and other charming idiosyncrasies of French life? My friend's call unleashed a baying pack of memories. How many years since that glorious plundering of the *chariot de desserts* in the Grand Monarque in Chartres, highlight of an autumn weekend raid that also featured a sublime *beurre blanc* on the banks of the Loire at Les Rosiers and a spectacular wine harvest festival party in a village hall near Chinon?

When did we last ski until the lifts closed, throw everything in the car and, still in our wet ski clothes, make tracks for the Jura to beat the dining-room deadline in Arbois? If we tore ourselves away from the slopes a little earlier, we could make it as far as Langres and drink flinty *vin nature de champagne* before unveiling the gooey delights of the not remotely grand Grand Hôtel de l'Europe's cheese board. It had been far too long. Was that France still there to be explored and enjoyed?

Cheap flights have done much to change our travel habits, and the shackles of family life, which I put on rather late, have further reduced room for manoeuvre. But there is a more general explanation, and that is, fashion has moved against the French touring holiday. Thirty years ago, eating and drinking and driving seemed the height of sophistication. As a formula it now seems to offend just about every fashionable preoccupation. If the roly-poly Michelin man was designed to set the wheels in motion and sell rubber, Mr Blow-Out has spare tyres and liver damage on his conscience now. Not even the invention of Nouvelle Cuisine – expensive food for consumers without an appetite – could save the gastro-nomadic experience.

Yet the great French restaurant and the family-run country hotel are cultural treasures worth celebrating, along with *Bonjour Tristesse* and *Impression, Sunrise*.

The answer, of course, is the bicycle. "Meet the future!" as Butch Cassidy declared, popping Sundance's girlfriend on the crossbar. On our bikes, we can rediscover rural France and do justice to the national gastronomy without guilt or increased risk of *crise de foie*; pig out, and still come home from holiday fitter and lighter. This would be our project: France on a bicycle, or the Michelin Star weight loss diet.

We agreed on a week in September and, miraculously, just about everything else. We wouldn't do Lycra, sponsorship, cycling shoes, iPods, main roads, sat-nav, support vehicles or big towns (except Chartres). We would not deny ourselves wine with lunch and we would walk up hills if we jolly well felt like it. Selecting only roads coloured yellow or white on the Michelin map – ideally those tinged with green, for scenic value – we would stay cheaply, share a room and spend our money on a good supper.

"We'll be so shattered, we won't notice the bedroom," said my friend.

Even our machines were well matched – a Dawes Galaxy and its stable mate the Super Galaxy. Any kind of Galaxy is a prince among touring bikes; light yet solid enough for a long journey with two saddle bags – panniers, we call them – slung over the back wheel.

"No bigger than 20 litres," advised my friend, the more experienced cyclist of the pair of us, "or you'll regret it." My panniers exceeded the approved size, but all the gadgets – lights, camera, batteries, chargers, adapters – left precious little room for clothing, and none for a book. In the bedroom that we would be too shattered to notice, we would be too shattered to read.

Galaxy announced his intention to cycle in brogues. "They're my most comfortable shoes, so it makes sense, don't you think?" It sounded a heavy choice for one so concerned to keep his load to a minimum, and I was not surprised when he turned up in trainers – a word I'm sure he deplores. Tennis shoes, then.

Over the question of helmets, we dithered. "Perhaps I'll wear it for going downhill, but not on the flat or when we're climbing," suggested Galaxy.

This did not seem the most logical approach, and we would not cycle many miles in France before the first impatient farmer overtook us on a blind corner. After that we found ourselves wearing the helmet more often.

After reversing our route to suit Galaxy's summer holiday schedule in his Swiss bolthole, we each unrolled the map of France on our kitchen tables and pored over it with magnifying glass and highlighter pen, like generals preparing an invasion.

Our route more or less drew itself: up and over the Jura by the lowest pass we could find, through the Burgundy hills to hit the Loire south of Orléans, via some wine-tasting on the Côte de Nuits near Beaune, and Châteauneuf-en-Auxois (request stop), where Galaxy and Mrs G decided to form a team, all those years ago. I am not the only one with happy French-pottering memories.

After an easy day on the river bank we would push north for Chartres, the Normandy Beaches and home. Sixty-odd miles (100km) a day would take us from Lake Geneva to the Channel in a week: seven full days in the saddle, plus half a day at each end. This was not a Tour de France, but a crossing; an old-fashioned raid, or, as our ancestors used to say, une chevauchée, without the rape and pillage.

Why? For the simple pleasure of rolling slowly through a beautiful country, feeling its contours and enjoying its changes of colour, stone, cheese and wine.

I don't think the question of cycling compatibility occurred to either of us, although it certainly should have. We had never cycled together, in more than 30 years of a typical gamesy male friendship that has flourished on tennis courts, golf courses and ski slopes. Walking up Etna on skis, we fell in step quite effortlessly, neither holding up the other. Why would a cycling tour be any different?

Periods of tension between us have never lasted long or required discussion, and mostly concerned control of the in-car sound system. Music would not be an issue on a cycling trip.

From my days on the guidebook trail, I consider myself a pretty good plotter of routes through France. Give me a map and a red Michelin guide, perhaps supplemented by the Gault-Millau if I am feeling greedy, and I can sniff out a good stopover like a pig after a truffle. It is not just a question of combing the book for rosettes, toques or luxury. At a more modest level, you develop a sense about places listed with no special mention, and learn how to read the rich language of Michelin's time-honoured hieroglyphics.

Michelin now includes descriptions of the establishments it lists. To my mind this adds little to the information value of the guide, dilutes the code-breaking fun of using it and reminds us that it is put together by humans, as likely as the rest of us to lapse into formulaic repetition (*décor dans l'air du temps ... cuisine au goût du jour ...*) and the clichés of descriptive summary.

But this was Galaxy's show, and I decided not to interfere. His bible for stopover selection is what he calls the Logis de France "guide" – catalogue, I prefer – which he likes because it is (a) free and (b) a lot lighter than the Michelin. I have my doubts about the reliability of Logis de France, but resolved to keep quiet about them. I knew he was choosing cheaper hotels than he would if travelling with Mrs G, for my sake. He was generous enough not to mention this.

It was obviously important to train while Galaxy was away plying the Swiss hairpins at rarefied altitude, and I trialled the Super Galaxy on our annual family holiday in Wales. The saddle felt horribly hard, and after many years on a mountain bike the low-slung road bike position seemed unnatural and contorted.

Craning my neck to see the road ahead, I found it hard to imagine spending long hours like this. At the end of the day I would be holding the newspaper above my head in order to read it, like Michelangelo after a day at work on the Sistine ceiling.

I soon worked out how to change gear and brake while sitting up, and rode without mishap to the sea and back, via a short sharp hill which I was relieved to find I could manage. Much-loved roads of which I thought I knew every inch I saw afresh, observing gradations in the landscape as I climbed slowly from the sea, smelling the Welsh bracken and feeling a chill on my face as I cycled alongside a fast-running stream. As I rolled down to the small market town near our house, the sudden warmth of the air hit me, with a vinegary whiff of fish and chips.

I remember reading Lawrence Durrell in a book about the Greek islands, recalling how he could smell the citrus groves long before the island of Chios came in sight. Come off it, Larry, I thought at the time. Now I am not so sure. The practice rides made me think: why aren't we doing the bike tour in Wales? The weather might have something to do with it.

Morges to Malbuisson: 57km

I would have preferred to travel to Switzerland by train, but at the time Eurostar single fares to Paris were overpriced so I flew to Geneva with British Airways for £50, with no extra charge for the bicycle – well done, BA. The thing must admittedly be dismantled and packed in a "recognisable bicycle bag", and this expensive and bulky item then has to be stowed and carried home by the already laden cyclist. I made do with two cardboard boxes generously donated by Ridgeway Cycles of Wantage, where, after much indecision and looking over my shoulder to check no one I knew was watching, I bought a pair of padded pants. I knew Galaxy would disapprove, doubtless preferring the prep schoolboy's defence against a beating: three silk handkerchiefs next to the skin. I bought a fingerless pair of cycling gloves too. Grazed palms could easily ruin the trip.

My feelings towards BA cooled markedly when it refused to accept my tightly bound panniers as a single item of hand luggage and then failed to load the checked pannier on my flight to Geneva. By the time I gave it up for lost, there was a long queue at Geneva airport's lost-luggage desk, and I missed not one train to Morges, where Galaxy was drumming his fingers on the table after lunch beside the lake, but two.

The delay was bad enough. Worse was the realisation that the tool I needed for reassembling the Super Galaxy was in the missing pannier. My padded pants were in there too.

On a brighter note, the bicycle itself had arrived undamaged, and I had a lighter load to haul over the Jura. Galaxy's Swiss Army knife was equal to most of the reassembly task, and a bike shop in Morges did the rest. They also agreed to dispose of my cardboard boxes, a problem I had not considered until it arose on the Place de la Gare in neat and tidy Switzerland.

The hills were alive with the sound of children on their way home from school before we were ready to set off, and our lakeside hotel on the French side of the mountain seemed a remote target. But Galaxy was in no mood for compromise. "If we get behind at this stage, we'll never catch up," he said grimly. I had eaten nothing more than a BA snack all day, but this was not the moment to suggest further delay. We needed to get going.

Pedalling across a Swiss hillside on a sunny afternoon, with vines to the left and sunflowers to the right, against a backdrop of Alpine peaks mirrored in the receding lake, ought to have been a heavenly experience. In fact it was hell. Having said we would not hurry, we were against the clock from the word go. That was one resolution broken, and we soon broke another, abandoning our empty yellow road for a busy red one that climbed more steadily and saved us... at least a mile.

The problem was, we were cycling into a brisk northeasterly. I had noticed white horses on the lake as we came in to land earlier in the day, and the wind had not abated. It would keep the sky clear for the next week, but gave us an early lesson in one of the hard realities of long-haul riding: it is not the hill climbs that get you, but the wind. Hills are finite, with a goal, if not in sight, at least in prospect; and what goes laboriously up usually comes joyfully down. A headwind just keeps blowing you backwards, and it eats into your soul. Note for future reference, if we ever do this kind of thing again: when planning a cycling itinerary, spare a thought for the prevailing wind.

It is true that cycling always seems to be into the wind, a natural effect of air resistance as we roll along. Galaxy calls this the anticyclone factor.

Progress improved as our route took a westward turn, but the light was fading fast when we pedalled over the border and hobbled into the first French café we saw. "How's your backside?" Galaxy asked. Not sure. I might have left it in Switzerland.

"To Malbuisson? Un bon petit bout ... at least another hour and a half," said a local soak who was pouring his own drinks from the Pernod bottle. So we put in a call to our hotel to make sure they would keep some food hot for us. "Ah, les cyclistes anglais," said the iron lady of the house. "We were wondering where you had got to. The kitchen closes in half an hour." We made it in 25 minutes, hurtling down through the gloaming like two cyclists of the Apocalypse. The final dash for dinner boosted our average speed to 15.6kph – almost 10mph – for the 57.2km ride from Morges, with a top speed of 48.1.

"The Englishman tells you how far he has ridden, the Frenchman tells you what he has seen," said Galaxy, quoting some sanctimonious cycling friend of his (French, obviously). I had seen a lot of my friend's increasingly sweaty back.

Galaxy disapproves of the speedometer – or computer, as we are supposed to call it – not wishing to become a slave to it. And it is true, you can spend a lot of time staring at the thing. I soon learned to manipulate my average speed by cycling fast for a while, and then stopping, instead of maintaining a steady pace. This was unsociable and ran contrary to the pro-tortoise, anti-hare idea of our trip. But I find it helpful to see the tenths of kilometre tick by, and watching the speedometer helps me up the hill. Galaxy prefers information in miles.

Do I need to point out that cycling is mostly an uphill activity? I may not be the only debutant who came to the ball imagining that the ups and downs of hill country – painful toil vs headlong freewheeling pleasure – would balance each other out, as they emphatically do not. It takes no great mathematical genius to work out that since climbing is slow and descending is fast, you will spend far more of the day going up than down. Nor do the ups and downs balance out in terms of average speed: you lose more time going up than you gain on the way down; stop more often, and arrive at your destination even later than your average speed would suggest.

Being the countryman that he is, Galaxy travels with a compass and altimeter; and the map, of course, crumpled in his pocket, whereas my swatch of pages cut out of the road atlas sits in a see-through plastic pouch on the handlebar, where I can glance at it while cycling.

I am not sure that we ever needed the compass, although Galaxy was always alert to the potential for engineering a situation where he might be able to whip it out and say: Aha! good job we brought this little chap along.

The altimeter, on the other hand, turned out to be a surprisingly good friend. Our Michelin maps rarely indicate the exact length of each hill, but often mark a spot height at the top. So it is helpful to have a companion calling out the altitude as you break through the invisible

Our route more or less drew itself

contour lines, even if he does it in feet. Another phenomenon that regular cyclists may recognise is that of struggling to make headway on a road that looks completely flat or even slightly downward-sloping, but is in fact an ascent, as confirmed by the altimeter.

Few words were exchanged over supper, but a sense of achievement hovered above the table like a halo. In difficult circumstances, we felt we had not done too badly. Many tiring hills lay ahead of us, but surely nothing to compare with our conquest of the Jura's mighty Col de Jougne (1008m), a watershed between the drainage basins of the Rhine and Rhône. Beneath the table, it was a relief to be able to feel my chair. I had done my prep on the subject of cycling and penile numbness, and if my

23

pants failed to turn up, Willie Walsh might have an ugly lawsuit on his hands.

In the small hours I could sense Galaxy fretting about the prospect of another delayed start in the morning. It was a relief to hear a horn at the door at dawn and pull back the curtains to witness the delivery of one small black bag, with its precious cargo of protective underwear. We were ready to go.

The hotel we stayed in at Malbuisson has since closed, but the lakeside resort makes a good target for a half day's ride from Lausanne or thereabouts. We would stay there again, ideally at Le Bon Accueil, a converted farmhouse with a Michelin star for the cuisine, and a promising bunch-of-grapes symbol for its list of Arbois and other Jura wines.

Malbuisson to Pierre-de-Bresse: about 100km

All morning we cruised effortlessly downhill, not in one headlong rush but in rolling stages, with changes of landscape as we lost height, from forest and timber mills to vineyards and vegetable gardens. Nor were we the slowest road users out on this sunny September morning: near the *département* boundary between Doubs and Jura we overtook a horse-drawn holiday caravan, and punched the air as we passed.

On the final long run down to Arbois the Super Galaxy hit a new top speed of 62.3kph, and kept it going into the built-up area for the puerile thrill of breaking the speed limit on a bicycle. Galaxy rested his case for the prosecution about the evils of the computer.

Not the slowest on the road

September is a busy time for rural festivals in France. We were a day too late for the descent of the cows from the high pastures on the ski slopes of Métabief, and in Arbois we just missed the *Fête du Bouis* wine harvest festival, when local *vignerons* carry their finest grapes to St Just's church, and string them up all together in the crossing, a giant grape chandelier – the *Bouis* – that hangs there for weeks, buzzing with wasps and slowly rotting. Newly hung, the *Bouis* was gleaming and resplendent when we walked stiffly up the aisle to admire it, before a good lunch at La Cuisance.

Internet translation websites have a lot of confusion to answer for, and a few good jokes. I am not the kind of tourist who brings chortle-inducing menu translations

Jura wines

Drinking local wine that we don't find at home is an old-fashioned treat that adds to the pleasure of a visit to a beautiful region, especially when the wine is good. *Vin jaune* is the pride of the Jura cellar, and *poulet au vin jaune* a signature dish. There is nowhere better to eat and drink it than Jean-Paul Jeunet's hotel/restaurant on the Rue Grande in Arbois. Jeunet has two Michelin stars, so you will be in for a pound, not a penny.

Vin jaune matures for at least six years and three months in barrels which are not topped up in the usual way, a film of yeast forming on the surface to stop oxidisation and the production of vinegar. A complex wine emerges, often likened to sherry, but unfortified. It is bottled in 62cl *clavelins,* the difference between 62 and the conventional 75cl representing the so-called "angels' share". *Vin jaune* is at its best ten years after bottling, but keeps much longer, is expensive, and needs a few hours to breathe. Most restaurants serve it by the glass. Drink with Comté cheese or a local chicken dish.

Château-Chalon is the most prestigious name in Jura wine, and a beautiful village to visit. All its wine is *vin jaune,* and those words do not appear on the Château-Chalon label. Visit Berthet-Bondet by prior appointment; www.berthet-bondet.net, 0033 384446048.

Another Jura speciality, *vin de paille* is a sweet wine produced by drying the grapes for at least six weeks traditionally but not necessarily on a bed of straw, and aged in the barrel for three years. It is often served chilled with foie gras or as a pudding wine. Arbois rosé is a more affordable treat: connoisseurs who take a dim view of rosé in general make an exception for it, for the good reason that it is red wine, unusually pale in colour. Other Jura drinks include *Macvin,* a liqueur wine fortified with *marc du Jura;* and *crémant du Jura,* fizzy white or rosé.

back from holiday to share with long-suffering friends at home, but it would not be fair to leave La Cuisance without saluting this collector's item, from the English version of the restaurant's website.

"Located on the river bank, in the historic center of the village of Arbois, we invite you to add to the pleasure of the puck, lulled by the singing of The Cuisance." The explanation for this bizarre formulation may be a confusion between the French words *palet* – a puck, as smacked about in a game of hockey – and *palais* (palate). So it is not really the fault of the internet, but a spelling mistake by the French inputter.

Cuisance is not an olde worlde word for cookery, but the local river, a tributary of the Loue and thus a sub-tributary of the Doubs. It is hard to think of a French river with an ugly name, although the Meuse sounds a bit brown and lugubrious, and the Cuisance must be one of the prettiest of them all. It has twin sources in a nearby *reculée* – the geomorphological *spécialité du pays*, a bit like a box canyon, of which we had admired a fine example before hurtling down to town in the morning – and flushes into the Loue, so to speak, after a mere 20 miles (35km) of rapid and exuberant life.

The name Arbois has a nice ring to it too, and it is one of my favourite French towns, a grey-gold place where the rugged honesty of the Franche-Comté meets the opulent *savoir-vivre* of Burgundy; of rhythmic arcades, solid belfries and interesting local wines and cheeses that rarely make their way abroad. Unpretentious but not in the least dull, good-looking but not too pretty, Arbois is just right. Louis Pasteur grew up there and never lost his attachment to the place and his beloved Cuisance, understandably enough. His simple town house is a small and in a quiet way rather touching museum; a good introduction, as they say, to the man and his work, which was rooted in the *terroir jurassien*.

Lons-le-Saunier, Salins-les-Bains... Franche-Comté is rich in saline springs, and salt was a pillar of the local economy from the early Middle Ages, extracted not by natural evaporation but in boilers. In an ideal world, our itinerary would have included a salt detour to see the utopian 18th-century architect Claude-Nicolas Ledoux's ideal city at Arc-et-Senans: brave new world industrial architecture, much influenced by the ideas of Rousseau, with warehouses and offices built like Greek temples and now offering an unusual style of B&B. Ledoux placed his royal salt factory close to the source of fuel for the boilers, the forest of Chaux, and built wooden aqueducts (*saumoducs*) to bring the saline water (*saumure*) from Salins-les-Bains. Salins has charm and is also worth a visit, with a new salt museum in its factory, *la Grande Saline*).

From Arbois to Salins-les-Bains is a ride of 14km, and the same again from Salins to Arc-et-Senans, via Galaxy's favourite French hotel, the Chateau de Germigney at Port-Lesney. Mention his name and you will be well received, and he and Mrs G may find an upgraded bottle of wine waiting in their usual suite when they next visit.

Ignoring Ledoux and the blandishments of Germigney, we pursued our blinkered course out into La Bresse, a marshy region best known for its chickens, which wear the proud badge of their own *Appellation Contrôlée*. There are few great sights but plenty of lesser treats for the passing cyclist to enjoy: barns the size of churches, colourfully tiled roofs, an abundance of wildlife, and no hills.

Pierre-de-Bresse is not a village I would ever have expected to visit, but we arrived in time to tour the château and its local museum gave us insight into life in this quiet corner of *la France profonde*. Facing the château, the Hôtel de la Poste fitted the bill exactly: decoratively challenged and not exactly the last word in luxury, but friendly, cheap, and run by every member of a busy family, with a good chef among them who turned out an excellent *poulet aux girolles*. Hotels like this used to be at the heart of the pleasure of exploring France. If only there were more of them left.

Flat out in flat country

Poulet de Bresse

The cornerstone of classical French cuisine is not the fattened goose liver, the truffle or the crayfish tail, but the Bresse chicken, described by Brillat-Savarin in *La Physiologie du Goût* (1825) as *"reine des volailles, volaille des rois"*. The proud Bressans believe it was a stay in their region and a chicken dinner that provoked good king Henri IV to express the noble wish that all his French subjects should be able to enjoy *"poule au pot"*.

After the farmers of La Bresse took legal action to defend their product against cheap and unworthy imitations, a rectangle of about 100 x 40km in Ain, Saône-et-Loire and Jura *départements* won *appellation d'origine contrôlée* status in 1957. Two hundred poultry farms produce one million chickens a year, less than 10% for export.

The Bresse chicken is a white bird of the Gauloise race, with a red crest and blue feet. Every aspect of its diet, development and living space is controlled. At five weeks old it is allowed out of doors to forage and build up its strength, and at four months, fully grown and well muscled, it moves back inside to grow fat in a wooden cage (*épinette*), having had its nails cut to prevent self-harm by scratching. Two weeks later, smooth and white of flesh, firm, fat and succulent, it is ready for the *poulailler* and the pot. The rules are slightly different for the *poularde* (a fatty young hen) and the *chapon* (capon – castrated young cockerel) which is traditionally served at Christmas.

Every December sees a round of competitive fairs in the region – *Les Glorieuses de la Bresse* – at Louhans, Bourg-en-Bresse, Pont-de-Vaux and Montrevel, with the winning *chapons* despatched to the Elysée and Matignon palaces. For more information and recipes see www.pouletdebresse.fr

Pierre-de-Bresse to Châteauneuf-en-Auxois: about 80km

In no hurry to say goodbye to the Bresse, we pedalled slowly away through the autumn morning and paused on a bridge to watch a family of swans fight the powerful Doubs, seven cygnets lined up in their mother's slipstream, while a kingfisher flashed across the water, working the banks. The Doubs had grown up a lot in the 24 hours since we crossed an infant stream feeding the lake at Malbuisson.

Coiled in the eastern corner of France, the Doubs travels nearly 300 miles/500km to cover the short distance from its source to its confluence with the Saône not far from where we stood. If we had thrown in a twig at Malbuisson, would we have beaten it to this bridge? My powers of mental arithmetic admitted defeat.

Galaxy was on a mission to swim in every possible major river on our route, and this was our chance to tick off the Doubs, although our hands were still cold and the river's strong current and steep banks would dissuade all but the most determined bathers. But the river-bathing ritual is a baptismal homage to nature more than a cooling-down exercise. Via the front lawn of a static caravan, we made our way to the river bank. Galaxy took the plunge, Super Galaxy selflessly holding the towel.

The Saône was next on our hit list, and Galaxy had scarcely dried off before we reached Seurre, which proudly advertises its *tourisme fluvial, activités nautiques, restaurant de la plage, port de plaisance* etc. The restaurant looked thoroughly depressed, a large boulder blocked the bottom of a cracked concrete slide and a rusty notice informed us of a bathing ban imposed in 1995.

Not wishing to flout the law in so public a place, we pedalled up stream for a few minutes and found a path down to the water at Pouilly-sur-Saône. If there was a *Baignade Interdite* sign here, we looked the other way, and relied on the villagers to do the same as we found a quiet spot for a furtive dip, without disturbing the Phoenician barges which are said to lie at rest on the river bed. The Saône is a quieter river than the Doubs, and Pouilly would be a pleasant place to drop anchor. Its website humbly alerts the visitor to the possibility of renting a pitch at *le camping municipal* by the year, to fish or do nothing.

As well as its Hôtel de la Poste, its *piste de pétanque* and its Bar des Sports, the French village of our imagination comes with a sweet-smelling *boulangerie* where the whole world passes through the door each morning to discuss their ailments and collect the *pain quotidien* – with the request "*pas trop cuit, s'il vous plaît*" (not too well cooked) solemnly repeated as if the thought had occurred that very morning; and an *alimentation générale* where under one roof we find all we need for the perfect picnic: cheese, pâté, fruit, wine. All we need now is a penknife with a sharp blade and a corkscrew; and our plastic cup overfloweth.

Sad to report, the French rural economy has been through the same convulsions as ours, and for the same reasons. Cycling along the back roads, we crossed village after lifeless village with no commercial activity whatever. For picnic provisions, we would have to divert to the main road and edge-of-town hypermarkets. How sad is that?

Between Pierre-de-Bresse and Aloxe-Corton we passed not a single shop, and arrived in the wine village thirsty and resigned to our not-so-terrible fate of another restaurant lunch. As the church clock wound up to strike one, we made straight for the wine *dégustation* booth, only to have the door slammed in our faces without apology. "It was the *paulée* last night, and *maman* is tired," said a sour-faced child, referring to the village knees-up at the end of the wine harvest. So: another local festival missed, and our fantasies of naked grape-trampling would have to be shelved for another year.

There was, of course, another explanation for the failure of *maman*'s hospitality. "I expect they saw our helmets," I said. What cyclist would ever buy wine? "This one," said Galaxy, who would collect his purchases on the next return journey from Switzerland in the Subaru.

With a hilly afternoon in prospect, we had been counting on Aloxe-Corton to come to our aid in the puck-pleasuring department, and were disappointed to find it had nothing to offer, not even a café. So much for wine villages. The sound and sight of their names set such delightful hormones coursing around our system, we expected the places themselves to be delightful too. But once we got over the thrill of seeing the famous name on a sign beside the road, and had taken our pictures of it, they were mostly grey and dull places, where serious business was done behind closed doors.

The nearby town of Beaune is no mere wine village but a *haut lieu* of Burgundian culture, a luxuriant weave of medieval art and good living. In a car, we could have driven there in ten minutes and had any number of restaurants to choose from. On a bicycle, it would have meant an extra hour's hard labour.

There was nothing for it. Slinging a weary leg over the cross-bar we set off through the hateful and overpriced vineyards, swearing that never again would a drop of Aloxe-Corton, nor even the great and self-important Corton, pass our lips. That'll teach them.

At which point Le Charlemagne hove into view – a roadside restaurant, out on its own, near the wine village of Pernand-Vergelesses. Never mind what sort of restaurant: if it served food, we were keener than Dijon mustard. A spotty teenage waitress intercepted us at the door and looked us up and down with a sceptical eye. "Are you sure you want to eat here? We have a Michelin star, you know."

34

Art and wine in Beaune

Half a day in downtown Beaune is all it takes to see and taste the best of Burgundy.

The sightseeing part of the experience is the Hôtel Dieu, a hospital founded in 1443 by Nicolas Rolin, chancellor of Burgundy, for the benefit of the poor of the here and now, and himself later. The visit takes about an hour and its highlights are the superb gabled courtyard with its timbered galleries and the definitive Burgundian roof of geometrically patterned coloured tiles; the 50-metre great ward or *"salle des pauvres"* with double beds and chapel; and Roger van der Weyden's polyptych of the Last Judgement, which originally stood in the chapel.

The hospital has been and still is funded by charitable donations, notably of prime local vineyards of which it now possesses more than 60 hectares. Revenue from wine sales and tourist visits helps the cause. The Hospices de Beaune wine auction, conducted by Christie's every November, is the focus of the three-day event, *Les Trois Glorieuses*. In 2011, 618 barrels of wine (228 litres each) raised more than five million euros.

From the Hôtel Dieu it is a short walk to the monastery church of the Cordeliers, which now houses the *marché aux vins*. On payment of a small entrance fee you can wander at leisure through the beautiful vaulted spaces tasting as you go, from white burgundy and cheerful Beaujolais to the big reds of the Côte de Nuits, using a *tastevin* which is yours to keep. The wines are available for sale, and the list ranges from humble *aligoté* (the basis for the abominable kir) to magnums of Corton costing more than £1000 apiece. Not all are open for tasting, but the selection always includes some top wines. There is no pressure to spit out the wine, but if you want to appreciate the best offerings, don't be carried away in the early stages.

Yes, and we have a credit card. We have cycled all morning, and we are hungry. Reluctantly the girl pointed us towards the lavatory, which was black and shiny, with orchids.

At such moments one could easily feel victimised. It was not as if we were caked in dust and oil. In tennis shirts and what golfers describe as tailored shorts, we would have passed muster at the stuffiest country club in the land. The waitress had simply observed our bicycles and made the assumption that we belonged with football supporters and people who travel in coaches, in the broad category of those who are unsuitable. Cyclists do not buy wine, and they do not eat in Michelin-starred restaurants. Well, sorry, these two did.

A good lunch it was too, in a trendy Asian-fusion style that set us up nicely for the rigours in store. We tackled the steep vineyard *côte* in the heat of the afternoon and after nearly an hour's toil dismounted at the village of Fussey to find the Marcillet family enjoying a pause in their seasonal labour: they had just finished the *vendange* in their lower vineyards, and were about to start on the upper slopes. We paused too, and in the cool of their vaulted *cave* recovered our strength and our faith in French hospitality, sipping and mostly spitting Bourgogne Chardonnay, Hautes Côtes de Nuits and Savigny-lès-Beaune, priced between five and ten euros a bottle; not forgetting the new-season *moux*, fizzy and already alcoholic after a few days in the vat. Madame Marcillet noted our order in a leather-bound ledger for payment on collection, as and when;

at the end of the next ski season, probably. No deposit required.

Many ups and downs later we reached the fortress village of Châteauneuf-en-Auxois, where a young British couple has realised the dream of a new life in *la belle France*. In their spotless B&B, they gave us a fine example of the love-hate relationship that persists between our nations.

"Yes, we absolutely love it here," the owner told me, "but have you heard the great news?" I knew exactly what he was referring to: France's defeat at rugby the previous evening, by Argentina. Why is that great news? Looking into the murky depths of my twisted soul, I won't deny that traces of atavistic anti-French sentiment are to be detected. But surely we ought to make some effort to bury them.

Châteauneuf-en-Auxois to Vézelay: about 90km

Cycling alongside the Canal de Bourgogne in the morning, we called a cheerful *bonjour* to fishermen who had been out in the chilly autumn mist all night and, to judge from their non-committal reaction to our greeting, not catching much. We soon had to leave the canal and cross a busy *Route Nationale*: a terrifying moment. Two hedgehogs on the motorway, we nervously tightened our chin straps before wobbling out into the traffic storm. Somehow it spared us, and we disappeared gratefully into the hinterland once more.

In the first village we reached after crossing *la Nationale*, a lady of advancing years was busy with the important task of sweeping up dust in the road. Placing one hand in the small of her back, she straightened up to greet us. "*Bonjour, messieurs!*" she sang out, her voice a joyful peal of bells. "*Vous allez loin?*"

"*La Manche!*" we called back, wondering if she had been one of the young beauties who showered kisses on the liberating army in '44.

"*O là là!*"

Her laughter followed us to the edge of the village, where a large Charolais cow also raised its head to watch us go by. Wide-eyed and unblinking, it walked along the fence beside us until it ran out of field. If people wonder what you actually see when cycling through France on the back roads, the answer is: cows. You also see houses and front gardens, and occasional glimpses of laundry. There are lots of barking dogs too.

The French – sorry: many French people – consider it quite appropriate to leave a dog alone all day in the garden with nothing to do but race up and down the fence, baying hostility at passing strollers and cyclists and hurling itself at the gate with a heart-stopping howl of fury. The dogs that sniff you coming and start barking well in advance are fine. The terrifying ones are those that lie low until you are just passing the gate, no more than a few feet from its bars, dreaming of lunch or old girl friends, and then... Crash! After you recover your composure, having just avoided wobbling into the path of an oncoming truck, you swear you will never again let a dog surprise you. But you will. They can sense unreadiness, and pounce. Some of the dogs we passed

38

may have a collection of scalps in the kennel, of their cyclist victims sent skeetering across the road. Result!

Cycling and motoring itineraries differ in this respect: car tours are constructed around points of special interest; on a bike ride you see things, and eat and sleep in places, that happen to be on the way. Both kinds of itinerary lead to the hill of Vézelay, which wins three stars from the green Michelin for its 12th-century pilgrimage basilica and the same in my red bible for Marc Meneau's gastro-nomic pilgrimage hotel L'Espérance. Vézelay marked the exact mid-point of the line we had drawn across France. L'Espérance would be our halfway house.

Like pilgrims of old, we saw the church towers from afar and watched them fail to grow appreciably larger as we toiled along. After a hard afternoon in the Morvan hills it was a relief to find L'Espérance on the valley floor, dump our bikes and go for a walk. Nor were we the first pilgrims to check into a cheap B&B hotel across the road from L'Espérance. Running such establishments in walking distance of trophy restaurants must be a good business. They are rather like the birds that live on the backs of hippos, grooming them and feasting on their bugs. If the Meneaux found them too annoying, they could always open a cheap annexe of their own.

"Would you like to meet my husband?" Madame Meneau asked, when we presented ourselves for dinner. It was an unexpected honour, and a slightly disconcerting one, to have the great man sit down to watch us eat.

"*Pas comme ça!*" M Meneau said severely, when I dipped the flesh of an oyster in the mound of rock salt on which it had been served. "The salt is for decoration." Oops.

We had warned the Meneaux that we were arriving by bike, hoping that they would look kindly on the shortcomings of our travelling wardrobe. Marc Meneau had constructed a special menu for us, starting with a sumptuous thick soup, as he explained, "to rebuild your strength at the beginning of the meal". The soup did the job, and we attacked the ensuing banquet with gusto, drinking his brother's Vézelay rouge ("much better than mine!") while the chef expounded his culinary theories and reminisced about catering for private hunting parties with royal guests from England.

"Like you they are *sportif* and they have a real appetite," he said appreciatively. "It's a rare thing these days. Most of the time here we are cooking for the eye and the mind, not the stomach." M Meneau's exploding foie gras balls were a spectacular treat for the mouth, and we would still taste them as we pedalled up to Vézelay the following morning.

When it comes to rolling the eyes, talking rubbish and nodding off during dinner, I have previous. At one time, waking to the noise of angry restaurateurs or dining companions hammering on the lavatory door was a regular part of my life. The problem is less acute now, but I was still worried about staying awake through the evening. It had been a long day in the saddle and our sightseeing stroll up the hill had left no time to regroup, horizontally, before dinner.

I don't know if it was M Meneau's brilliant menu planning, or the invigorating effect of exercise; but to my relief the upper lids defied gravity without the aid of matchsticks or an emergency dash for *le petit coin*. And Galaxy was on top conversational form, quizzing Meneau tirelessly about game – how to translate it, kill it and cook it. The two sportsmen discussed woodcock for ages, after a lively display of animal charades to establish that they were talking about the same bird. It may not be true that you learn something new every day, but that day we learned the word *bécasse*.

St-Père-sous-Vézelay to Ousson-sur-Loire: about 100km

Burgundy, the Loire, the Dordogne... these treasures of France we know well, and love, of course. But what about the unsung areas that lie in between? "It's 100km from here to the Loire," said Marc Meneau, "and it's called La Puisaye. There's nothing. It's *bocage*, really."

By *bocage* we understood a region of woodland and small-time farming. That sounded like good cycling country, and so it proved. Of half a dozen possible routes through La Puisaye we chose the one with the prettiest-sounding villages. Lucy-sur-Yonne and Druyes-les-Belles-Fontaines lived up to the promise of their seductive names,

Druyes-les-Belles-Fontaines

and Guédelon gave us our sightseeing surprise of the week: a medieval castle under construction in the middle of nowhere, using only medieval materials and methods, and scheduled for completion in 2023, unless they introduce the 35-hour week before the end of the 13th century.

Medieval builders evidently liked a well-appointed picnic area, and we gratefully borrowed their bench and table for our lunch, polishing off a whole bottle of wine before embarking on our site tour. This revealed stone cutters and rope-makers busy at their work stations, a

Guédelon

Guédelon is not a film set, a restoration project or a theme park. It has been described as "archaeology in reverse" – learning about the past not by digging it up, but by building it and confronting the same problems. Historians and archaeologists report that the exercise has given much new insight.

Guédelon has been conceived, very specifically, as a small-scale second-division residential castle, notionally "set" in 1228, during a period of peace between crusades, with the ravages of the Black Death and the Hundred Years War still some way off.

Puisaye was border country between France and Burgundy, and this place was chosen because most of the required materials were available locally – oak, stone, clay, sand and water. Many tools are made on site: mortar, ropes, nails, saws, roof tiles, lifting-engines.

The 50-odd labourers work in medieval clothes and the "tavern" serves medieval dishes. Of course there are compromises. Hard hats may be worn, and you may catch a worker sneaking off for a smoke. Anachronistic scaffolding is erected, to satisfy the demands of health and safety.

The rear defensive wall and two towers are almost complete, as are the great hall and VIP guest room. The roof of the living quarters is almost finished: the first rib-vaulted roof made using medieval techniques for 600 years. At least as interesting as the fort is the surrounding village, with a forge, rope-maker, carpenter, stone masons, and a weaver. There are interactive tours for children, and a chance to meet the workers.

Guédelon is a fascinating history lesson, but in ten years or so it will be a fully-fledged repro castle with a moat and battlements. What will be the point of it then? Perhaps they could re-enact a siege and work out how to demolish it in the most authentic way.

Maryline Martin, the director of the project, wants to paint the finished castle in bright colours. "We think of medieval buildings as being exposed stonework. They weren't," she asserts. "They were painted white or, in some cases, brightly coloured." So why do all the castles in medieval illuminated manuscripts look stone grey?

Guédelon is closed on Wednesdays, except in July and August.

man working a treadwheel or "squirrel cage" to hoist building blocks, and a splendid menagerie of pot-bellied pigs and other denizens of the medieval *basse cour*.

One beaker too many and a headwind conspired to leave me drained of all energy by late afternoon, and I cycled the last ten miles more or less oblivious to my surroundings, like an infantryman asleep on the march. At one point I came to with a start, convinced that I had just cycled across a main road without pausing to look right and left for traffic. But perhaps it was a dream. Our first view of the Loire was a glint of water between two towers belching vapour. *"La Loire – fleuve nucléaire"*, is EDF's proud boast.

Our overnight destination, Ousson-sur-Loire, sounded promising, and we were delighted to find a rough grey village, by-passed by the main road, with historic flood levels etched in the walls of its old houses. This pictur-esque scene cried out for a creeper-clad riverside hotel and restaurant terrace from which to watch the swifts darting about at dusk, and other nesting birds that enjoy life on Ousson island, the largest in the Loire. But there was no sign of one.

We pedalled up and down and around and about, with the floodwaters of irritation rising fast, before calling our hotel in desperation. Where the hell are you? Beside the N7, was the depressing answer. A tarty pavilion in an artificial garden, Ousson's Logis would have been a serious disappointment had we not been too shattered to care. I fell on to my bed, and Galaxy had great difficulty getting me off it in time for supper. I'm not sure the food was worth it.

Ousson-sur-Loire to Artenay: about 110km

I have heard it said before, and it bears saying again. If a village on the Michelin map is not underlined in red – indicating an entry in the red guide – there is usually a good reason. (Unfortunately, that reason may be the fact that you are using an up-to-date map. Why Michelin gave up the extremely useful red underline, I have no idea. Can we have it back, please?)

And if cycling the Loire is a slightly hackneyed holiday concept, there is a good reason for that too. Flat but never dull, it is the perfect context for happy pedalling, with a main road along one bank and an empty minor one on the other side, and long stretches of towpath on a raised embankment giving river views denied to motorists. Bathing places are easy enough to find but the river is so shallow, paddling is about as far as it goes. We found a beach at Cuissy, but did not stay long after solitary middle-aged men began emerging from the bushes. Cuissy may have a hidden agenda.

The big-name Loire châteaux lay downstream, beyond Orléans, but our quiet section of France's greatest river gave us plenty to see: the splendid *pont canal* at Briare, over which we ought to have cycled, and would have, had we known it was *cyclable*; pepper-pot towers, crenellations and swans on the moat at Sully, a château vision lifted straight from a Book of Hours; golden mosaics at Germigny-des-Prés, perhaps the oldest church in France; Romanesque carvings at St-Benoît-sur-Loire, and lunch. We had done with chicken and full-bodied Burgundian fare. Now we had entered *beurre blanc* and *chabichou* country. For the perfect fish lunch, rounded off with a small disc of goat's cheese from the abbey farm, seek out Au Grand Benoît.

Ousson reinforced a long-held suspicion of mine, that the Logis de France guide is not, as Francophile orthodoxy holds, a foolproof way to find the traditional family-run French country *auberge* offering good food and amazing value. It is a starting point, but there are plenty of duds in its collection of 3000 hotels. Another is the Hôtel de la Fontaine in Artenay, where *"Madame et Monsieur Fleuridas vous réserveront un accueil particulièrement chaleureux"* (warm welcome guaranteed), according to its entry on the Logis de France website. Our experience was rather different.

Having failed to book a room and been redirected to the neighbouring As' Hotel *(formule rapide et pizzas)*, we cycled past the Fontaine and put our heads inside to reserve a table for supper. "No problem," we were told; "we serve from 7.30 till nine." When we reappeared at twenty to, chairs were on tables. *"C'est terminé,"* Fleuridas said bluntly. "There was no one, so we sent the chef home early."

"Je regrette" or *"désolé, messieurs"* would have been nice, but the French don't do apologies, do they? Fortunately, the As' Hotel serves late as well as fast, and its formula of pizza, barmaids in black leather and football on big-screen TV scoops up the local and passing *routiers* trade. And there you have another depressing vignette of modern French country life. On our return I wrote to Logis de

Sully-sur-Loire

Romanesque carvings at St-Benoît-sur-Loire

France about the Fontaine in Artenay, and received no answer, not even an automated email response of the kind Thames Water can manage.

Artenay to Senonches: about 100km

Every journey has its low point, and we bottomed out on our way through the granary of France, the flatlands known as the Beauce, so named, according to Rabelais, because Gargantua took one look at it and exclaimed, "*Je trouve beau, ce!*" Even if we allow that Renaissance ogres may have expressed themselves in this clumsy and ungrammatical manner, it did not seem beautiful to us, merely big and bottom-numbingly dull, with cathedral-sized silos and fields that stretched to the horizon, with not a hedge nor a wild flower in sight.

We had been on holiday until we left the Loire at Châteauneuf. Now we were cycling back from holiday, and the road to Chartres felt like the prairies of Saskatchewan. Pushing the wheels round is a repetitive business that provokes a repetitive train of thought, and the mantra of the morning was: why had we not stayed on the Loire and followed it to the Atlantic? What a nice ride that would be. We had heaved a sigh of relief at the end of the Burgundy hills, but now a few ups and downs would be welcome. A bend in the road, even. Anything to break the monotony. Cyclists rave about Holland and Denmark, because they are so flat. Give me the undulations of France any day.

We made it to Chartres in the end, and the cathedral's stained glass lifted our spirits; that, and a good lunch at

Le Moulin de Ponceau, a converted watermill near the cathedral, among businessmen and elegant ladies who looked askance at our dusty panniers plonked on the floor; not to mention us. The countryside improved as we left the featureless fertility of the Beauce behind us and entered the Perche. Rattling through the woods on a bridle path that saved two sides of a triangle – a triumph for Galaxy's inspired compass-assisted navigation/guesswork – we were back in our stride.

Almost all those we met along the road were gratifyingly impressed when they asked where we were going and we replied proudly *"La Manche!"* or (less truthfully) *"Angleterre!"* But the world does not lack small people eager to belittle the efforts of others and at the Hôtel Pomme de Pin in the pretty village of Senonches we found one.

"Caen!" we declared, like dogs wagging their tails for a pat, when our hotelier popped the question.

"Quite an easy day's ride," was all he could say, with a dismissive shrug; "about 150km." He went on to entertain us with details of his cycling exploits, which include regular afternoon rides to Deauville (125km) for an evening at the Casino; and a recent trip to the Pyrenees, 850km and into the wind all the way. Well, good for you, *monsieur*. One hundred kilometres a day will do us.

Senonches to St-Julien-le-Faucon: about 115km

In Normandy, we felt almost home; and at home, in a familiar landscape of orchards and thoroughbreds and timbered manor houses – Sussex with *savoir-vivre*. But there are thorns in these hedgerows. In the region that suffered the brunt of the D-Day onslaught, the smallest hamlet has its war memorial inscribed with a sombre roll call of loss, the same family names repeated over and again. *Henri Lenormand, tué en combat … Thierry Lenormand, deporté et fusillé … Aimée Lenormand, victime civile …*

Remembrance is good, but there is no point in brooding. We found a field overlooking the Touques valley, where an Impressionist landscape painter might well have planted an easel; ripped up our last baguette and stuffed it with Pont l'Evêque. There is nothing quite like a local one, low on food miles and guzzled in situ. "Are you thinking what I'm thinking?" said Galaxy.

I was. Lying on the grass in the warm sun, with a cup of wine and only a few miles to go, happiness would have been almost complete, with a different companion, of the opposite sex. Normandy is Flaubert country, and our secluded picnic spot would have been just the sort of place the loathsome Rodolphe Boulanger would have programmed in his sat-nav, for the seduction of Emma Bovary and other willing victims. We giggled like school-boys at the absurdity of the thought, creaked to our feet and pedalled on.

Normandy reminded us of home in another way: we stayed in a B&B and went out to supper in a nearby restaurant in the village of St-Julien-le-Faucon. It is a typically English formula, apart from the food in the Auberge de la Levrette, which was several notches higher than any country pub grub near us.

Our B&B was a comfortable if not stylish home in the best Blackpool landlady tradition, and the breakfast

Coupesarte: Sussex with savoir-vivre

The Madame Bovary trail

The small village of Ry, near Rouen, was Flaubert's model for Yonville in *Madame Bovary*, that everyday tale of middle-class adultery and suicide in 19th-century Normandy. On its one street – "long as a rifle shot" – Le Bovary occupies the premises of Flaubert's Lion d'Or. Its rival, L'Hirondelle, takes its name from the diligence that transported Emma every Thursday to her 'piano lessons' in Rouen, where "she discovered in adultery all the platitudes of marriage".

Villagers drink at Le Flaubert and buy their smalls from the sublimely named Rêve Ry, a *jeu de mots* that may allude to Emma's romantic aspiration, wherein lie the seeds of her downfall. Rêve Ry's *patronne* seems obliging enough, but then so did the insinuating draper and moneylender Lheureux, whose merciless demands provoke the novel's grisly dénouement. A plaque above the toy shop door confirms the site of the chemist Homais's *officine*. We can find the Bovarys' two houses and look for the window where Emma leaned out after being jilted by Rodolphe on the day of their planned elopement. She thought about jumping, but didn't. Good decision: from that height, you would be lucky to break an ankle.

Flaubert did not choose Ry with a hatpin. In the shadow of the old church, two stones – one contemporary, the other installed recently by a Flaubert Society – remember the village doctor Eugène Delamare and his wife Delphine, who took a lover, ran up debts and poisoned herself in 1848 at the age of 26, using arsenic stolen from the village chemist, leaving a young child and an inconsolable husband. Like Charles Bovary, Eugène Delamare followed his wife to the grave in less than a year.

"This is the shelf where the real Madame Bovary found the arsenic," explains the keeper of the Galerie Bovary, a museum chiefly devoted to a display of mechanical automata that act out scenes from the novel. Mercifully, the display does not include "pickled foetuses decaying in their jars of viscous alcohol".

At the attendant's flick of a switch, tiny dolls whir into action. The young Madame Bovary dances with le Vicomte. Emma swoons on receipt of the termination letter that Rodolphe has sent in a basket of apricots, hidden beneath a layer of vine leaves. And there they are, a cluster of ball bearings painted orange and glued in a miniature basket.

The Galerie does not spare us the detail, any more than Flaubert did. We see the famous cab ride through Rouen, when Emma and Léon get it together in the confessional-like intimacy of the shuttered cab, and in the next scene the Emma doll reveals all – at least, the top half of all. "She flung off her clothes with a sort of brutal violence, tearing at her thin stay so that it hissed about her hips like a slithering snake."

Naturally, Ry's neighbours are in on the Bovary act. We can follow a Circuit Emma Bovary, touring country lanes in search of La Huchette, Rodolphe's home, the obvious candidate being the Château de Gratianville, home of Delphine Delamare's lover Louis Campion, two kilometres south of Ry. On a hilltop we will pause to look down on Ry, as Rodolphe and Emma did when out riding one misty morning in early October.

"Never had the wretched village where she lived seemed so small… The horses breathed noisily, the saddle leathers creaked. 'Where are we going?' To this question he made no reply. She was panting slightly. Rodolphe looked about him, gnawing his moustache.' We know the rest. A few short paragraphs later Rodolphe has a cigar between this teeth, after the act, and in 40 pages the apricots and vine leaves will be on their way.

served by our hostess may well have had a full English option, or Canadian waffles and maple syrup – I honestly can't remember. My only vivid memory of the place is of a nasty moment in the pink bathroom, when I realised in mid-stream that the piece of pink flesh I was aiming at the pink porcelain bowl was, in point of fact, numb.

I said nothing to Galaxy or anyone else about this, until the symptoms wore off a few days later, by which time I was quite the expert on nether numbness. I have no idea why serious cyclists prefer a hard narrow saddle to a broad soft one, but they do. It could be an indication of the chronic masochism that many attribute to cyclists, perhaps rightly. Be that as it may, I decided my saddle would have to be swapped for something less like an instrument of medieval torture.

St-Julien-le-Faucon to Ouistreham: about 55km

Down to the coast we rolled in the morning – standing in the stirrups, in my case – on the warpath in reverse. It took us over Pegasus Bridge to Bénouville and easily along the towpath to the ferry port at Ouistreham, where we stripped on the sands of Riva Bella, formerly Sword Beach, and threw ourselves into the waves.

We were not the only cyclists lined up on the quay among the heavy divisions of mobile homes and estate cars loaded with wine. Most of our fellow two-wheelers had camping gear piled high and bulging panniers front and back, and looked very weary indeed. If we looked like dilettanti cyclists to them, too bad. We were glad to have travelled light.

In my arrogant youth I used to reflect that I would know when I was getting old when I took longer over a walk – from a roadside car park, typically, to a hilltop *table d'orientation* – than the estimate in the Michelin green guide.

Now I am relieved to find that our average speed of 18kph (11mph) for the journey from Morges to Caen was slightly faster than the 14kph assumed by the ViaMichelin route-planning website. Most keen cyclists would find this laughably slow, but it is our pace, and it suits us.

The computer told us we had cycled 821.6 km, without let, hindrance, puncture, rainfall or serious argument (too shattered for that). Our belts told us we had lost weight, although we had eaten like greedy princes along the way. And what had we seen? A small *tranche* of France. Plenty left for the next *chevauchée*.

Hotels (with restaurants unless stated)

* = cheap, ***** = expensive

***   Malbuisson, Le Bon Accueil:
     www.le-bon-accueil.fr   0033 381693058

****   Arbois, Jean-Paul Jeunet
     www.jeanpauljeunet.com   0033 384660567

**   Arbois, Messageries (B&B)
     www.hoteldesmessageries.com   0033 384661545

**   Arc-et-Senans, Salines
     www.salineroyale.com   0033 381544517

***** Port-Lesney, Château de Germigney
www.chateaudegermigney.com 0033 384738585

** Pierre-de-Bresse, Hôtel de la Poste
www.hoteldelaposte.free.fr 0033 385762447

*** Châteauneuf-en-Auxois, Hostellerie du Château
www.hostellerie-de-chateauneuf.com 0033 380492200

***** St-Père-sous-Vézelay, L'Espérance
www.marc-meneau-esperance.com 0033 386333910

* St-Père-sous-Vézelay, La Renommée (B&B)
http://la.renommee.pagesperso-orange.fr 00 33 386332134

** St-Benoît-sur-Loire, Le Labrador
www.hoteldulabrador.fr 0033 238357438

**** Chartres, Le Grand Monarque
www.bw-grand-monarque.com 0033 237181515

** Senonches, La Pomme de Pin
www.restaurant-pommedepin.com 0033 237377662

Restaurants

* Arbois, La Cuisance 0033 384374074

**** Pernand-Vergelesses, Le Charlemagne 0033 380215145

*** Beaune, La Ciboulette 0033 380247072

** St-Benoît-sur-Loire, Au Grand St Benoît 0033 238351192

*** Chartres, Le Moulin de Ponceau 0033 237353005

*** St-Julien-le-Faucon, La Levrette 0033 231638120

Information

Jura www.franche-comte.org

Burgundy www.crt-bourgogne.fr

Loire www.visaloire.com

Normandy www.normandie-tourisme.fr

Swiss trains www.sbb.ch

Ferries www.brittany-ferries.co.uk

ROUTE 2

UP THE UPPER ALLIER, DOWN THE UPPER LOIRE

A circuit in the Massif Central from
Vichy to Roanne (about 550km,
including 50km by car in the middle)
September 2009

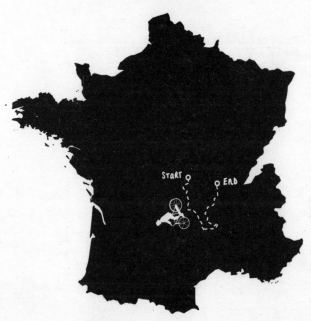

Allier River
Loire River
Start
Vichy
End
Roanne
Clermont-Ferrand
Puy de Dôme
Bort L'Etang
Feurs
Issoire
Chambles
Ste Etienne
Brioude
Vorey
Langeac
St-Arcons
Prades
Le Puy en Velay
Pont d'Alleyras
Goudet
Gerbier de Jonc
Ste Eulalie
Barrage de Naussac
Langogne
Auberge de Peyrebeille

My turn. Can't wait to unfold the map, roll up my sleeves and get stuck into the logistics of a good itinerary.

Galaxy had dropped hints about an Atlantic to Mediterranean ride but, revisiting the train of thought that had kept me going through the tedious fertility of La Beauce, I was not to be deflected from a return to the Loire. Cycling along rivers appeals as a way of seeing countries and hilly regions, because the gradient is by definition gentle (I assumed wrongly) and, if we ride downstream, it ought to be in our favour, on balance. Rivers are almost always of interest: scenically and as a focus for history, châteaux, wildlife and life itself, to say nothing of exciting opportunities to disregard *Baignade Interdite* notices which, roughly translated, mean A Popular Place to Swim.

At more than 1000km from Ardèche to the Atlantic, France's greatest river is too long for us to manage in one ride, so it seemed logical to start at the beginning and tackle the first half which, unlike the more famous Orléans to Angers stretch, I hardly knew at all, beyond the memory of a long-lost coffee-table guide to the Loire. The image that stuck in my mind was of Arlempdes, a wild and Romantic scene of rusty grey castle ruins perched atop steepling volcanic-rock formations above the infant stream. Walter Scott, in a better climate.

The question was, how to reach the source, nearly 1500m up among the volcanic plugs, lava domes and other igneous summits of the Mont Mézenc? In his book *Cycling The River Loire*, John Higginson starts from Orange in the Rhône Valley and pedals up from there, covering more than 200km before he reaches the source. This was too tough and time-consuming for us, and I came up with an alternative plan using the "Cévenol" highland railway line which runs north-south over the Massif Central between Clermont-Ferrand and Nîmes.

With our bikes in the back of Galaxy's car we would catch an overnight ferry to Le Havre, hammer the motorways for a morning, leave the car at Sancerre – or its station on the Burgundy bank, Tracy-sur-Loire – and travel south by train to Langogne via Clermont, a famously beautiful train ride through the gorges of the Allier; all this being achievable in one long day.

Langogne is about 50km away from, and 500m below, the source of the Loire: a great improvement on Orange, with the added attraction of counting among its 3200 residents an ex-au pair of ours. Emilie declared herself willing to drive us to the Gerbier de Jonc, and from there we would cycle back to the car in a short week, following the river and leaving half a day at the end to buy wine in Sancerre before driving home.

Unfortunately, my research failed to unearth the fact that the Allier Gorges section of the Cévenol railway line closes from time to time for maintenance, and our September trip coincided with such a period.

So much for my logistical skills. I had to rethink the whole trip, and came up with the idea of a circuit from Vichy – up the Allier to Langogne, and down the Loire as far as Roanne, returning to Vichy from there by train or, if we had the energy, by cycling over the hills. Emilie could still be pressed into service, so to speak, and on the way home we would still have time to call in at Sancerre.

The revised itinerary raised a few problems, chief of which was the inescapable fact that going up the Allier would be uphill, which was not part of our plan. Also, beyond Langeac the road does not follow the Allier closely: there are multiple ups and downs, so we would be doing many times the climb from Langeac's altitude (496m) to Langogne's (910m). The same goes for the top of the Loire: there is no road along it, so the idea of cruising down a country lane beside the stream is fantasy. This was obviously going to be an arduous ride, and – small point – Galaxy had had a heart attack in the intervening period.

In fact, the trip proved a great success, and probably more satisfying than the journey I had originally planned. Cycling up the Allier was as beautiful as anything we have done, and I would not want to have missed it. If you asked me which ride I would recommend: down the Loire from Roanne to Sancerre, or up the Allier from Brioude to Langogne, the Allier takes it by a distance. Down the Allier from Langogne to Brioude would be even better.

The Massif Central translates conveniently as the Central Massif. It really ought to be called the South Central Massif, since its place on the map is below the centre of the country and its walls drop steeply to the Mediterranean behind Nîmes and Montpellier.

There are many different ranges and high plateaux, but I think of it as a Massif of two halves: my bit and her bit. This goes back to the research effort for the Which? guide, when the editor and I divided our labours, she touring the southern part of the Massif Central while I concentrated on the Auvergne proper. Comparing notes afterwards, we argued endlessly about the relative merits of her bit and my bit, I arguing for the supremacy of the Auvergne on the grounds of its shapely volcanic pimples or "puys"; its churches, where the decorative possibilities of the colourful black and red volcanic rock are so beautifully explored; and its higher summits. My bit peaks at nearly 1900m, whereas hers scarcely manages a paltry 1800.

She would make the case for the south as the last best place in France, a rugged wilderness where wolves stalk the forests and naked canoeists (a particular interest of hers) sunbathe on rocks in the Ardèche canyon. Compared with the exciting storms and baking summer heat of the Cévennes, she considers the Auvergne grey and gloomy, and she may have a point. Julian Barnes writes of a region where, in our minds, "small mahogany cows jig on the slopes of extinct volcanoes to the music of local bagpipes", but where the visitor's lasting memories are more likely to boil down to two things: rain and cheese.

Our circuit would start in my bit but spend most of its time in hers.

"C'est jolie l'Auvergne, mais il y a trop de vert," wrote the young George Sand after ten days at le Mont Dore in 1827. (The Auvergne is pretty but too green). Nearly half a century later she returned to write an article for the newly

founded Club Alpin Français of which she was one of only seven female members.

"Auvergne involves neither great exertion nor great danger," she now wrote more appreciatively. "People may consider it beneath them to explore a region where anyone can go so easily. But age brings if not more humility to the mind at least more wisdom to the legs and one falls back on charming Auvergne with a sense of ingratitude to be rectified. One goes up these hills without vertigo or exhaustion, like someone going to the top of the house to look out over the garden. The Alps and Pyrenees are our outer walls; the Auvergne is our fortress." Words of beauty, wisdom and relevance to cyclists like us.

If we had embarked on these French tours in our youth, sooner or later we would have targeted the Alps and Pyrenees, as keen cyclists do. But the Massif Central is more to our measure. We can make it to the top without busting a lung and feel … not proud of ourselves, but lucky. "Why do we do this?" I asked Galaxy, halfway up some hellish hill. "Because we can," he replied.

Two years had elapsed since our ride back from Switzerland. Galaxy had acquired a bicycle computer, I noticed, as well as a bumbag for his drugs and an emergency resuscitation spray in the use of which – under the tongue, for quick absorption into the blood stream – he instructed me. He seemed pretty fit, but it was nice to know he was well equipped to resuscitate me.

In order to cut down on socks and smelly foot syndrome I decided to trial cycling in plastic beach sandals. I was not 100% confident that Crocs would be suitable for a long bike ride and took along an old pair of trainers for back-up. But two pairs of day footwear is an unjustifiable extravagance in terms of pannier space, and one pair would have to go. Which would it be?

Our experiences in Burgundy – being turned away from wine-tasting and sneered at in smart restaurants, and our memorable evening at L'Espérance in Vézelay – had made me think: why do people assume cyclists are shoestring travellers? With the rigours of our route up the Allier in mind, we planned two spoiling stopovers in top-end hotels of unashamed luxury: Château de Codignat near Clermont-Ferrand, and Les Deux Abbesses, at St-Arcons, near Langeac.

Codignat was our first port of call, but first we had to find somewhere to leave the car for a week. In a mood of nostalgia for the days when we could identify hotels whose entry in the red Michelin included a picture of a Maigret-black Citroën traction, wave the guide book – current edition only – and claim a free parking space, I telephoned several hotels and restaurants in Vichy suggesting that if we stayed the night or ate lunch they might like to look after our car for a week. None of them leaped at the idea and, as Galaxy pointed out, did we actually want to spend a night or eat an expensive lunch in Vichy? Probably not.

We drove to the centre of the wartime capital of a vanquished nation and found a wide boulevard near the Parc des Sources with plenty of parking spaces and no sign of restrictions. "Can we park our car here for a week?" we asked a respectable-looking man in a trench coat who was out for a stroll in the curative air. "Certainly," he replied, "but don't expect to find much of it when you come back."

So we scuttled off to the reassuring haven of the station car park and the peace of mind payment would bring. The car might not be any safer there, but at least we would be able to blame someone else.

Vichy to Bort-l'Etang: about 50km

The afternoon ride was straightforward enough. The Allier skirts Clermont-Ferrand to the east, and after crossing the river – good swimming at Joze – we kept to the east of the Allier. Our route was pleasantly rural throughout, with good views of the peaky volcanic landscape of the Chaîne des Puys, a miniature mountain range to the west; the Monts de la Madeleine to the east; and no hills at all dead ahead obstructing our progress. What a fine idea to follow the river.

This happy state of affairs lasted a couple of hours, until we reached Lezoux, where, after a pause at a small hotel (Les Voyageurs – a good alternative stopover to Codignat on a less self-indulgent itinerary), we began to climb.

If you were building a château in the Auvergne, you would be unlikely to site it on the river bank or in a road-side village for the convenience of cyclists. The Château de Codignat is not a hotel that tries to impress by calling itself a château, but a real castle that has turned itself into a hotel. It was built half a millennium ago on the site of an earlier fortress, and its builders chose a hill where they would not be flooded, overlooked in the swimming pool or overrun by revolting peasants. Pushing up

Château de Codignat: upscale, uphill

the long, steep drive, I found myself formulating hostile thoughts towards the Château de Codignat, but it was hardly fair to do so.

"Can I send someone for the rest of your luggage, sir?" said a smart young woman in a shining silver trouser suit that went well with all the polished breastplates and pikestaffs hanging from the walls.

"This is all of it." The memory of the receptionist's horrified reaction delights me still.

Our maid in shining armour led the way up a spiral stone staircase in a round tower to a bedroom with a fleur-de-lys canopy, damask hangings, missals and tassels and a window seat where I could read my prayer book by the light of the moon and imagine myself in a wimple making a tapestry. It was a complete and convincing reconstruction of a medieval bedroom, in all respects but comfort, which was considerable (and most welcome). I poured myself a drink, walked up three stairs to a steaming bathroom and lay down for a soak.

The château-hotel experience was instructive and not entirely satisfactory. Because of our regime – not punishing, but time-consuming – we arrived in time for dinner, tired; and left after breakfast in the morning, having spent eight out of fourteen hours asleep.

Quality of sleep is important, but we could not help thinking we were making less than the most of our stay in an expensive multi-facility hotel with tennis court, swimming pool and extensive parc. In future we should make an effort to arrive earlier, leave later and spend more time awake. A shorter cycling day – 60km instead of 100km – would be one way to achieve this. Another would be to stay two nights in each place.

Château de Codignat would be a fine base for excursions, and is not too far from Clermont-Ferrand for a cycling day out to see the Puy de Dôme (using the new mountain railway, probably); the black cathedral and its more appealing neighbour Notre Dame du Port; and the Aventure Michelin museum, which opened in 2009. Considering the important part Michelin has played in my cultural and corporeal life, I feel I owe it a visit. All who love France would surely feel the same.

Le Puy de Dôme à vélo

Auvergne's most picturesque volcanoes are the Monts Dôme, which line up to the west of Clermont-Ferrand in a 40km chain of cones bursting through the skin of a high plateau by a few hundred metres. The best known and biggest of them is the Puy de Dôme (1464m), a lava dome with a Gallo-Roman temple on top and a spiral toll road which issues a famously punishing challenge to the cyclist. Fernand Ladoux was the first to cycle up it, in 1892. In the 1964 Tour de France, Raymond Poulidor and Jacques Anquetil duelled all the way to the top, Poulidor winning the climb but Anquetil retaining the race lead by 14 seconds.

The road has been closed for a while, but is due to reopen – O lucky reader – sometime in 2012. Assuming the same schedule applies, it is reserved for cyclists from May to September on Wednesday and Sunday mornings (leave the car park between 7.00 and 8.30).

Purists start (early) from Clermont-Ferrand: 9km to the car park, for a 500m altitude gain. From here it is 4.5km to the top with an average gradient of 11%. The fastest cyclists knock it off in half an hour. Tempted? Bear in mind that descending by bike is not allowed. You have to come down by train.

Château de Codignat to St-Arcons-d'Allier: about 115km (including 6km by car)

Another vindication for Galaxy's approach to route planning over mine. My better half draws his line on the map, revises it to avoid steep hills, puts a full stop on it where he thinks we will have cycled enough and books the nearest hotel (within reason). Going roughly in the right direction, I find two places I like the look of, and if they are a bit further apart than we might like, I reckon we have what it takes to go the extra mile. In France, as in life, Galaxy knows better how to get from A to B.

Soon after leaving Codignat we faced a long climb to the Col de Potey (583m), welcoming us to the Auvergne proper, the Auvergne *musclée*. What strategy did we employ?

Some cyclists count the pedal revolutions or watch the computer, trying to maintain a certain speed. I find myself singing hymns or reciting poems, and trying to guess at the bottom how many times I will get through it before the top. It is never as many as you think. This works well for me, or would do, if only I had a wider repertoire.

A few months before this trip I had helped my son learn the "Jabberwocky" for school, so I knew most of that, although I had trouble making the transition from the frumious Bandersnatch to the Tumtum tree.

About the only thing I find I can almost always manage, from start to finish – proudly singing chariot when all around me sing chariots – is "Jerusalem", which takes me about two minutes, including the organ solo between verses (but not the introit). The Col de Potey is a hill of about six Jerusalems and one verse in length. At the top there is a lovely flower meadow.

There is a problem with river valleys through hilly regions, I now know. If the valley is wide enough, it is a natural thoroughfare and the road will be busy. Think of the Rhône Valley, the Isère... and the Allier, north of Issoire.

After collecting and congratulating ourselves at the pass, we sped happily down to the Allier, admired it, and pulled out our maps. A motorway roars along the river to Issoire in no time at all, but the only road we could find was fiddly, hilly, tiring and slow. If I was doing it again, I would pre-research train times from the station near the bridge, Parent-Coudes-Champeix, and take the train to Issoire. It takes 11 minutes, and would save at least an hour.

I might even continue by train to Brioude, but that would be lazy, and it would be a shame not to see St Austremoine, most callipygian of the Auvergne's great churches, with lively painted capitals inside and carved signs of the zodiac decorating the shapely back end.

The lurid colour scheme may shock those who like their churches grey, but it does make the carvings easy to read.

Leaving Issoire is not easy, because of the motorway and railway, but eventually we found our way across the river and slogged in considerable heat up to the village of Nonette, which is indeed finely set, but... Galaxy thought *Non, merci* might be a better name.

It was footwear decision time and, after a successful morning in the Crocs, I bravely threw the trainers in the bin at our picnic spot beside the Allier, beneath the Pont Pakowski, along with some cheese parings and an empty wine bottle. From now on, I was committed to my crocs and I hoped they would not let me down. Nor have they. The beach sandals turned out to be ideal for bathing, as they should be, protecting my feet against broken glass or sharp stones and giving extra buoyancy. They are also good for cycling in the rain. My feet get wet, then quickly dry off.

In the context of the day our progress was slightly disappointing, and it would soon be time for the first phone call of the afternoon, alerting Les Deux Abbesses to the fact that we were running late.

At the end of the day it is important to relax, refresh, reflect and loosen the legs, which are terribly tight after hours of pedalling. We like to arrive by 6.30 at the latest and when reserving a room I always make this clear.

"If we're going to be any later than 6.30, I'll phone to let you know," I say, having been brought up to understand that French hoteliers grow increasingly twitchy as this hour approaches, and if an ad hoc turns up requesting a room, they will be sorely tempted to let him have it.

The result of my policy is an expensive phone bill. Every afternoon around four, when the hopelessness of our situation becomes clear, there is a great scrabbling around for telephone numbers, and the call must be made. "When do you stop serving dinner?" Further calls may be required. "Could you save us some cold food?"

The lady at Les Deux Abbesses sounded extremely doubtful. "You can't possibly arrive here by bicycle," said Mother Superior. "We're in a remote mountain village, you know. It's far too steep." Did she know she was dealing with two conquerors of the Col de Potey?

I said I had looked at the map and thought we could manage the 6km ride from Langeac to St-Arcons, even if it took us a long time. "No, we'll just have to come down to Langeac and pick you up." She sounded quite cross.

Mother Superior wanted to know when we would reach Langeac. Good lord, we hadn't even reached Brioude yet. "I'll ring you nearer the time," I said. "Would 7.30 be all right?"

No, it would not. "We close the village before then." What is this, a hotel or a boarding school?

We made up some time on the road to Brioude, and I was glad because it is a favourite of mine. A century ago, it was a fishing resort of global renown, but these days only a few hundred salmon manage the long migration from Greenland to their spawning grounds at the top of the river. I love the way the huge church is open on both sides with market stalls all around. You can buy your tomatoes and cheese, stroll across the cobbled aisle, come out the other side and pick up a loaf. The church really is at the heart of all the things that matter. Its interior is not painted in the manner of Issoire, thank goodness. It doesn't need to be, so warmly coloured and good to stroke are its polished stones. The nearby village of Lavaudieu is just as good: as heavenly as the name suggests.

At Vieille Brioude we left the main road and followed the river through an ideal landscape: small road, pretty views, perched villages, afternoon sun on the water. We did not have much time to explore, nor did we feel the need. The countryside could not have looked better than from where we sat on our bicycles.

"It's another world up there," said the barmaid in Langeac, where we waited for our taxi ride to Les Deux Abbesses.

Viewed from the plush leather surrounds of Mother Superior Laurence's super-jeep, the road to St-Arcons looked perfectly manageable.

Les Deux Abbesses (named after two aristocratic nuns of the Lafayette dynasty) is not a school but a hotel village whose owner, Laurence, has bought up empty houses and saved St-Arcons from becoming a ghost village. From 250 in the 1950s, its population had declined to 12 when she arrived in 1998. This is a bold and noble enterprise in which one can only wish her success. "It's a crazy bet that this beautiful nature needs a luxury hotel," she told us. Crazy: her word, not mine.

The small houses have been meticulously restored using scrupulously authentic materials, decorated in an achingly elegant stripped style for which the word may be *gustavien*, and furnished with art books and antique volumes of philosophy. This was the first wooden bath tub I have ever slept in, and the experience was beautiful.

Les Deux Abbesses

HÔTEL ÉCLATÉ LES DEUX ABBESSES
Quand les ruelles du village sont les couloirs de l'hôtel

Jeudi 24 Septembre 2009

3 Parfums de terre en Cappuccino
Lentille, Melanosporum, Pomme

Chaud, Froid, Glacé
Le Foie Gras varie
Sur une gelée écarlate

Voyage d'un Bar
d'Atlantique en Chine
Entre Citronnelle et Riz Vénéré

Les Fraises s'épanouissent
en Vacherin déstructuré
aux senteurs de Violette

Chef : Nicolas Picaud
Pierre Hermet vous conseille les vins
Servi avec le sourire par
Carolle, Cindy & Sabrina

Le château 43300 Saint-Arcons d'Allier • Tél : (33) 0 471 740 306 • Fax : (33) 0 471 740 530
web : www.lesdeuxabbesses.com • email : abbesses@relaischateaux.com
sarl (24h au capital de 180000 euros • rcs le Puy en velay • siret 423 721 265 00019
tva intra : FR50 423 721 265 00019

The main "château" has a pretty garden and a treatment cottage which was closed long before we arrived and not yet open when we left.

The whole world is into extreme sports. Extreme hiking, extreme skiing, extreme potholing. People come to Les Deux Abbesses – mainly from Paris, I suspect – for extreme rustication: an extreme escape.

If the style of Les Deux Abbesses is in some respects one of recherché minimalism, in others it might seem a bit too much.

I don't mind being asked before I go to bed if I want tea or coffee for breakfast, because this is an easy question to which I know the answer: coffee, unless hung-over, in which case tea, unless badly hung-over, in which case tea with an additional something to take the taste away, and something else – a cushion, perhaps – to reduce the noise of the cup landing on the table.

But when asked, before supper, what kind of bread I want for breakfast, what kind of fruit juice and what kind of honey – they have at least six – I want to scream: too many questions!

The produce, when it arrives, is exquisite. But who needs six kinds of honey? Impossibly refined Parisian consumers of extreme rustication, and Americans with

St-Ilpize

six kinds of allergy. Will there be enough of them, to make a go of it? I hope so. The hotel is close to Le Puy and also attracts a few pilgrims, eight hours in to their long walk to Compostela. In fact, for the £200-a-night pilgrimage market, there is really nowhere else in the frame.

St-Arcons to Langogne: about 85km

With two years of perspective, it seems to me that cycling up the Upper Allier was if anything more beautiful than cycling down the Upper Loire. One reason for this may be that we cycled up the Allier very slowly, with many stops to take pictures; and rode down the Loire quite quickly. Photography is a form of note-taking, and my Loire notes are a bit sketchy.

But another part of me thinks my impression may actually be right. The road from Brioude – Vieille Brioude, to be exact – to Langogne through places such as St-Ilpize (my screensaver), St-Arcons, St-Didier and St-Haon is as good as it gets.

At Prades the going got tough – 4.5km of hell from the bridge below the organ-pipe basalt rock formations where *baignade* is not merely *interdite* but "*formellement interdite*". Soon after the spectacular view of St-Didier (perched turret house outlined against the wild and woolly forest), we fed chocolate to a troika of fine horses who appeared out of the woods to greet us in the most charming way.

High above the dam we sat for a moment among the pines (alternative screensaver), looking down on a

St-Didier

couple of canoeists and listening to the sound of work
on the line.

So much climbing... and we gave it all back in a
moment, spinning down to the river at Alleyras, and the
oasis of M Philippe Brun's Michelin-starred Hôtel Haut-
Allier, to which we long to return but probably won't.
No photograph required to remember Galaxy's look
of disbelief at my route-planning incompetence. How
could anyone not call a halt at this beautiful property?
Four hours to relax before dinner – why ever not?

From Alleyras we began to climb once more, and
stopped for a breather in a lay-by halfway up a long hill
(beyond Jerusalem). A man of a certain weight who had
overtaken us near the bottom in his big camper van was

also having a rest in the same place. He was tired, just driving up, and the camper van looked tired too.

At St-Haon we had a cup of tea and could have had a second while waiting for a herd of cows blocking the road. Jonchères's iron bridge was the last we saw of the Allier.

From the iron bridge we had just a little more climbing to do before reaching a pass at 1012m. Then down we joyously flew to the Barrage de Naussac and sprinted flat out along the lakeside and on down to Langogne – 8km in record time. Langogne's situation, lurking beneath its lake, is an unusual one. If the dam ever broke, heaven help it.

How we managed this ride from Brioude in a day and a bit beats me. When I look at all the wiggles on the map,

St-Haon, rush hour

and all the arrows, mostly pointing the wrong way, it looks like the work of a week.

Of course it was damned hard work (and the next day would have been a damned sight harder without Emilie). But it was worth every bead of sweat, and I think Galaxy feels the same.

The au pair relationship is a two-way thing. I taught Emilie much of the English she knows; she taught Galaxy and me how to say Le Puy, our destination for the next day and the much-anticipated highlight of the Loire half of our circuit. It is not Le Pwee, which is hard, if not impossible, for a non-French person – this one, at least – to say in such a way that a local person will understand. You have to say "*Pionvlay*"(Puy-en-Velay) very fast. The speed is crucial and the "*le*" is understood, coming into play only if you are in or going to Le Puy, in which case you say not *à Pionvlay* but *au Pionvlay*.

Emilie had booked us into Langogne's Hôtel de la Poste, its bar the meeting place of Langogne society, such as it is. She sat politely toying with a salad in an au pairish way while G and I chomped our way through a hefty supper, until I thanked her for agreeing to be our *chauffeuse*, at which she looked startled, upped and left.

"Did I say something wrong?" I asked Galaxy. "That depends what you meant," he replied. "*Chauffeuse* means someone who keeps you warm at night."

I have my doubts about this, and think he may have been pulling my leg. But he swears by his understanding of *chauffeuse*, and Emilie's reaction suggests there may be something in it.

Gerbier de Jonc to Vorey: about 95km (including 4km by car)

We have often told ourselves that we could have managed the 50ish-km ride from Langogne to the source of the Loire, and that may be true. But we would not have enjoyed it much: Langogne was shrouded in pre-autumnal mist when Emilie appeared in her father's Renault Scenic in the morning and the mist thickened as we climbed, soon becoming cloud. We would not have seen a thing, and it was cold too.

The source of the Loire is a holy place much visited, remote though it is. Early on a foggy morning in September, however, the souvenir stalls had yet to open and there were few people around paying their respects to the life-giving springs which bubble magically from the spongy meadows. I write springs, because there are several of them and after much argument I think they have agreed to share the glory of being the Source. In a barn which declares itself to be *la Source Géographique de la Loire* – as distinct from the nearby *source authentique* and not very far away *source véritable* – we did not even have to queue to fill our water bottles from the spout.

The Gerbier de Jonc (1550m) is a phonolitic peak. It looks less like a mountain than a large cairn, a heap of stones that someone has piled up, as well they might, to mark the birthplace of France's senior river. It is not enormous, and in other circumstances Galaxy and I might have clambered up for the view and the satisfaction of summiting. But the fog was not inviting, and Crocs are not well suited to this kind of expedition.

The Loire and the Aigue Nègre

At this pretty confluence of streams just below the Gerbier de Jonc, which branch is the Loire? Wrong: it's the stream on the right. The left-hand branch is the Aigue Nègre (black water), which looks more like the senior partner, and so it is, its source being 4km away, to the Loire's 2.5km. It also brings a greater volume of water to the marriage, so, according to all the rules of geography, logic and fair play, either the stream on the left ought to be the Loire or the river that runs into the Atlantic at St-Nazaire ought to be the Aigue Nègre. But neither is the case. The Châteaux of the Aigue Nègre has an exciting ring to it, and might work rather well as the title of a Tintin adventure.

It is their greatest drawback. A stroll, yes. A rocky scramble, no.

Emilie took a picture of me sitting at the foot of the Gerbier de Jonc beside my bicycle, looking weary and for all the world as though I had pedalled up from Orange. In fact, I felt a little carsick.

Nearby – at the top of the road by which we would have approached if we *had* cycled up from Orange – we found a road sign marking the Mediterranean/Atlantic watershed, and took some more pictures there before saying goodbye and thank you to Emilie. The fog was breaking up and making way for a beautiful autumn day.

From its source the Loire flows south-west for a few kilometres before recalculating – "turn around when possible" – and heading north for Le Puy.

No road follows its early contortions closely, so after inspecting the river's first confluence, a pretty scene with autumn colours and many rowans in berry, we awarded ourselves coffee at the Hôtel du Nord in Ste-Eulalie, the first sur-Loire village, and clattered off down the mountain by the D122, not stopping until we reached the small volcanic Lac d'Issarlès.

This lake is so perfectly round, a good aerial photograph is guaranteed to make you stop and say: "Wow! Amazing!" The view from the bank lacks the same wow factor. The perfect roundness is not so easy to appreciate from ground level, and when we saw it the water level was low. As our garden pond reminds me, when water and surrounding sward do not meet but are separated by a

Our chauffeuse, Emilie

strip of bare mud, the effect is poor. In summer, bathing and watersports take over from hydroelectric service and the tidal effect may be less noticeable.

Issarlès is a popular excursion target, easily combined with the source of the Loire. It has accommodation and the simple Panoramic would be a good halt at the end of a hard day's ride from Langogne. The Hôtel du Nord in Ste-Eulalie would be better still.

All the ups and downs of our route were a matter of some concern to my companion, and debate between us. Galaxy was always looking at the map in the evening, finding an alternative route that climbed or descended more steadily, away from the river. Yes: it's called the main road. I wanted to stay with the rivers, which were the "idea" of the trip. This tension came to a head above the riverside village of Goudet, when we stood at a fork in the road, dithering pig-headedly, if that is possible, and nearly went our separate ways.

It was obvious from the map that the road I wanted to take descended steeply to Goudet and ascended steeply on the other side, to St-Martin-de-Fugères. G could see a flatter way and wanted to take it. I was not for turning, because the road down to Goudet might take us past Arlempdes, the first château on the Loire. I also thought we would be more likely to find a restaurant in Goudet than in St-Martin, and the time was right for one. Mention of lunch swung it, and G reluctantly turned his bike through 180 degrees and followed me down the hill. It was a hard pill for him to swallow, and it was a gamble for me. I knew if it failed he would be one angry man on the road to St-Martin.

We were on the wrong side of the river to see Arlempdes at its best, but Goudet's castle ruins were no less fine and Walter Scottish. Imagine my relief to find the solid and reassuring grey fabric of the hotel-restaurant de la Loire beside the bridge. Joy died a swift and painful death when we read the sign on the door: *Fermeture Exceptionnelle.*

I am not always the best at asking for directions, but this was an emergency. Surely, there had to be some-where in Goudet where we could get a sandwich. Goudet is on the Robert Louis Stevenson donkey trail, for heaven's sake. (This is my cue for an ambitious manoeuvre, the cross-reference. See Chapter 3.)

Spying a small green sign to the Ferme Auberge du Pipet, we found a teenager cutting the grass. He gave no answer, but ran off. A woman appeared at her door. "I'm sorry," she said. "I can't help you. All I have is a small amount of *charcuterie* and a bit of cheese."

In no time we were installed on this fine woman's porch, which turned out to be the Ferme Auberge. She brought piles of meat and cheese, plus a bottomless vat of soup, an embarrassment of salad, enough wine to be going on with and a surfeit of bread. There may have been a pudding too. It was a feast.

Her husband drove up and introduced himself as Massebeuf Jean-Claude. We chatted about our trip and discussed the suitability of his daughter Ludovine – "a good worker" – as our next au pair. Then Galaxy spoke.

"How far is it to St-Martin?" he asked casually.

"Only 4km," said Massebeuf Jean-Claude. "But it's a different country up there. Often snowy."

"That's a nice van you've got," said Galaxy.

"Yes. It's a Renault."

"A good size. I bet you can carry lots of useful stuff in it."

"Yes. Not bad."

"I wouldn't be surprised if you could fit a couple of bicycles in the back, and a couple of cyclists."

Eventually Massebeuf Jean-Claude caught on.

Above Le Puy

"I thought you said you were cyclists, not hitch hikers."
To think, he had considered entrusting his daughter to
one of these charlatans.

"Of course we would prefer to cycle up the hill to St
Martin," Galaxy said, and I swear I almost believed him.
"But we really want to visit Pionvlay and if we cycle up
the hill to St-Martin, we won't have time. Everyone says
Pionvlay is one of the most beautiful towns in France."

I have had many occasions to congratulate myself on
my choice of travelling companion. This was his finest
hour.

Massebeuf Jean-Claude's van was not as comfortable
as Laurence's super-jeep, but it saved us more pain. It
brought us to a land of broad open highlands, and we
fairly raced to Le Puy.

Le Puy-en-Velay, to give the capital of Haute-Loire its full title, owes its fame to its remarkable setting on and among spiky volcanic spurs and plugs; the hot eruptive colour of its burnt stones; the healing powers of the Black Virgin in its extraordinary cathedral, which is as stripy as a Buchanan's humbug; its lace and its lentils.

Other attractions include an immense statue of the Virgin made from melted-down Russian artillery pieces from the Siege of Sebastopol (1855). This monument, Notre Dame de France, can be visited, with a lift and a viewpoint at the top. My imagination, normally quiescent, runs riot at the thought of riding up the inside of the Virgin, exploring the cranial cavity and looking out through her cannon-ball eye, to say nothing of the exciting treats on the way up. A window in the navel, perhaps?

We also hoped to visit Le Puy's lace museum (Musée Crozatier) which I have enjoyed before; but missed that too. The lace industry was at its peak in the mid-19th century, and with a workforce of 80,000 *dentellières* contributed much to women's emancipation. There is a lace-making school in Le Puy and "learn to" holidays can be arranged.

The heart of the old city is tortuous, steep and cobbled, and the cathedral itself a confusing building of many layers, projecting from the top of the Rocher Corneille, as the core hill is known, like a humbug-striped baseball cap. As the swell of pilgrims grew, the cathedral needed successive extensions, and the only way to extend it was outwards.

Le Puy is the starting point of the most popular pilgrimage route to Compostela, and every morning a crowd of pilgrims assembles to be sent on its way with the bishop's blessing. Thanks to the Black Virgin, the cathedral itself is an important shrine and even at the end of the day it was thronged with the faithful, shuffling patiently through.

The present Virgin is a replica of an 11th-century wooden figure which was publicly burned on June 9th 1794. In the heat of the moment a secret door in the Virgin's back popped open, and a roll of parchment fell out. It too was consumed by the flames.

After climbing the stairs to the most giddily perched of Le Puy's monuments, St Michel de l'Aiguilhe, we made our way out of town and found the road south, flagged on the map for scenic value and entitled Les Gorges de la Loire. This sounded promising and had we been travelling up the river instead of down we might have appreciated the scenery more, if not the slope. But compared with the wilds through which we had ridden (and been driven) for the last two days, our route along the Loire Gorge seemed like a busy main road. It would make a more enjoyable sightseeing drive than scenic bike ride, we thought. Perhaps we were suffering from cycling Stendhal's Syndrome – excessive intake of beauty.

At Vorey we found the Hotel Rives de l'Arzon, a cheerful place full of local gossip and laughter, with football on TV in the bar and the chef's speciality trout and lentils on the menu.

St Michel de l'Aiguilhe, Le Puy

Vorey to Feurs: about 110km

After all our exertions in the hills, a pleasantly unde-
manding Sunday morning ride gave us good river views
among other incidental pleasures of French country life.
At Beauzac we paused to browse market stalls, drink
coffee and watch the village *flonflon* band march past.

Aurec painted a pretty picture, with allotments beside the river and small boats pulled up on the bank. In deference to the French Sunday lunch, we stopped at the first likely looking restaurant we found, with a sunny terrace: Les Oliviers, not worthy of a pilgrimage but good to know about if you're passing. Empty when we dropped anchor, it was gratifyingly packed half an hour later. Three courses and wine set us back less than 15 euros each, and set us up for our last big climb, eight kilometres from the Loire at Le Perthuiset to the hilltop fortress village, belvedere and Sunday afternoon beauty spot of Chambles.

At the bottom of the hill we found ourselves waiting at a traffic light beside a rusty van held together by psychedelic paint. A weirdo with a mangy dog on his lap stuck his head out of the window and with a hysterical laugh offered a handful of unwrapped sweets. Beware freaks bearing gifts: the pastilles might easily contain dangerous intoxicating substances. Unfortunately, they were only sweets.

The Loire cuts a deep wide trench to the west of the city of St-Etienne, and looks more like a mountain lake than a river. The view from Chambles is splendid, and only G of our peloton felt the need to scamper up the round tower and add another 20 metres of verticality to the view.

A helter-skelter descent from Chambles brought us out of the hills and down to the wide Forez plain, a definitive change of landscape. Keeping the Loire between us and St-Etienne until we were well past its sprawl (which includes Andrézieux), we found a small road leading north and recrossed the Loire south of Montrond-les-Bains. La Poularde is a gastro-hotel of long-standing repute, but the atmosphere at Montrond is subdued, to put it politely. If there's anything duller than a big spa town, it's a small one.

Nor did the agricultural factory town of Feurs set the heart racing, but the Hôtel l'Etésia at Feurs was where our day's pedalling reached the end of its allotted span, and there we stopped. A low-slung modern building near a roundabout on the outskirts of town, it looks made for the VRP (commercial traveller) market, and probably is. But with clouds menacing, we went in and were glad to have done so when the monsoon broke five minutes later.

The rain showed no sign of letting up, the fires of hunger were burning bright, and the Etésia has no restaurant. We asked the management to call a taxi for us. She refused. "Mon mari will drive you whenever you are ready," she said. When we wanted to leave the restaurant we had only to call, and mon mari would come and fetch us.

It is often said that the French go out of their way to treat cyclists with respect and, while I could introduce you to a few who don't, the Etésia certainly took hospitality beyond the call of duty. La Bonne Franquette was the restaurant we found. It was much livelier than we expected of a Sunday evening in a town like Feurs, and its south-western specialities (cassoulet, confit de canard, madiran) went down well. Mon mari was waiting outside for us, engine purring.

Feurs to Roanne: about 55km

In a straight line this journey is a mere 38km, but a small road – white with a green stripe on the Michelin system – wiggles along the Loire, crying out for cyclists, so we took it. The Château de la Roche was the Lac d'Issarlès revisited: the camera loves it, but the reality was disappointing. Viewed from close up, the castle is an obvious fake, and the water level was extremely low. The ride as a whole was beautiful, though: well worth the extra kilometres, especially the run down to and over the Villerest dam.

Roanne was as far as our journey down the Loire would take us for now. I am not sure we deserved a good lunch, but we were going to have one.

If the Maison Troisgros was surprised to see two dusty cyclists at the door, it was far too polite to say so, and as it happens, I doubt we were a rarity. Roanne is the Compostela of the food world and gastro-pilgrims must arrive from all corners, by every means of locomotion: on horseback, by 2CV and on all fours.

Or, more comfortably, by train: Troisgros commands the space traditionally occupied by the great provincial hotel-restaurants of France, the Place de la Gare. In Roanne it is now called the Place Jean Troisgros in honest recognition of the town's debt to its star family. Let us hear it once more: three Michelin *macarons, sans interruption*, since Danny le Rouge and co were ripping out the railings and manning the barricades on the Boulevard St Michel.

"How many tourists visit Roanne for reasons other than Troisgros?" I asked the maître d'hôtel. "None," he said.

Politely we were shown the underground car park –
henceforth also bicycle park – and from there a secret
passage led directly to the bathroom and fitness suite.
Our evening outfit was perhaps a little crumpled but
I like to think we scrubbed up all right and emerged
fit for purpose. There followed an aperitif moment in
the calm of the Japanese garden before we received the
summons to a room of quiet earth colours balanced by
the subdued hum of lunchers happily absorbed in quiet
mastication.

Troisgros is not a solemn experience, but a serious
one. A floppy fair-haired gentleman with a pale-blue
cashmere pullover thrown over his shoulders, and long
fingers that have never seen harder work than dismem-
bering a crab, looked slowly up from his plate, raised
one eyebrow, gave the faintest hint of a nod and went
back to his lunch.

The Monday lunch menu was 33 words long. It
contained no spectacular flights of exotic fantasy,
nor did it take us on a journey across the Pacific
Ocean. Who could stomach such a thing, at lunchtime on Monday? We began with soup – *velouté de
potimarron à l'amande* (a dream) – followed by lobster
with consommé, rabbit and ceps, goat's cheese
cannelloni, strawberry and mint tart, a few sweet
titbits, and then, Amen. There was also a cheese
board, and it needed two grown men to carry it.
Jean Jacques the sommelier advised Menetou Salon
if we wanted something to go with the lobster,
Côte Rotie for the rabbit, and either Montagny or

Meursault for the goat's cheese cannelloni. We went for the Montagny.

A distinguished art historian once told an uppity classmate of mine: "Kindly remember you are studying the work of a genius. Your job is to appreciate and try to understand, not to criticise. Never suggest – never even think – that Dürer made a mistake."

I realise that down this road the emperor's new clothes lie, but if I was an emperor and Michel Troisgros was my tailor, I would take the risk. Troisgros was not having us on, and it was not two naked men who pushed their bicycles across the Place Jean Troisgros in an unseemly rush to catch the 15.39 service to Vichy.

A good lunch enjoyed if not deserved

Auberge de Peyrebeille: the serial killer hoteliers

Above Langogne on the high road from Le Puy to Aubenas, where the wind howls and snowdrifts tower over the heads of grown men, the Auberge de Peyrebeille was more mountain refuge than roadside inn. On a stormy night, the 19th-century traveller must have breathed a sigh of relief at the sight of it. Unsaddling gratefully, he would hurry inside, banging the snow off his feet and little suspecting, as the innkeeper closed the door and bolted it shut, the terminal nature of the hospitality in store.

Over a period of a quarter of a century (1805–31) Pierre Martin, his wife Marie Breysse and their servant Jean Rochette (nicknamed Fétiche), are said to have robbed and murdered some 50 guests: knocking them over the head, emptying their pockets and burning their bodies in the oven.

Local suspicion grew, and the three were convicted on the evidence of a drunkard they had booted out because he could not pay for his bed – not worth murdering. On October 2nd 1833 they were guillotined on the forecourt of their inn in front of a bloodthirsty crowd of 30,000 spectators, the spot now marked by a stone smeared with a bloody cross. Court papers went missing, and the legend grew far beyond any basis in fact. It has inspired novelists, film-makers and investigative crime writers, many of whom think the Martins were innocent.

I had no idea of this story when I drove past some years ago. There was something about the place that made us pull over and take a look. It wasn't in the Michelin guide and was therefore not on my list of places to visit. But my companion, who had a limited appetite for tympanums and historiated capitals, perked up at the prospect of a visit with some narrative interest, and wanted to go in.

A beady-eyed toothless hunchback answered the door. Show you round? Oh, yes, I'll show you round. I'll show you round, all right.

And in the blood-curdling tones of a pantomime villain, he declaimed the terrible story of Pierre and Marie Martin, always walking behind us, pushing us forward from one room to the next. Down the stone stairs we gingerly stepped, towards the oven. "And it was right here, m'sieu' – 'dame, that Pierre Martin took his mallet out from under his coat, and… " The bludgeon did not come down on our heads, but Peyrebeille made quite an impact. There is now a motel (0033 466694751) next door to the original "Auberge Rouge". Sweet dreams.

Hotels (with restaurants unless stated)
* = cheap, ***** = expensive

***** Bort-L'Etang, Château de Codignat
www.codignat.com   0033 473684303
* Lezoux, Les Voyageurs   0033 473731049
** Brioude, Poste et Champanne
www.hotel-de-la-poste-brioude.com   0033 471501462
***** St-Arcons-d'Allier, Les Deux Abbesses
www.lesdeuxabbesses.com 0033 471740308
*** Alleyras, Le Haut Allier
www.hotel-lehautallier.com   0033 471575763
** Langogne, la Poste
www.hotel-poste.fr   0033 466690002
** Ste-Eulalie, du Nord
www.hoteldunord-ardeche.com   0033 475388009

* Lac d'Issarlès, Le Panoramic
  www.lepanoramicissarles.com   0033 466462165
* Goudet, Ferme Auberge du Pipet
  http://lesgitesdupipet.pagesperso-orange.fr   0033 471571805
* Goudet, la Loire   0033 471571841
** Vorey, Les Rives de l'Arzon
  www.hotel-rives-arzon.fr   0033 471011399
** Feurs, L'Etésia (B&B)
  www.hotel-etesia.fr   0033 477270777
***** Roanne, Troisgros
  www.troisgros.com   0033 477716697
** Roanne, Grand Hotel (B&B)
  www.grand-hotel-roanne.com   0033 477714882

Restaurants
* Aurec-sur-Loire, Les Oliviers   0033 477354434
** Feurs, la Bonne Franquette
  www.bonnefranquette.com   0033 477261953
***** Roanne, Maison Troisgros
  www.troisgros.com   0033 477716697

Information
Auvergne   www.auvergne-tourisme.info
Languedoc-Roussillon   www.sunfrance.com
Rhône-Alpes   www.rhonealpes-tourisme.com
Ferries: LD Lines (Portsmouth – Le Havre)   www.ldlines.co.uk

ROUTE 3

FROM THE CEVENNES TO THE ATLANTIC

La Bastide to Arcachon via the
Stevenson Trail, the Tarn Gorges, a little
of the Lot and a soupçon of Sauternes
(about 710km)
May 2011

BORDEAUX

Le Teich
Arcachon
Duna de Pilat

La Réole
duRas
Montflanquin
Puy L'évêque

Sauternes

Le Puy

START

La Bastide
Le Bleymard
Col de
Finiels

Peche Merle

CAHORS

LOT RIVER

Ste Enimie

Le Pont
de Mont Vert

FLORAC

St Cira
Lapopie

St Rome De Tarn

CORDES

Albi

TARN RIVER

Milau

ROQUEFORT

For variety of beautiful places and interesting stops, and brilliant May weather that built up to a heatwave as we approached the sea, we look back on this as the best of our rides. But it had its gruelling aspects, not least sorting out the travel arrangements.

All looked simple enough when I unrolled the map of France on my friend's dining table and outlined an idea that combined his desire to link the Mediterranean and the Atlantic and mine to revisit the Cévenol railway, which had thwarted us last time.

To recap: an improbable railway trundles over the empty highlands of the Massif Central, through some of the wildest country in France, between the lava-black city of Clermont-Ferrand and Nîmes, the dusty bull-fighting capital of Roman Provence. The great thing about this train is that, rather like a ski lift, it takes you up to a high place where you can jump out and head downhill.

I reckoned it should be possible to reach the highest stop on the Cévenol line – a station shared by La Bastide-Puylaurent and an old spa called St-Laurent-les-Bains, at an altitude of just over 1000m – by train, in a day.

La Bastide is an old staging post on the high road through that slightly magical mountain region – someone must surely have called it 'the water tower of France' – where half a dozen major rivers are born, their sources all within a few kilometres of each other. From adjacent hills not far from La Bastide, the Tarn and the Lot slip away to the west, the Allier and the Loire head north, and the Ardèche tumbles down through its great canyon to the south-east.

We had already explored, if that is the right word, the upper reaches of Allier and Loire. Now the water tower of France would make a good starting point for a ride down the Tarn Gorges and across to the Atlantic via Bordeaux wine country.

"Sounds great," said Galaxy. "Why don't we finish at Arcachon?" This sounded suspiciously like an agenda – to revisit a romantic adventure, perhaps, from his days as a carefree yellow-911-driving Kensington gadabout. I thought better of requesting more detail, with Mrs G in earshot.

Arcachon was fine by me. I imagined us rolling effortlessly through south-western France, downhill all the way, to a lazy afternoon at the foot of Europe's premier sand dune, followed by a plate of oysters and a bottle of Entre Deux Mers. The trip turned out rather differently from this, but not in a bad way.

Now I had to make it work. The quickest and cheapest way to get to La Bastide is via Paris and Nîmes, the 800km Paris-Nîmes leg of the journey being, to use one of Galaxy's catchphrases, the work of a moment – less than three hours. But Paris-Nîmes trains do not have bike spaces, and Galaxy balked at the idea of dismantling his bicycle and packing it in a bag. The slower Paris-Clermont-Ferrand train does accept bicycles, so we decided to approach La Bastide that way.

No accommodation guide that I could lay hands on had anything to say about La Bastide – although had I been more diligent in my googling, I might have been tempted by L'Etoile, a ramblers' refuge run by a Belgian-

Greek adventurer who certainly knows how to run a lively website. But I liked the sound of a Logis de France near the station in Issoire, about half an hour (by train, that is) south of Clermont-Ferrand.

No less a cultural icon than Jacques Brel stayed at the Hôtel du Parc for three months in the 1960s. Something told me the Parc would be rather fun: a bit of a find, for Alastair Campbell and other pillars of the Brel fan club. An early train next morning would get us to La Bastide by ten, and that was quite early enough for a warm-up day on the bike.

More work-out than warm-up, I realised, on looking more closely at the map. Our first *étape* would be a serious challenge: 48 kilometres from La Bastide to Le Pont-de-Montvert via two mountains with a combined ascent of 900 vertical metres. The Montagne du Goulet hosts the source of the Lot, the Mont Lozère, the source of the Tarn. Well, Galaxy had dragged me over the Jura on the first afternoon of our first ride. This beginning would have symmetry.

How to get to Paris? Eurostar is the quickest way, but rather than go to the trouble of lugging our bikes to St Pancras we decided to drive to Dover in comfort, leave a car there, catch a ferry in the traditional way and begin our high-speed rail journey in Calais. We calculated that we would be glad of the car on the way home.

Before embarking for France, I turned to noted Brelomane J Barnes for an aperitif. A short story called "Tunnel" mentions the "surprising banality" of the fact that for London residents Paris is closer than Glasgow:

in three hours our man can be heading down "the mild decline of the Boulevard de Magenta".

It took Galaxy and me 24 hours to reach the Boulevard de Magenta, via a car park in an industrial estate on the outskirts of Dover, a ferry and a night in the 240-year-old Hôtel Meurice in Calais – *ancien régime* accommodation for an old-fashioned itinerary.

It was not until G was comfortably installed on the ferry with a glass in one hand and his phone in the other – for ongoing berating of the builders he had left in charge at Galaxy Towers – that he took a closer look at our itinerary.

Ongoing builder bashing

"What's wrong with the road to Mende?" he asked helpfully. "It looks like the quickest way from La Bastide to the Gorges du Tarn, and we wouldn't have to go over those horrible mountains." And ... "Why can't we go and see the cathedral in Clermont-Ferrand? Didn't we visit the church in Issoire last time?"

I pointed out that staying in Issoire would mean half an hour longer in bed; and riding over the mountains would take us along the trail blazed by Robert Louis Stevenson and his she-ass Modestine in 1878, as described in his little book, *Travels with a Donkey in the Cévennes*, of which I had found a copy in Blackwell's the previous day. Mention of RLS mollified my companion, a great reader who loves schoolboy adventures and yarns from the days of Empire. It was time to disembark.

Calais's history is one of boom and blitz, England and France taking turns to attack it, starve it and blow it up, with episodes of ethnic cleansing, the Spanish weighing in at one point to put Calais to the sword as only they knew how, plus the Germans and Canadians at either end of World War II. As a final insult we bombed Calais by mistake in 1945, months after it had been liberated.

Such is the fate of strategic ports. The building style is post-war (obviously) and almost uniformly bleak, the main street is now quite seedy, and the town as a whole seems to cower, like a dog that spends its life wondering where the next kicking will come from.

We made for the Meurice, a great name in the history of French hotels. The name is more famously associated with the palace on the Rue de Rivoli, but the Calais

Meurice was the prototype. In the post-Napoleonic era a chain of Meurices studded the road south from Calais for the accommodation of eager English gentlemen with wild oats to sow in gay Paree.

The broom of change has not swept through the Meurice since I first stayed there in the 1980s, despite a change of owner and presumably several changes of dog. "*Le style cosy*" still prevails, the snug still has its louche Edwardian cartoons, and a framed newspaper cutting from 1909 still celebrates M Blériot's 37 minutes of fame.

The same gracious welcome, the same comfortable bedrooms and English country colour schemes, the same sofas and armchairs on the landing – for servants and bodyguards, of course. The house Weimaraner, Zeus, looked and smelt as though he had not moved from his throne for some years, but was also friendly in a lapidary kind of way. I like a hotel with a dog. It says: this is our home, not an outlet delivering a product in an industry. If you don't like dogs, stay somewhere else.

Not least among the hotel's attractions is the beautiful collection of vintage cars M Cossart keeps in the garage. We parked our bikes next to the racing-green Jag.

Finding the dining room occupied by a private party, we asked the girls at reception if the town had a decent restaurant they could recommend. They booked us a table at Le Channel, which considers itself rather smart, with a window in the floor, Blackpool Tower style, allowing one to hover above a cellar full of overpriced wine. We thought the food expensive too, but at least it was good, and the cheese board brought a reminder of how fiercely regionalistic France remains.

Galaxy is careful about his cheese intake these days, but in celebration of our return to the land of his Huguenot ancestors and the relaunch of our cycling project, he asked the waiter to cut him off a bit of something local. "Maroilles?" I piped up, keen to show off. The waiter looked horrified. "*Le Maroilles, c'est du 59,*" he explained gravely. "*Ici on est 62. Le fromage de la région, c'est le Bergues.*" Silly me.

Do French schoolchildren still learn their *département* numbers by rote, from 01 (Ain) to 95 (Val d'Oise)? I have long envied the French this facility and spent happy hours in the passenger seat studying the "*d'où vient cette auto?*" page of the red Michelin guide. (20? Trick question: there isn't one).

Now they have spoiled our sport by changing their number-plate system, thereby denying us the chance to pull over and avoid road hogs from Bordeaux at the first sight of a 33 plate charging up behind us, lights flashing furiously. Thanks to the cheese waiter at Le Channel, I will never have a problem remembering that 59 is Nord and 62 Pas-de-Calais.

Perhaps I am doing Calais an injustice. There is a new lace museum, and the restoration of Notre Dame, where de Gaulle married a Calais girl in 1921, is almost complete after 70-odd years. Always described as English in style – de Gaulle might not have approved – it is one of the few buildings to survive from the long period of English occupation (1347-1558), which began with the Battle of Crécy and a year-long siege. After the citizens of

Calais had eaten their horses, dogs, rats and mice, "and nothing remained but to eat one another" (as the town's governor wrote in an unsuccessful plea for help from the French king), the town's leading merchant Eustache de Saint Pierre and five fellow citizens offered themselves and the keys to the town to the English king Edward III in exchange for a promise to spare the town.

Rodin's larger-than-life group sculpture of the Calais Six was commissioned in the aftermath of the disastrous Franco-Prussian War and stands beneath the town hall, consoling all losers with the thought that defeat can be as heroic as victory.

After breakfast we gave Zeus a goodbye stroke and told the Meurice girls how sorry we were not to have been able to dine there. "You could have," they said: the hotel has a separate little restaurant, La Diligence, beyond the dining room, unnoticed by us.

We blushed, I hope, to think how cheerfully they had responded, when we marched up demanding that they find us "somewhere decent to eat in town". The Meurice is accustomed to boorish Brits. It may not be a palace, but it is a better hotel than Calais deserves.

Luckily, we left plenty of time for the ride to the TGV station at the French end of the Channel Tunnel, Calais Fréthun (which rhymes with Verdun, not Béthune). The local road signs are not geared towards people making this journey, but after ten kilometres of trial and error among waterways, roundabouts and hypermarkets, we found the station in time to achieve the ritual *compostage* of our tickets and with difficulty carry our bikes up

Lace-making and landscape painting

The first industrial lace machine was made in England in 1813, and met fierce opposition from factory workers. Although exporting the machines was illegal, three Nottingham lace-makers smuggled theirs to Calais and found a more co-operative labour force and new markets to exploit. The industry flourished and by the end of the 19th century employed 10,000 Calais men, women and doubtless children. That figure has now declined to 3000, but Calais still claims to be the world's leading producer of lace for lingerie, haute couture and wedding dresses. A museum dedicated to it, in an old factory on the Quai du Commerce, grandly calls itself La Cité Internationale de la Dentelle.

One of the three refugee lace-makers was the father of Richard Parkes Bonington (1802-28) who was saved from a career in the family business when a local artist recently returned from England, Louis Francia, spotted a talent. Francia encouraged the young Bonington's love of open-air landscape painting, taught him the ideas and techniques of Thomas Girtin and sent him to Paris with letters of introduction to important figures. Bonington was a great hit in France and his breezy beach scenes and seascapes influenced developments later in the century – Barbizon, Impressionism – thus earning Calais its place in the history of art as, most appropriately, a link between England and France.

and down several flights of steep stairs to reach our platform.

We must have looked tired because a railway official came up to show us where the train's bike carriage would stop, and asked where we had cycled from, obviously expecting an answer like Ventimiglia, or Tehran.

"Calais," we replied.

The SNCF man looked surprised. "Then why didn't you catch the train there?" It had not occurred to me that a TGV might start in town. We were able to smile at our stupidity: after all, we had not missed the train, merely cycled ten unnecessary kilometres and carried our bikes up and down unnecessary staircases.

This ought to have taught us not to assume that TGVs must necessarily be caught at TGV stations, but it failed to do so – to our considerable cost, a few months later. Now that I revisit the SNCF website, I can see why I made the mistake. When asked for morning trains from Calais (*toutes gares*) to Paris, it offers the 11.19 from Calais Fréthun (with bicycle spaces), with no mention of its departure from Calais Ville at 11.09. Could do better.

By one o'clock we were in Paris, fortunately on time, because our connection was tight: less than an hour to push our bikes through the crush at the Gare du Nord and find our way to the Gare de Bercy. This was our first tilt at Paris. Helmets on.

As almost all who try it agree, cycling through the capital was amazingly easy and enjoyable. This sunny spring lunchtime, traffic was light. Buses gave us a wide berth, no taxi driver cut us up, and pedestrians moved politely aside with none of the abuse and fist-shaking hostility that goes with the territory in London. Parisian cyclists zoomed about in great numbers, ignoring the rules in the carefree manner one would expect. All were bare-headed and several visits later I am still waiting to see my first Parisian cyclist in a helmet.

Down the mild decline of the Boulevard de Magenta we sailed, without hesitation or deviation, helped on our way by cycling signposts and cycle lanes that swung from pavement to bus lane and back. The Place de la République was a more serious adventure, and at Bastille our signposts ran out. A pedestrian pointed us in the right direction and Galaxy homed in on Bercy, carting his bike up an outdoor escalator. "Well done!" we told each other, swapping breathless high fives as the station clock moved past 13.45. We turned our attention to the display board for a platform announcement.

But there was no platform, merely a bald statement scrolling across the screen to the effect that an unexpected phenomenon – work – necessitated a change of scheduling and the 13.58 to Clermont-Ferrand would leave from the Gare de Lyon. *Sacré bleu.*

The two stations are not far apart but even so, we did well to find our train with, by our reckoning, two minutes to spare. As it happened, the train left fifteen minutes late and reached Clermont-Ferrand later than that; so it was lucky we had not booked La Bastide's Greek refuge, because we would certainly have missed that connection.

A few steps from Issoire station, overlooking the gardens from which it takes its name, and only a short stroll from St Austremoine's church, we found the Hôtel du Parc. It has a small terrace where one could happily wait for a train with a drink and a good book; or linger over dinner of a warm evening, hoping Jacques Brel might step out from the shadows for an impromptu "*Ne Me Quitte Pas*".

According to the Parc's owner M Robin, Brel did not sing for his supper, but divided his waking hours between learning to fly the small plane he had bought from Issoire Aviation, then known as Wassmer, and drinking whisky.

What was it like, having the great man in the house? M Robin shrugged. "It was under the previous owner," he said, and I was not surprised, because I doubt Brel would have put up with M Robin's pettifogging regime for three hours, let alone three months.

I raised my first eyebrow when he proposed to charge us eight euros (each, probably) for parking our bikes in his garage. There followed a long-winded tour of a small bedroom cluttered with gadgetry and notices detailing house rules and all the things guests are not allowed to do. Bizarrely, these include turning off the television. Bills are paid on the night of arrival. Wall-mounted machines dispense things that might otherwise be stolen: plastic cups, soap, paper bags, loo paper.

As he droned on, the strain of the day began to tell, and I reached out for support. "*Monsieur, s'il vous plaît!*" barked M Robin. "That's my paintwork you're touching!"

M Robin is one of those hoteliers – declining in number, thank goodness – who view every guest as a potential thief and devote their energies to foiling his plans. He ought to be a traffic warden, or a beater-down of insurance claims.

"When are you going to eat?" he wanted to know, reasonably enough. "Eight-thirty?" I ventured. "Oh no, no, no," said M Robin, "that's much too late!" We settled on eight o'clock, and obediently sat down on the dot, after an abbreviated visit to St Austremoine and the café opposite. Local customers were still drifting into the Parc for dinner at nine, without a murmur of complaint from our host. Madame Robin's food is not bad at all, but her husband charges city prices for modest local wine (St Pourçain).

At least that left us with plenty of time after supper to explore Issoire. "You will find the entry code for the back door written on the bill," said M Robin. (When you've paid it, he did not need to add.)

Exploring Issoire is the work of not many moments, and we were back before M Robin had finished barricading his fortress. I sat down to read a magazine leaving G *champ libre* in the bedroom to wash his socks and prepare for an early departure. "It's late," said M Robin. "*J'éteins*." (Lights out.)

The Auvergnat has a reputation for low cunning. I am not sure if he is local, but M Robin certainly fits in. To speed the parting guest, nothing is too much trouble, and he telephoned personally with a wake-up call we had not requested, half an hour before our alarm was set to go off.

He served breakfast in person too, cheered by the imminent prospect of our departure. One last thing: "Where's the key?"

In the bedroom door, we replied. M Robin snorted: did we expect him to fall for that one? So off I trotted to fetch the precious key, and, playing Eustache de St Pierre to his King Edward, delivered the same. His

Majesty was satisfied at last. "Thank you," he said. "Now I've got my key, you can have your bikes. *Au revoir, messieurs.*"

Adieu, M Robin.

Athough I was looking forward to our long-awaited appointment with the Cévenol railway, this was not a sentimental journey: we were using the rail network to take us and our bikes to a place we lacked the energy to reach under our own steam. It was not a means to an end but a means to a start.

For many others it is a destination in itself, combining the attractions of a wonder of the world and an endangered species. From all corners of the trainspotting world enthusiasts travel to Clermont-Ferrand or Nîmes. They take the Cévenol from one end of the line to the other, and travel home again. *Voilà*: travel.

"What makes the Cévenol so special is that it does not follow the course of any particular valley," I read on a website, "but incessantly crosses from one to another, cutting through the mountainsides, and stretching out over rivers and gorges on the way."

Railway buffs love the detail. The Cévenol boasts 106 tunnels. At Villefort, the highest stone viaduct in France, all 256km of it, crosses the river Altier at a height of 72m. The Chamborigaud viaduct is even longer, at 409m.

Galaxy and I settled down in a comfortable modern carriage to watch the beautiful countryside through which we had cycled 18 months before, go past. If we incessantly crossed from one valley to another, I am ashamed to say we did not notice.

He hung his damp socks out to dry; I caught up with Stevenson who, after escaping the clutches of a talkative Trappist at the monastery of Notre Dame des Neiges, shared a room with some railway engineers who were working on a viaduct between La Bastide and Mende. That branch line, another collector's item now known as the Translozérien, would open 24 years later.

Brioude, leafy. Langeac, long wait for train full of lumber coming in other direction. It was at Prades that our last bike ride had begun to climb seriously, and we peered up to see our road snaking up through the woods high above us. Did we really cycle up there?

We passed the lovely hotel Haut-Allier at Alleyras, surely the most remote Michelin-starred table in France, and recognised the iron bridge where we had said goodbye to the Allier. After Langogne, that town with the rare distinction of being overlooked by its lake, we entered a landscape that can only be described as sunny uplands. We had reached the top of the line, and La Bastide.

La Bastide to Cocurès: about 60km

No one who saw us finish one trip would have much difficulty recognising us at the start of another. We are creatures of habit, and part of the pleasure we derive from our jaunts is in the unrolling of the routine, the simplicity of it and the sticking to it. The same shorts and tubigrips, and the same shirts, his with a top pocket where the map lives, and whence it can be removed, unfolded dextrously with one hand and studied while riding along. (Don't try this at home.) I feel pretty confident that he has worn the same check shirt, cream coloured trousers and canvas boat shoes on every evening of every bike ride we have shared. He might say the same of me, though I am not quite so constant.

In deference to the Cévennes' proud boast to be the wettest place in France, I brought improved weatherproofing to this party. My panniers were now waterproof and rolled up inside them were new overshorts which, although not designed to accommodate undershorts bulging with train tickets, camera, phone, wallet, passport and toolkit, just about did; and a bright yellow rain jacket, by Scott, which would have clashed nicely with my old Crocs had I not retired them in favour of a blue pair.

Rolling through a warm and breezy morning that might have been made for cyclists, our happiness at having finally passed Go was compromised only by the knowledge that we would soon be sweating our way up a big hill. After synchronising our computers – his in miles, mine in kilometres – we were distressed to find ourselves losing altitude. There was no need for a computer to confirm that his trusty old bike, by now named Modestine, was still better at freewheeling than mine. It always has been, and he claims to have broken the mythic 40mph barrier on more than one occasion, as I never have. The Super Galaxy saves its best for uphill work, with an extra bottom gear that encourages me to dream that I am the superior climber of our team.

Thirteen kilometres to the turn-off for L'Estampe were all too quickly achieved.

The Montagne du Goulet (1463m) rose before us. Others have described it as a paradise of mushrooms and wild flowers, but for us it was just a big hill. Galaxy stripped for action.

This was where RLS had his only serious argument with Modestine, who objected to his choice of a short cut through the woods and his use of the goad. We stuck to the road and were ready for a pause when we came across a group of young hikers with two donkeys and a colourful drover. The children's faces told us it was a big hill for them too.

They were on a school outing from Montélimar and bound for the Col de Finiels, which they hoped to reach at the end of the next day. The donkeys seemed less heavily laden than the children and looked understandably chipper. Their names? Canelle and Mousse-Café. "They can't all be called Modestine," explained the drover, and the same goes for bicycles. The Super Galaxy, being brown, became Mousse-Café, henceforth and for evermore.

Stevenson did not let Modestine's displeasure on the way up the Goulet affect his mood.

"Beautiful and interesting sounds filled my heart with an unwonted expectation; and it appeared to me that, once past this range which I was mounting, I should descend into the garden of the world."

We had no such expectation of Le Bleymard, the village that lay between our two mountain climbs. But lunch would be good. We imagined a rustic inn where we might be greeted like true explorers and if lucky feast on cold meat and hard cheese. "On bicycles? No... really? Bravo! Come on in..."

Instead, Le Bleymard looked surprisingly prosperous and its hotel, La Remise, was a-clatter with profitable lunchtime trade, like a county town hotel on market day. We recognised a group of loggers we had passed on top of the Goulet, chainsaws buzzing, and were lucky to find a table. After spinning out our lunch with another glass of *picpoul* for the road, I asked the management what the bedrooms were like, as he raced by with a tray full of hard liquor for the chainsaw gang. "All full!" he called over his shoulder. Full up, on a weekday in May, in deepest Lozère? Impressive. The Chemin Stevenson industry is in full swing.

RLS was well aware that the railway would bring profound change to the region through which he was travelling, opening the door to the deadening influence of the wide world. How would he feel about his own influence?

A fine rain was falling as we crossed the Lot and pedalled slowly away from Le Bleymard in the direction of the Col de Finiels. Yonder dark hill looked a long way off, and a long way up.

Cycling up hills may be a bit like childbirth: all pain forgotten within moments of completing the job. Be that as it may, I don't remember suffering acutely on the long ascent to the Col de Finiels – 10.4km for a 472-vertical-metre ascent at an average slope of 4.5% and a

Travels with a Donkey in the Cévennes

Robert Louis Stevenson's little classic is the account of his two-week journey on foot from Le Monastier to Alès in September/October 1878. Stevenson was dogged by ill health throughout his short life, and does not spell out his motives for heading for the hills in the wettest part of France at the wettest time of year. He was attracted by the non-conformist tradition in the Cévennes, and his girlfriend Fanny had just left him for San Francisco. It was essentially a travel-writing exercise: an adventure to write up for money.

Stevenson decided, if not to camp, "at least to have the means of camping out"; not in a tent, which would mark him out as a camper to all passers-by, but in a sleeping bag, which would serve a double purpose – a bed by night, a bag by day.

He had a sack made in Le Puy, and slept in a fur cap with a hood to fold over his ears. His only defence against the rain was a "tentlet" made of his coat, three stones, and a bent branch.

To carry the sack he needed a beast of burden – "something cheap and small and hardy, and of a stolid and peaceful temper. All these requisites pointed to a donkey". The sack cost 80 francs and two glasses of beer, the donkey 65 francs and a brandy. "That was as it should be; for she was only an appurtenance of my mattress, or self-acting bedstead on four castors."

Stevenson made slow progress until an innkeeper made him a goad – "a plain wand, with an eighth of an inch of pin. Thenceforward Modestine was my slave."

Stevenson and Modestine did not spend every night under the stars. Encounters and conversations are brilliantly remembered, portraits sketched in a few sure phrases, but Stevenson is at his best on nature and his emotional response to it, especially at night. The darkness held no fear for him, unlike the confinement of a bedroom, which he found almost intolerable.

JA Hammerton was the first cyclist to follow in the footsteps of Stevenson and write about it (*In the Track of RL Stevenson*, 1907). He met a few people who remembered Stevenson and others who claimed to. One cleric whom the author tried to engage in serious conversation about religion and politics – à la Stevenson – talked about nothing but Stevenson. *Travels with a Donkey* is a small book that fits easily in the saddle bag, and even the map pouch.

maximum of 6.9%, according to a cycling cols website that ranks the Finiels not very high on a list of challenges. The gradient is not extreme; we paced ourselves and stopped periodically. Taking a photo or having a drink is the usual excuse, but we also had the lifts (unfortunately closed) and pistes of Le Bleymard's ski area to inspect. Viewed from above, the black run did not look too terrifying.

If we could manage the Col de Finiels, how about something stronger? The famous hairpin ascent to Alpe d'Huez, perhaps: only the other day I was reading an article by a middle-aged man who hired a workaday mountain bike in Bourg d'Oisans, hitched up his skirts and... but what am I thinking? This is dangerous talk.

The Finiels is not the most dramatic of passes, a long "faux plat" over the shoulder of the Mont Lozère, with no discernible crest. We were relieved to get there though, a day ahead of the Montélimar gang and spurred on by the sound of thunder rolling up behind us.

This is not to say our way was better than theirs. On the contrary, on foot is the true countryman's choice, wandering through the fields and woods on rough paths. If there are ceps to be picked and wild flowers not to be, they are the foot soldier's reward, not the cyclist's. On the way down, landscape rushes past the cyclist at 50kph: exhilarating stuff, but a bit of a blur. Of our ascent I remember scents and sounds, Alpine chalets, horses, foals and cowbells. At one point I was distracted by the sight of a mountain dog and its adorable brood of puppies. Several minutes later, after rounding the next hairpin, I looked down on the same family.

On the way down ... well, we did pause to talk to a man who had bravely taken the decision to stop work, having no desire to be a lightning conductor while erecting his fence. "Le Pont-de-Montvert? It's downhill from here," he said. We guessed that – 12km downhill, in fact, for a descent of 660 vertical metres. In 20 minutes we were down.

It is some consolation that Stevenson had the same feeling. "The whole descent is like a dream to me, so rapidly was it accomplished. I had scarcely left the summit ere the valley had closed round my path."

Stevenson detected in Le Pont-de-Montvert "an indescribable air of the south". If the sun had been out, and the air heavy with pastis and the click of boules, we might have felt the same. But the place looked damp and grey to us, and we ducked inside a café to escape the rain before introducing ourselves to the office of the Association Stevenson, which founded itself in 1994 to produce maps, brochures and postcards and whatever else it can think of to swell the tide of literary pilgrims. The Association also counts, and clocked 6140 tourists on the Stevenson trail in 2010, on foot (with or without

Le Pont-de-Montvert

donkey) or on bicycles. Would we count, for 2011? And if so, who counted us?

As our fellow wheelman Hammerton found more than a century ago, Le Pont-de-Montvert seems more interested in Stevenson than the historical events that brought him there. That may be understandable, because the history of religious conflict in France is no bedtime story. However, the bravery of the people of the Cévennes in fighting for their freedom of conscience is said to be integral to their character, so we ought to take an interest.

The murder of du Cheyla

(Quotations from RLS, Travels with a Donkey, *Chapter 12)*

After a century of religious tolerance, the Revocation of the Edict of Nantes in 1685 saw Protestants outlawed for their faith. Denied the right to practise their religion in church, the Cévennes protestants held outdoor assemblies. Their informal church was known as "le Désert", and their gatherings grew increasingly hysterical and extreme.

Louis XIV sent troops and inquisitors to enforce conversion, and the chief enforcer was Abbé du Cheyla, Inspector of Missions for the Cévennes. Du Cheyla used his house at Le Pont-de-Montvert as a prison and "closed the hands of his prisoners upon live coal to convince them that they were deceived."

Few were convinced. "A persecution unsurpassed in violence had lasted near a score of years; hanging, burning, breaking on the wheel, had been in vain; ...

not a thought was changed in the heart of any upright Protestant."

On July 24th 1702, at an assembly in the woods on Mont Bougès, a black-faced and toothless wool-carder called Pierre Séguier, known as Esprit (Spirit), declared in the name of God that the time for submission had passed, and the time to take up arms was upon them.

At ten o'clock that evening, du Cheyla was disturbed in his prison-house by the sound of a group of 50 psalm-singers, led by Séguier. They were at the door, "breathing death". Du Cheyla ordered his guards to open fire and a psalm-singer fell. His bloody shirt gave the Camisards their name.

Du Cheyla retreated upstairs with his men defending the staircase. Séguier's band set fire to the house. Du Cheyla and his men let themselves down to the garden on knotted sheets. Some escaped but du Cheyla broke a leg and could only drag himself under the hedge, where the light of the flames revealed him to his pursuers, fatally.

"One by one, Séguier first, the Camisards drew near and stabbed him. 'This,' they said, 'is for my father broken on the wheel. This for my brother in the galleys. That for my mother or my sister imprisoned in your cursed convents.' Each gave his blow and his reason; and then all kneeled and sang psalms around the body till the dawn." They left du Cheyla's prison-house in ruins, "and his body pierced with two-and-fifty wounds upon the public place. 'Tis a wild night's work, with its accompaniment of psalms; and it seems as if a psalm must always have a sound of threatening in that town upon the Tarn."

Séguier was burned alive three weeks later. The Camisards achieved a few victories and much slaughter, but as their leaders were captured, killed or chased from the country, the cause lost momentum. The insurgency was over by 1705, with sporadic outbreaks of violence continuing until 1715.

In the early-evening rain we followed the young Tarn through the twists and rocky turns of its woodland gorge from Le Pont-de-Montvert to Cocurès. Stevenson was reminded of the pass of Killiecrankie at this point, and in the midst of so much beauty, "a humble sketcher laid down his pencil in despair". A humble reader knows that feeling.

If we needed an antidote to Issoire, to restore our faith in French hotel-keeping, La Lozerette at Cocurès was the perfect port of call. Downing pestle and mortar, Pierrette (Agulhon) welcomed us in from the rain, wiped her hands on her apron, took our wet clothes off us – not literally – and threw them straight in the drier. Bikes? In the garage at the back.

At supper Pierrette took control, asking politely if we were quite sure when we ordered a wine from far-off Cahors and proposing instead something cheaper and more local, to go with the treats of the *terroir* she had in mind for us. We had crossed an important watershed and were now in Languedoc wine country – the South of France! I sensed my companion bristle slightly, but we were glad we agreed to her recommendations. Pierrette was Veuve Clicquot's pin-up *Femme de Vin* 1994, and she knows her stuff.

With a long ride ahead of us, we asked for an early breakfast, and Pierrette was there in her dressing gown first thing, grinding the coffee beans and dishing out her home-made cherry jam.

Cocurès to Millau: about 100km

Florac is the authorised start of the Tarn Gorge – or finish, depending on which way you tackle it – although we felt we had seen some Tarn Gorge already, and the river that rushes past Florac is not the Tarn, but the Tarnon.

We made the short detour necessary from the Tarn and found the little town, strung out beneath the limestone wall of the Causse Méjean, busily preparing for market day. It had the makings of a colourful scene, with Breton-smocked artists, booted hikers wielding ski sticks, dreadlocked downshifters and other alternative types selling honey and morally superior bread. Plane trees shade the local crackshot *tireurs* and *pointeurs* on the *piste de pétanque*, and Florac really does have that southern something. We would have liked to hang around for a bit, before saying goodbye to RLS.

The ride down the Tarn Gorge to Millau took us all day. We had a light breeze in our faces but the slope was with us, and in places it seemed quite steep, considering the road basically follows the river. We crossed many more cyclists on the way up than passed us going down, and felt sorry for them (momentarily). Although not a main road it is a busy tourist thoroughfare and we were glad not to be riding it in summer. Already there were more than enough camper vans trundling along and barging past us on blind corners. We tried crossing the river once or twice in search of a viable track along the other bank, but without success.

In a car, you can add another dimension to the spectacle by tackling the hairpin roads that snake up to the *causse* at various points, making it possible to alternate between low road and high road with giddy views down into the gorge. The contrast between the landscapes is extreme, the *causse* windswept, sparse and often cold, the bottom of the gorge sheltered, lush and balmy – a different season altogether. We were quite happy on the low road.

The walls are impressive but it is not a dark or austere landscape. On the contrary, every spare patch of ground is taken up with an orchard or some vines. We were passing through at the right time of year for cherries, which are a Tarn speciality.

We left the road to inspect the small village of Ispagnac, formerly (pre-phylloxera) a wine village supplying consolation to the shivering inhabitants of mountainous Gévaudan. There are roses around every doorway and a pleasing thick-walled Romanesque church overlooks the boules pitch and Boulodrome café. The dimly lit golden interior (of the church, not the café) seemed perfectly conducive to meditation. Galaxy spent a long time inside – several minutes, in fact – and declared emphatically on emerging that he liked it very much "as a place of worship".

I wondered if there was something slightly pointed about this remark, his drift perhaps being that to judge a church on any other criterion, such as beauty or historic interest, is somehow missing the point. I suppose he is right. The remark has come up again a few times since then, he pronouncing for my heathen benefit on churches "as places of worship". Most of them compare unfavourably with Ispagnac.

There are three villages at road or valley junctions along the gorge: Ste-Enimie, La Malène and Le Rozier. Ste-Enimie is the pick of them, in our view, and the pick of its cluster of hotels and restaurants is the very friendly Auberge du Moulin, which had wet feet when I stayed there one rainy autumn night. It looks down on the water from a respectful height, and advisedly so, because flash floods can be extremely destructive in the confinement of this long narrow canyon. If the weather suggests there is any risk, don't park your donkey in the waterside car park. For a treat, the place to stay would be the Château de la Caze, midway between Ste-Enimie and La Malène, just below the village of St-Chély.

On a more leisurely cycling schedule it would be good to make room for a boat trip. La Malène is the traditional place for a guided cruise through the narrows (Les Détroits) courtesy of Les Bateliers; alternatively, there are numerous stony "beaches" with operators offering

St-Chély-de-Tarn

canoe hire and a lift back from a pre-ordained pick-up point further downstream.

After Le Rozier the valley opens up, and all is fruitful. The rains of the Cévennes had given way to sun and heat, and 16km short of Millau we decided we needed a rest. Stopping nowhere in particular beside a village called Boyne, G lay down on the grass and I wandered across the road to look at the window of a wine shop. It was closed, but a woman saw me loitering, jumped up from her day bed and opened the door.

"Don't worry," I said, "we aren't going to buy anything; you might as well go back to bed." Not at all: the woman wanted us inside. Fruits of the earth were there in abundance – nuts, cherries, vinegar, wine and combinations of the above: cherry vinegar, cherries in red wine, cherry, or walnut-flavoured aperitif wine... and if we weren't buying, at the very least we should agree to taste. It was a good rest. Le Domaine du Vieux Noyer: recommended, not as a place of worship, but as a place of refreshment.

And so to Millau, the glove box of France. The town won a place in my heart some years ago when I visited one of its last remaining glove manufacturers: Lavabre-Cadet.

In a high-ceilinged town house with distressed stucco and echoing floorboards, among designers, cutters, stretchers and stitchers, a man explained to me how the gloving industry grew up as a by-product of Roquefort cheese, which required lambs to be removed from their mothers at an extra-tender age and thus produced an abundant supply of extra-soft leather. The glover was proud of his *beau métier*. "I am my own master," he told me. "When the weather is good and there are mushrooms to be picked, I am free to go out and pick them." Thank the Lord, he had never had to work in a factory or a hypermarket.

Two weeks later a shining pair of soft black leather gloves arrived in the post. I have rarely worn them. They are the sort of gloves one sees dandyish characters in Oscar Wilde plays peel off, finger by finger, before helping themselves to a muffin, and such engagements do not feature prominently on my calendar. But I have managed not to lose the gloves, and if I ever take up cat-burgling they may come in useful.

I was conscious at the time that Millau's gloving days were numbered and that I should treasure the memory of my visit, as indeed I have. So it was a surprise to return to Millau and find the fashion glove business not dead at all but in full swing. Lavabre-Cadet is still there but the big name in town these days is Causse.

Founded in 1892, Causse now employs 30 craftsmen who make 20,000 pairs of gloves a year. A bright spark of the family has decided to push the brand and to that end has opened a Causse shop on the *très chic* Rue de Castiglione in Paris and a new Causse factory/showroom/shop in Millau. G and I enjoyed our visit so much he was almost moved to buy a pair for Mrs G, but in the end decided that gloves might be a less suitable present than a pair of espadrilles from Arcachon. This may have had something to do with the price.

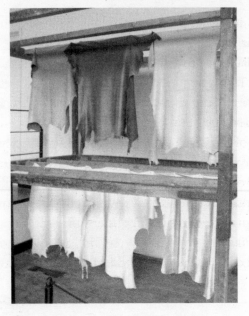

Causse – next stop, Rue de Castiglione

And Millau's revival may have something to do with the motorway, which crosses the Tarn a few miles west of town by means of a record-breaking bridge designed by, among others, Norman Foster. I say bridge. It is always called a viaduct, or *le Viaduc*, which sounds more impressive.

Le Viaduc is said to be world's tallest bridge, but (somehow) not the highest. It opened in 2004, forming the last link in the motorway from Clermont-Ferrand to Montpellier and putting Millau back on the map of the road from Paris to Spain.

In the run-up to construction plenty of doom mongers predicted that *le Viaduc* would be the death of Millau, but such is its fame, people make long detours to include it on their route.

Millau used to boast about its situation as a gateway to the Tarn gorge. Its proudest claim now is that it is close to *le Viaduc*: a gateway to the motorway. Only the most privileged houses and hotels can offer their visitors a view of the Tarn, but few are the Millavois who do not enjoy a view of *le Viaduc*. Our hotel, a colony of flimsy chalets on an unpleasantly steep hill above Millau Plage (a campsite) to the east of town, wasn't up to much, but it had an excellent view of Foster's bridge.

Thanks to *le Viaduc*, Millau is cool, or hot; a town to be reckoned with, and included in lists of places we should

Le Viaduc de Millau

be ashamed of not visiting. All of a sudden Millau is the best place in France for hang-gliding, as well as being a hot spot for climbing, via ferrata-ing, hiking, biking and cherries. Is Millau a brand? Quite possibly. Has Norman Foster's bridge fuelled the revival of the glove industry? I think it has.

We just missed Millau's *Fête du Vélo*, and were sorry not to be able to enter its "slow cycling race", the winner being he or she who completes the course in the longest time – presumably without stopping or going round in circles. This sounds rather fun, and we might have been quite competitive.

One brand that remains bigger than Millau is Roquefort, the blue sheep's cheese – blue cheese made from sheep's milk, that is – from the village of Roquefort-sur-Soulzon and its limestone caves, which were formed by the partial collapse of the Combalou plateau on the Causse du Larzac.

Pliny the Elder acquired the taste and 2011 marked the sexcentenary of Charles VI's confirmation of the rights of the villagers to ripen their creamy cheese. *Appellation contrôlée* status came later and fixed the rules of production. If the right Lacaune ewe hasn't grazed the correct field, and the curd hasn't been fertilised by the appropriate strain of *Penicilium roquefortii* and sat for three weeks in the designated cave followed by several months of slower maturation wrapped in silver paper in the fridge ... Roquefort, it ain't.

Production is controlled by seven companies, of which the largest is Société (64% of the market, five euros for a

cave tour). You won't find people selling *Roquefort fermier* beside the road. Variations of bacteria from cave to cave account for slight differences between the cheeses. Société has three: 1863 or Cave des Abeilles is the usual (or "classic") Roquefort, Cave des Templiers the strongest, Baragnaudes the creamiest and most complex.

Unfortunately for us cyclists, the 25km ride from Millau to Roquefort is mostly uphill. Rather than slog up there to visit the Combalou caves, Galaxy and I found a cheese specialist to bring some Roquefort down to Millau for us to taste there. He confirmed that the best thing to drink with Roquefort is a good Sauternes, but all we had was red Gaillac, so we drank that, and it was fine. On a worrying note, Roquefort, unlike Millau, may be going out of fashion. "Young people today want a milder, easier cheese," said the cheese expert. How depressing.

Millau to Ambialet: about 100km

Below Millau, the Tarn enters a more pastoral phase. Or so we thought, for most of the morning. After riding beneath the viaduct and not being hit by any

Orangina cans or fag packets jettisoned from a height of 270m, butterflies and rolling meadows were our companions. The village of Peyre looked down on us declaring itself to be one of "*les Plus Beaux Villages de France*" a title that fills me with suspicion, for no better reason than deep-veined scepticism. If I were to own up to my suspicion, which may be unfounded, it would have something to do with payment, and exchanging the cheerful mess of village life for shutters and front doors of conforming colour, neat window boxes and knick-knackeries selling pot pourri and scented candles.

St-Rome-de-Tarn stands on what guidebooks call an eminence – a hill, in other words – above the river. G decided to stay down below and swim while I slogged up the eminence to have a look at the village and its hotel, Les Raspes, which is a beautifully converted private schoolhouse with a swimming pool in its garden. The classroom makes a good dining room, and there is a river beach to wander down to, with boating and a waterfall. St-Rome must have been an enchanting place to go to school, and Les Raspes is a better hotel than anything on offer in Millau.

When the village clock struck one, I realised we had not bought our picnic. Looking at the map, I could not see any likely villages coming up and thought it would be prudent to buy sandwiches from the village café. This is an expensive approach to picnicking, and when I found him at the bridge, G seemed quite cross about it. "I was looking forward to a nice *plat du jour*," he said. The sandwiches were mine to carry and, if he had his way, they would be mine to eat.

If we thought we had left gorges and steep scenery behind, we were mistaken. Les Raspes du Tarn, as the section of the river between St-Rome and Brousse-le-Château is known, is as wild and shaggy as anything upstream, with the difference that there is no road at river level, but a succession of punishing ups and short downs, which in the early-afternoon heat took any remaining wind out of our sails.

We said at the outset that if ever we felt like walking up hills, we would. But dismounting is never less than a capitulation and is not a decision taken gladly. Pushing the thing up a hill is no fun, but when a walker overtakes you, or the speedometer suggests that one easily might, what is the point of struggling on?

I forget how many times we sped down to a dammed stretch of the river ("*Baignade Interdite*") only to have to toil back up another torrid hill. But it was more than once, and we were hot and hungry.

I kept suggesting a sandwich break, and G kept refusing, determined that around the next corner he would find vindication in the form of a tempting *plat du jour*. We were both getting a little tetchy, as happens when the fuel gauge nears empty.

Eventually he agreed to eat in a place beside the river with brambles and a dog barking at us from its tether outside an empty house. And inevitably, within minutes of moving on we came to a village with the perfect lunch spot: the Auberge du Truel, run by an old-car enthusiast from Dieppe whose prices are about as up to date as his TR3. He recognised in me, and I in him, a kindred Croc-wearer.

"*C'est les meilleurs pneus* (the best tyres), *n'est ce pas?*" he said, and I had to agree, keeping to myself any reservations I may have had about my sole mate's choice of white, with matching socks.

We treated ourselves to a huge ice cream and marvelled at the cost of living, *au Truel*: £30 per person per night, half-board, including wine and coffee. Galaxy did the maths and decided the Auberge du Truel would be much cheaper than living at home. "Do you mind if I move in?" he asked. Away from the tourist zone of the well-known gorges, this corner of France offers a rare combination of beautiful places and low prices.

We were closing in on Brousse-le-Château, another of the prettiest villages in France – and only a hardened churl could argue with that claim – but before that we had to survive the most terrifying experience yet to confront us: a tunnel.

It was on the D200 beside the Tarn below the village of Broquiès, and we would have plunged gaily into it had there not been a traffic light at the entrance, with a notice inviting cyclists to press a button on entering and leaving the tunnel. How quaint! We pressed the button, let a delivery van go ahead of us and set off behind it.

Moments later we were enveloped by a darkness more profoundly black than any night endured by Stevenson on one of his mountains. The tunnel was completely unlit. We couldn't see the road surface, the walls or the roof, only the delivery van's rapidly disappearing rear lights. Galaxy was in front, but I couldn't see him either. All my instincts wanted to stop, get off and walk, or scrabble around in the panniers for my lights, but then I really would have been in the dark. The only thing for it was to ride as fast as possible towards two pinpricks of red light, hoping not to collide with my friend, a pothole, or anything else. It was an Indiana Jones moment.

The map suggests that the tunnel is less than a kilometre long, but it felt like miles. At the end we collapsed beside the road, laughing stupidly like two baby turtles that have reached the sea against all odds. In Brousse-le-Château we awarded ourselves a cup of tea.

A rocky spur with castle ruins atop a tangle of old houses; a narrow cobbled bridge over a rushing stream; flowers in window boxes; tiny patches of vegetable garden. Brousse-le-Château is a picture. Take it, and move on.

An alternative approach would be to schedule a night there, in the Relays du Chasteau, which looks up at the narrow cobbled bridge and castle ruins. The name may be off-puttingly twee, but that's what you get in one of Les Plus Beaux Villages de France. And there is nothing else remotely twee about the hotel, which is quite simple and extremely cheap. If the ground-floor décor seems to take simple to the verge of basic, the reason may be frequent flooding. "The water doesn't usually rise higher than the ceiling," said Madame Sénégas, with equanimity. When the autumn storms break over the Cévennes, there is only so much the dams can do.

Ambialet is famous for its meander and the rocky peninsula it all but encircles: a geography textbook demonstration of the final stages of an oxbow lake in the making. Pity the poor trout, who must swim 6km for less than one hundred metres of progress.

Ambialet also has the Hôtel du Pont which is at least as good a reason to break a journey. Two centuries will soon have passed since a veteran of Napoleon's Russian campaign, Jean-Pierre Saysset, retired from active service to this grassy bank beside the Tarn and set up his son in the Hôtel du Pont. Seven generations later the Saysset family is still there – dozens of them, black-haired, busy and welcoming. It may have been the sixth generation when I first visited, and while a few details of the hotel have naturally been updated, its style and essential character have not changed a bit.

When the young generation takes over, it is only natural for the new incumbent or his pushy wife to want change: sack the cook, revamp the décor, open a spa, take the whole thing upmarket. At Ambialet this has not happened. The Hôtel du Pont knows its place – in the local community and the tourism firmament – and is happy there, and I hope future Saysset generations keep the faith. Any attempt to upgrade in a quest for stars and a bigger spending clientele would be, if not doomed, a great shame. My room had a writing desk in the window, looking out over the Tarn, and I can think of few places where I would rather spend time chewing a biro.

It was time to talk strategy. In my wisdom I had decided not to continue along the Tarn from Albi to the old abbey of Moissac, the confluence with the Garonne, and on to the sea; but instead had drawn a line northwards from Albi to rejoin the Lot – last seen at Le Bleymard – via Cordes.

Galaxy thought this diversion from the straight line was mad, but Albi and Cordes are two of every francophile's favourite places in the south-west, and in my mind they are inseparable, like apri and cot. Also, I liked the idea of the Lot (countrified) more than the Garonne (built up). The artists' village of St-Cirq-Lapopie, on the Lot, is another favourite place and by my reckoning any cyclist who knocks off Albi, Cordes and St-Cirq in a day, or even two days, has a full cup.

The problem had been finding a good place to spend the next night, Cordes being not quite far enough, St-Cirq-Lapopie a little too far. The Oustal del Barry is a beautiful hotel at Najac, but it would mean a diversion, and even in a car one notices the steepness of the hills around Najac. It is a typical problem for the cyclist who is a bit fussy about his choice of stopover. In the end I had opted for St-Cirq-Lapopie, and it meant a hard day's ride through hilly country. We could save more than an hour if we by-passed Albi.

"We can't do this trip and not visit Albi," said Galaxy. "The important thing is to have a plan, and stick to it." This was his plan. Leave early, make sure we leave Albi by 9.30, Cordes by 11.15, and so on, until, miraculously, we would reach St-Cirq-Lapopie at 6.30, in time for G to do his laundry, lie down on his bed and read his book for half an hour before springing into action with his

customary "I'll be the good-looking blond at the bar."
Good plan.

Ambialet to St-Cirq-Lapopie: about 125km

Unfortunately, the boy with the key to Modestine and
Mousse-Café's stable overslept and kept us pacing the
bridge for half an hour. Then, midway between Ambialet
and Albi – via a tiny road along the right bank, a gorgeous
country ride on a misty morning – Modestine started
playing up; something to do with a bracket. After a spell
of roadside tinkering, G declared that he needed to visit
a bike shop in Albi.

We crossed the Tarn at St-Juéry and pedalled through
dreary suburbs that seemed to go on for miles. But they
came up with a bike shop and it mended G's gears (no
charge). A mechanic, grim-faced as a vet who has bad
news about your very old Labrador, handed Modestine
carefully back to her owner with this gloomy pronounce-
ment: *"L'ensemble du vélo est très fatigué. À changer!"* (The bike's
knackered. Change it.) This was indeed a blow, and it
was in a sombre mood that we pedalled towards the city
centre and its famous ensemble of historic buildings.

Albi is a town of red brick. Houses, streets, cathedral,
archbishop's palace, bridge over the Tarn – all brick.
Even the buses are brick-coloured. Not London-bus red,
but warm dark pink, the colour of Petra. To the short-
stay visitor it all looks wonderfully harmonious, but one
might tire of Albi's bricks before very long.

The palace has a Toulouse-Lautrec museum, the little
Pigalle master being of noble Albigeois stock, and the

cathedral rises like a nuclear submarine surfacing in the Red Sea, the very image of the medieval church militant. Inside, it has a particularly gory Last Judgement mural and a beautiful gallery of late Gothic prophets and sexy sybils around the choir.

Galaxy took against the cathedral, "as a place of worship". We were so far behind his schedule, he was itching to be out of there and there was no point suggesting a tour of the choir (extra charge).

Cordes was still 25km away: 25km of a busier road than we were used to, starting with a steep hill – two arrows on the Michelin torture scale. The steep bit was mercifully short, and after that came a series of switch-backs. "What a lovely road..." said Galaxy, who was enjoying the sensation of making some progress at last, "... for someone in a fast car."

It was gone midday before we were seated in a café at the top of Cordes-sur-Ciel, to give the town its graphic but not entirely convincing full name, in front of two expensive glasses of rosé, dithering about lunch.

We had parked our bikes at the bottom and walked up through the citadel village by Cordes-style stairways to heaven. I don't, by the way, think it's possible to go on a French cycling tour and operate on the basis that panniers are likely to be stolen if left unattended for an hour. No doubt it does happen, but carrying them around is simply not practical. I would like to think the tempted passer-by might take a sniff and reconsider.

The Hostellerie du Vieux Cordes represented extreme temptation, with its seductive courtyard shaded by a tricentennial wisteria, and its giddy terrace suspended above hundreds of feet of air. "In an ideal world, this is where we would spend the night," said G. Midday is a perfectly good time to eat in France, but Galaxy's Law states that you must complete 60% of your miles before stopping for lunch, and we were nowhere near that.

We held the line, descended from heavenly Cordes unlunched and did not stop until we reached the Cistercian abbey of Beaulieu-en-Rouergue, not even for a swim in the Aveyron which we crossed and followed for a few hundred metres before continuing north.

Beaulieu is well named, a place of such spell-binding calm and loveliness, one could envy the monks their

Beaulieu-en-Rouergue

quiet life there, if there were any. The abbey was in decline before the Revolution brought the curtain down on its spiritual life. Its restored buildings now house a modern art museum, one of the best in the west.

Eventually, after several more hills and an absurd 91 kilometres of cycling before lunch, we reached the high ground of the Causse de Limogne, found a tree shading a patch of grass with a low wall to lean against, on the edge of a village (Puylagarde), and fell to the ground. It was so late, the shops had reopened for the evening. The spread was our usual: pâté, bread, cheese, melon, wine, not in that order.

From the pool in the garden on the other side of the wall we heard splashing and ladylike laughter. In a different version of this story, a beautiful encounter might have led who knows where, but in this version it didn't.

The *causses* are high limestone plateaux that occupy much of central south-western France, slashed by rivers such as the Dordogne, Lot and Tarn. In a landscape of scrubby oaks and low, lichen-covered walls of rough grey stone, we stopped at Limogne-de-Quercy, whose famous winter truffle markets interested us less than the ice cream counter at Le Galopin, before an exciting run down to the Lot at Cénevières. After a quick look at the château we sank into the river from a convenient slipway. The Lot moves slowly compared with the Tarn, and felt a bit slimy, but still good.

To describe St-Cirq-Lapopie's perch above this lazy river as an eminence does not do it justice. It clings to the side of a small mountain, in the shape of a cliff. "You never know," said G, "the Auberge du Sombral might be at the bottom." Alas, it is at the top.

Very few hotels would be worth pedalling up that hill for, but the Sombral is one of them. It was worth every painful revolution. The house is small and the family that runs it – a couple of a certain age and their daughter were the only members we saw, but the daughter has a *conjoint* in the kitchen – is modest and unassuming. But everything about the place breathes goodness and quality – furniture, fabrics, china, paintings… and food, naturally. This feeling, a kind of wholeness, is what drew people to the Lot and the Dordogne two generations ago. Surely it must be long lost beneath the tramp of beauty-spot tourism and expats? Not quite.

Father Sombral (I don't know the name) has retired from front-of-house duties and busies himself, like a monk illuminating a manuscript, extracting non-existent weeds from tiny patches of flower bed. The only place to store our bikes under cover was in his garden shed, a space of extreme confinement like everywhere else in this cliff village. Staying at St-Cirq-Lapopie is a bit like spending the night on a ledge of the Eiger. With permission, we manoeuvred our bikes and placed them carefully so as not to disturb any tools; and as usual Galaxy strung a bungee between the bikes to use as a washing line for his underwear.

In the morning, Father Sombral needed access to his place of work. I watched him dismantle the washing line, carry the bikes out into the street one at a time, take the utensils he needed, carry the bikes back into the shed,

St-Cirq-Lapopie

then carefully re-erect the washing line with its drapery exactly as before. He might have been replacing priceless china figurines after dusting the mantelpiece.

"Of course we can dry your clothes for you in the machine if you like," he told me afterwards. "But I think perhaps you prefer them like that, on the line." Galaxy's pants, a work of art.

St-Cirq-Lapopie to Puy-l'Evêque: about 85km

In the morning we had a date with the nearby cave paintings of Pech-Merle, on the other side of the river at Cabrerets.

Nearby... at... One says these things casually, thinking as a motorist, for whom the transfer from the Sombral to Pech-Merle would indeed be the work of a moment. On a bike it is the work of several moments and needs planning, because the number of visitors admitted to painted caves is strictly limited, and we had reserved spaces on the first tour of the day. Hurtle down to the Lot, 90 seconds flat. Rattle along the Lot Valley, ten minutes. Ride up the valley of the Célé as far as Cabrerets and proceed to the cave entrance. How long would that take?

Mother Sombral smiled and inclined her arm steeply towards the ceiling. As steep as that? Could Cro-Magnon not have chosen a cave by the river? Did the leaves of his prehistoric infusion not warn him about Galaxy's heart attack? The paintings are in point of fact not very high up, Mother Sombral explained in Cro-Magnon's defence. It was the entrance to the cave we had to worry about, and that is an invention of modern man.

Since we would later be returning to the Lot by the same route, we craftily left our panniers at a canoeing centre beside the main road and, unweighted, positively flew up the valley to Cabrerets. The remaining 3km ascent was less swift, but we checked in with a couple of minutes to spare, puffing and perspiring.

"It's cold in the cave," the guide told his assembled group, "make sure you have warm clothes." Now where were those jackets of ours? The guide peeled off one of his many layers and waved it in my direction. "Thanks very much," I said, reaching out, but it was not an offer of a loan, merely a demonstration of the item I needed, in case I had not understood the words *"vêtement"* and *"chaud"*.

Being underdressed in no way compromised our enjoyment of the hour-long tour of the cave, which

combines spectacular natural rock formations – concre-
tions, if you insist – and a dazzling gallery of wall
paintings and drawings, well presented by our guide,
who used his laser torch to point out the animal shapes
scratched, drawn and painted on the wall over a long
period (10,000-25,000 years ago).

A handprint in negative, as painted by every child in
nursery school. The head of a bear. A child's footprints
in the mud. Beautiful deer, horses and hairy mammoths.
The leopard-spotted horses, we now know, are not
imagined but faithful representations of spotted horses
that cantered and galloped in Cro-Magnon's garden. The
painter, possibly the child who left the footprints, mixed
the paint in the mouth, made an O with one hand and
spat/blew the paint through the O on to the wall. At
Pech-Merle the direct connection down the millennia is
extraordinarily strong.

At midday on a sunny Sunday the road along the Lot
was busier than we were used to. "I feel like a trout,"
said Galaxy. By one of those happy coincidences, on a
roundabout outside a riverside village called Vers we saw
a hotel sign: "La Truite Dorée". We glanced at the menu
and simultaneously thought, sod it. We may not have
ridden 60% or even 25% of our daily tread. But it was
Sunday, and on Sunday the French do lunch. *Cadurcien*
society was already streaming through the door in its
Sunday best, the brigade already looked rushed off its
feet and of course the dining room was fully booked.
What were we thinking? It was Sunday lunch, *amour de
Dieu*. But if we promised to eat quickly, Madame would

rig up a table for us outside. All was well, in the best of all possible worlds.

The 22-euro lunch menu included the desired trout, and eventually some wine, after a false start when G thought he was ordering a local wine, from the Lot Valley, and Madame Rushed-off-her-feet thought he wanted water (de l'eau).

The swimming pool in the garden next to our table exerted a strong gravitational pull, and the temptation to slide from coffee on to a chair beside it was intense. We nearly did but we didn't. Win some, lose some. The Golden Trout was a great victory.

The Lot snakes along in such an indecisive meandering way, if you tried it in a boat you wouldn't get anywhere fast. Grab hold of the river by its tail and pull, and it would stretch all the way to Italy.

Cahors fills one of the river's most dilatory meanders and it is the perfect town for a cycling tour. There is only one thing to see, and we can ride over it. It is the magnificent Pont Valentré, a fortified medieval bridge over the Lot. A viaduct, no less.

We did our best to find other things to see in Cahors, but the cathedral was only mildly rewarding and l'Amphithéâtre, which we diligently hunted down, turned out to be an underground car park.

From the west end of the bridge a signed cycling route led us out into Cahors wine country. The landscape improved after a long hill at Douelle and we were pottering happily through the vineyards when the rearguard noticed that Modestine's back wheel

Devil's Bridge

The construction of the Valentré Bridge took most of the 14th century, and gave rise to a popular story that may ring a bell with those who have had trouble with builders, or others who miss deadlines. Legend has it that the architect, in desperation, made a pact with the devil, who agreed to help him get the bridge finished in exchange for the architect's soul. But if the devil failed to execute any task, he would forfeit all rights of soul ownership. When the bridge was almost ready, the architect gave the devil a sieve and told him to fetch water from the well, for the masons to make the mortar for the last stone. The devil tried twenty times, but the sieve would not hold water. The devil admitted defeat but swore vengeance, and when the masons came to put the finishing touches to the central tower, the last stone kept coming unstuck during the night. The 19th-century restorer of the bridge added a carving of the devil pulling a stone from the top of the tower.

The early stages of the bridge's construction coincided with the pontificate of a notorious son of Cahors, Jacques Duèze, Pope John XXII, a man remembered as spectacularly depraved, even by the standards of the high Middle Ages. Based in the comfortable surroundings of Avignon, he opposed the spiritual Franciscans on the question of poverty – he was against it – and used his considerable ingenuity to raise vast sums for the Church and amass a personal fortune. This controversy is the background to Umberto Eco's novel *The Name of the Rose*.

Accused by his enemies of alchemy, fornication, adultery, incest, sodomy, simony, cannibalism and murder, John XXII is also held responsible for the fact that the papacy had to wait another six centuries before the name John was chosen again. But that may not have been his fault. (There was an anti-pope John XXIII in the 15th century.) A more balanced view may be that Pope John XXII was an energetic administrator and hard-liner who shared the plum jobs out among his Gascon friends, and in this way made enemies.

Le Pont Valentré, Cahors

was wobbling badly. Galaxy spotted a car maintenance enthusiast's garden with a garage open wide, and walked right in. It was all there: an inspection pit, a rack with every size of spanner neatly labelled and a Chippendales calendar.

The lady mechanic was working in her garden and told Galaxy to help himself to any tools and do what he liked with Modestine: jack her up, lie underneath her and tinker away to his heart's content, enjoying the sensual drip of 3-in-1 on his face. Even when he dropped a spanner (*clef*) down the drain, our hostess was not remotely put out, but whipped out a different spanner to dismantle the drain, *et voilà*. G made a stop-gap repair, mainly consisting of a dismantled back brake. It would see us to Puy-l'Evêque, the lady mechanic reckoned, no brakes front or rear being necessary for the short journey, which goes only one way.

Puy means hill and the Hôtel Bellevue is sited, as its name would suggest, on top.

The Bellevue's Christophe Lasmaries is one of the brightest chefs in all the Lot, and gives an oriental twist and spin to his creations in the hotel's colourful and panoramic Côté Lot restaurant. I say this because I have read it on good authority, seen the primary colours of the room and admired the view over the Lot. But I have not tasted the orientally spun creations, because I had foolishly booked us into this gourmet pilgrimage hotel on a Sunday evening when the Côté Lot restaurant is closed, as is the bistro (Côté Route). Duh. At least we had had a good lunch.

"You might get *steack frites* at the campsite," said Madame Lasmaries, a cool blonde who is in no imminent danger of developing a lined complexion from too much smiling. In our evening finery we felt like gentleman travellers, not scruffy cyclists, as we ambled down through the village and over the bridge. But the campsite diner was full, and we counted ourselves lucky, after nine on a Sunday evening, to find a restaurant open beside the river, if being forced to sup at a restaurant with *moules au foie gras* as its blackboard speciality can count as luck. I had the *canardburger* and to be fair it was not that bad.

Puy-l'Evêque to Duras: about 105km

On a lovely morning we followed the Lot through mist-veiled vineyards along the left bank as far as Fumel and then struck out across open country. It was a slightly giddy feeling, having no river to follow and no particular fixed points all the way to Sauternes, but it would not be true to say that our day was aimless: we had a hotel room booked at Duras.

Drawing a line across the map revealed a succession of villages with a lumpy theme: Monsempron, Monségur, Monflanquin, Montignac, Monbahus, Miramont. Hill villages one and all, poking up at regular intervals to punctuate hours of gently undulating fertility. In many regions of France, one has open fields to survey and grazing animals to commune with. In the south-west, it's wall-to-wall crops: maize, vines and masses of fruit. Cancon, *capitale de la noisette*. When the heat became too much, we paused on the side of the road and waited for the sprinkler to give us a cold shower.

The Haut Agenais is *bastide* country. In a process not unlike the planting of pine forest to stabilise the shifting sands of Les Landes, English and French monarchs planted new villages in defensible places, populated them with their supporters and gave them special privileges in an attempt to bolster their control of disputed territory. Much the prettiest of the *bastides* on our route was Monflanquin, a 13th-century foundation with an arcaded square that cries out for an artist's easel. Of the restaurants under the arches, which was it to be: Le Prince Noir or La Grappe de Raisins?

Neither: we were drawn instead to a hotel in a less picturesque spot, La Bastide des Oliviers, and would have settled for its 12.5-euro lunch menu had Galaxy's Law not been invoked, limiting our intake to a small drink. The waitress asked us where it was that we were going that so regrettably prevented us from staying for the lunch we so obviously needed. Had we been a little less sweaty and a lot younger, we might have imagined she was flirting with us. The Hostellerie des Ducs in Duras, we said. She was impressed. "You will be well received there: a beautiful swimming pool!" This was good news, because the mercury was nudging 30°C.

The lunch moment would come 20km and more than an hour later, at Monbahus, where the only man out and about in the heat was of course English. He told us in a very loud voice that if we wanted some lunch the only place in town was Maria's café and Maria would see us right.

Maria is Portuguese and possibly a bit deaf, or so we deduced from the fact that she had the TV tuned to a Portuguese channel at incredibly high volume. Could that explain why the Englishman – who obviously likes the ambience at Maria's – shouted at us? Are they all deaf shouters at Monbahus, from having to drink and swap gossip at deafening Maria's? Her ham baguette was all right, as far as it went, but as the focal point of our day it fell short. Emerging into the searing heat once more, we moved off and were glad to see the back of Monbahus, a loud and slightly deranged place.

Miramont was the next clinic for the limping Modestine, who had needed careful nursing through all the hill villages, with only the front brakes to hold her steady.

Thank goodness, Cycles Meca came up with a more specific and less terminal diagnosis for Modestine's malaise than Cycles Celestin of Albi's "*ensemble du vélo fatigué*". She had four broken spokes (*rayons*). G travels with a couple of spares taped to the frame, as every good cyclist should, and M Meca foraged around in his spare spoke bin and by some miracle pulled out two that fitted. And in no time at all he handed Modestine back to her owner with a smile, not a sad shake of the head. There: as good as new, or near enough. Galaxy lifted her up, turned the pedal and watched the back wheel spin free, fast and true. There would be no holding her now.

Although Duras does not have Mont in its name, it also stands at the top of a stiff climb, with a fine château looking out over the Gascon plain. We did not know it at the time, but the ascent to Duras was our last climb of the trip. A happy moment, if only we had been aware of it. The Hostellerie des Ducs was as good as our non-lunch waitress's word, with not only a lovely pool to collapse in, but also air-conditioning in the bedroom and a special parking facility for bicycles. We felt that we had found a true home.

L'Hostellerie is in fact the home of four generations of the Blanchet family, from Marcel, whose diplomas and membership certificates of this and that orotund gastronomic *confrérie* festoon the walls, to six-year-old Hugo, who has his sights set on a career as a cook. Hugo's grandfather (and Marcel's son) Jean-Francois looks after the *terrine de foie gras*.

I would be failing in my duty as a critic if I suggested that l'Hostellerie strikes no false notes. The background music – sounds of the 70s with Amazon pipes – was much too loud, the bedroom walls are abrasive enough to inflict a nasty graze and the mineral water provenance is North Wales or Denmark. G and I are not the most militant eco-warriors, but this does seem a waste of petrol.

The pluses greatly outweighed the minuses, however, and high on the list of pluses were *émincé de canard* and an inexpensive Côtes de Duras red recommended by Madame Blanchet.

Duras to Le Barp: about 105km

We had moved into serious wine country, and in the morning set off with Sauternes in our sights. Before crossing the Garonne at La Réole, we passed a pilgrim on the hard road from Vézelay, making his way towards the Garonne bridge, the Pyrenees and Spain. In heavy boots, beneath a heavy pack, he clumped through the warm morning. His journey looked hard work compared with our easy ride, but the pilgrim would wish it no other way. *Buen Camino!*

After passing La Réole's grassy airstrip we found the Canal du Midi towpath, and for 40 happy minutes followed it, up or down the canal to its source, or possibly its mouth; to its end, at any rate, where a last (or first) lock overlooks the Garonne.

A nearby village shop sold a Bordeaux *clairet*, and we bought it for our picnic out of historical curiosity, *clairet* being the old Bordeaux wine word that gave us "claret". It was a light rosé and we didn't think much of it. Lunch was a hurried affair, because we had a hot date at Château d'Yquem.

Is Yquem the greatest of all wines? The château is certainly outstanding and no one who has seen a picture of it would have any trouble picking it out from afar, riding the crest of its 189 hectares of priceless manicured vineyards and surveying the neatly combed Sauternes landscape with magnificent hauteur. It would in fact be advisable to memorise an image of the château, because there are no road signs to Yquem that we could find, and the map – our map, at least – made it not at all clear from which side to approach. This should not be taken to indicate that Yquem is in any way unwelcoming. On the contrary, if you ask nicely and give a reasonable amount of notice, they are pleased to receive visitors.

"Yes, we are aware that there is an abundance of road signs to every other château around here," a woman explained when we finally penetrated Yquem's defences, pushing our bikes up a rough track between the vines

Yquem

and puffing into the courtyard only fifteen minutes late, which is pretty good by our standards. "But as soon as we put one up, someone steals it."

The Bordelais are a posh crowd, and our guide Anne wore a smart claret-coloured suit and spoke the language of Racine with cut-glass precision. A leading lady on the boards of the Comédie Française could not have done better, but it was not clear enough for one half of the Belgian couple with whom we shared our visit; her husband had to translate Anne's beautiful words into a porridgey Flemish spittle that she could understand. It seemed a violation, like translating Mozart into rap.

Many good things come to those who wait, and Anne made us wait for a taste of the hallowed nectar. Through spotless cellars filled with immaculate barrels we walked, absorbing much historical and technical detail about grape varietals, fossilised oyster beds, peculiarities of terroir and the noble rot. Through many stages the quantity is reduced and reduced, in a quest for concentrated quality. The vines are cut low and the grapes allowed to shrink, until one plant produces one precious glass of wine. All six tasters – four men and two women – must agree that it is worthy of the great name, if the wine is not to be sold off on the cheap as mere Sauternes.

At last we came to the holy of holies, the tasting room. A bottle of 2007 stood on the counter. Anne opened it, and poured. Not a communion-sized sip with a wafer, but a glass of generous proportion. Anne invited us to find hints of mango, passion fruit, vanilla and honey. There was another taste that came through strongly: money.

"The top red wines always fetch more than top vins liquoreux," Anne said bitterly. "It's just pudding wine prejudice. Please don't call it a pudding wine! You should try it with Stilton, or foie gras, or Roquefort, or lobster – or a simple gâteau basque." Almost anything, in fact... "except chocolate. Quelle horreur!"

After the rarefied thrill of Yquem, Sauternes itself seemed a dull village with expensive wine shops and tea rooms trading on the name.

From there we moved quickly – which is to say at our usual sluggish pace, but it did not take long – into the great forest of pine trees that covers the south-western corner of France, from Bordeaux to Bayonne: the Landes. This region is in my mind forever associated with a truly horrible novel I had to read at school, *Thérèse Desqueyroux*. If not one of the most depressing books ever written, it is in my experience certainly the most depressing ever read – all oppressive heat, maddening mosquitos and screaming cicadas. Exactly like the Landes on a sweltering afternoon of unseasonal *canicule*, in fact.

We made our way as quickly as possible to the crossroads village of Le Barp, where the low-slung hotel Le Résinier had just what we needed: a pool, a colourful and comfortable bedroom and a very good supper. The atmosphere is young, laid-back and relaxed, with a hint of South Seas exoticism that suits the Landes perfectly.

Le Barp to Arcachon: about 30km

The Landes is unlike the rest of France in that it seems to have no history, although of course it does. Medieval pilgrims dreaded their crossing of this region of malarial marshes and unbridled piracy. Shifting sand dunes soon buried any churches they erected.

In the 19th century the pine forest was planted to stabilise and drain the land, and allow economic life to take root. It still has the new-world feeling of a raw country where pioneers stake their claim, clear their patch, build a little house and plant some subsistence crops. Oil rigs bob up and down to hypnotic effect. The houses are low and have no view. You can't see the sea when you get there, because a great barrier of sand dunes hides it. It is not just that the Landes is like nowhere else in France – any region can claim that. The Landes is like nowhere.

Because it is so different, the Landes is not without interest. It has its own wildlife, and its own folklore: a memory of peasants on stilts, tapping the bark of pine trees for resin. There are *landais* costumes, *landais* clogs and bloodless *landais* bull-fights. Little rivers (*courants*), almost uniquely clear and free of pollution, trickle secretly through the woods towards the ocean, where, blocked by the mountain of sand, they make lakes. Only one of these lakes is open to the ocean: the vast Arcachon Basin, full of oysters and bird life. In the Leyre Delta – the word gives the basin its due – Le Teich ornithological park is one of the bird-watching destinations of Europe.

The unique *landais* way of life is quite fascinating in its way, and well presented at the Marquèze Ecomuseum. "The fauna of the Landes is very rich," I was told. "But it is mostly small, shy and nocturnal." Not recommended for a safari holiday.

With so much forest, safe bathing in the lakes and hundreds of kilometres of unbroken sand, the Landes is a great place for camping, canoeing and surfing. And cycling?

Theoretically, yes. The Landes is flat and empty, with long stretches of cycle piste. I am told that the local cyclist likes nothing better of a Sunday than to take a train south (to Sabres, typically) and spend the day riding back through the forest. Combined canoeing and cycling excursions are possible too. Galaxy and I found one of these cycle pistes and followed a longish stretch of it on our way from Le Barp to the Bassin d'Arcachon at Le Teich. It was flat and straight and monotonous. But then, the roads through the Landes are like that and at least the piste had no cars on it. We felt that our taste of the Landes – a late-afternoon ride from Sauternes, an overnight stay in a really good little hotel and a short morning ride to Arcachon – was just about right. A little of the Landes goes a long way.

After lunch in the bird reserve cafeteria at Le Teich (excellent), we followed a rough path around the perimeter of the reserve, looking out for godwits, squacco herons, Napoleon's gulls and black-winged stilts, and closed in on Arcachon.

Our hotel was in the middle of town, but we rode on through, as far as the garden hotels and smart villas of Pyla-sur-Mer which, unlike Arcachon, looks out to the open sea. Galaxy had the memory of a romantic adventure from his gadabout youth to revisit, and the opposite number turned out to be none other than his future bride.

Le Teich bird reserve

He could not identify the hotel with 100% certainty, or was not willing to, but the search brought us to the most elegant beach bar-restaurant (and the most expensive beer) on the Atlantic Coast: La Co(o)rniche, at the shoulder of Europe's biggest sand hill, the mighty Dune du Pilat (103m). Don't ask me what the brackets are for. Cool niche would make sense, because it is one.

From the bar we found a staircase down to the water, walked along to the beach at the foot of the great dune, stripped off – in my case among the concrete blocks of the sea wall – and had our long-anticipated swim in the Atlantic. It was a fine way to end a hot day and a long ride, or would have been, if a sandal had not slipped from my grasp and disappeared between the blocks of concrete. It might have been a crevasse in an Alpine glacier, for all the hope I had of recovering the missing shoe. I tiptoed back to terra firma, glad to be still in possession of shorts, camera, wallet and train tickets.

Dune du Pilat

The semi-barefoot ride back to Arcachon was not my idea of comfort-zone cycling. Fortunately, the Cabane d'Aiguillon – known to all simply as La Cabane – is one of Arcachon's less elegant bars, an oyster farmer's wharf near the Pointe de l'Aiguillon. It took my blood-stained hopalong appearance in its stride and may be the best place in the world for oysters and Entre Deux Mers at sundown – well worth the considerable effort of finding it.

We rounded off the day with a feast of seafood Chez Pierre, looking across the bay from Arcachon's beautiful *Front de Mer*. There was something about the evening sky that suggested a change in the weather.

Above the breakfast buffet at the Hôtel de la Plage hovered a small cloud, in the form of a pair of espadrilles for Mrs G. Would it be the rubber-soled pair (6 euros) from E Leclerc or "*cousus main*" (hand-stitched, 16 euros) from the fashion boutique on the Boulevard de la Plage? I think we all knew G would make the right decision in the end, and we also suspected it would take several changes of heart and a last-minute dash when we ought to have been on our way to the station.

Emerging from Montparnasse station to face the tumult of the Parisian afternoon, I am ashamed to admit – as a onetime Paris resident – I had not the faintest idea which way to turn. It was the moment G had been waiting for, to whip out our old friend his compass and follow its magnetic nose to the Gare du Nord.

The TGV moved slowly through the northern suburbs, beneath the cheerful outline of Sacré Coeur and past

St-Denis before throwing off the shackles and acceler-ating away from Parc Astérix. As we raced towards the Channel, the weather took a turn for the worse. We asked if our train to Fréthun was by any chance continuing to Calais Ville, but it wasn't.

The road from Fréthun station to Calais starts off in a northerly direction. With a 40-knot westerly howling across it, and a stream of cars and trucks hurrying past in no mood to leave wobble room, it was no place for a cyclist. Sucked this way and blown that way as each truck lumbered by, we fought for balance and endured a frightening few minutes: as bad, in its way, as the tunnel below Broquiès. Then we came to a roundabout, turned right, and the gale blew us to Calais in double-quick time. We were late, as usual, and in grave danger of missing our ferry. But there was no need to worry. The gale had made a mess of the schedules, and we had more than an hour to cool our heels on the quay, shivering in the cold evening behind a concrete pillar. The heat of Aquitaine was a distant memory.

———————

Hotels (with restaurants unless stated)
* = cheap, ***** = expensive

***   Calais, Meurice
      www.hotel-meurice.fr   0033 321345703
*   Le Bleymard, La Remise
      www.hotel-laremise.com   0033 466486580

***   Cocurès, La Lozerette
www.lalozerette.com   0033 466450604

**   Ste-Enimie, Auberge du Moulin
www.aubergedumoulin.free.fr   0033 466485308

****   La Malène, Château de La Caze
www.chateaudelacaze.com   0033 466485101

***   Millau, Le Château de Creissels
www.chateau-de-creissels.com   0033 565601659

**   St-Rome-de-Tarn, Les Raspes   0033 565581144

*   Le Truel, Auberge du Truel   0033 565464298

*   Brousse-le-Château, Le Relays du Chasteau
www.le-relays-du-chasteau.com   0033 565994015

**   Ambialet, Hotel du Pont
www.hotel-du-pont.fr   0033 563553207

***   Cordes, Hostellerie du Vieux Cordes
www.vieuxcordes.fr   0033 563537920

***   St-Cirq-Lapopie, Le Sombral
www.lesombral.com   0033 565312608

**   Vers, la Truite Dorée
www.latruitedoree.fr   0033 565314151

***   Puy-L'Evêque, Le Bellevue
www.hotelbellevue-puyleveque.com   0033 565360660

**   Monflanquin, La Bastide des Oliviers   0033 553364001

***   Duras, L'Hostellerie des Ducs
www.hostellerieducs-duras.com   0033 553837458

***   Le Barp, Le Résinier
www.leresinier.com   0033 556886007

***   Arcachon, Hotel de la Plage (B&B)
www.hotelarcachon.com   0033 556830623

*****   Pyla-sur-Mer, La Co(o)rniche
www.lacoorniche-pyla.com   0033 556227211

Restaurants
***   Calais, Le Channel   0033 321344230

****   Arcachon, Chez Pierre   0033 556225294

**   Arcachon, La Cabane de l'Aiguillon   0033 556548820 / 0033 686579242

Information
Nord/Pas-de-Calais   www.northernfrance-tourism.com

Auvergne   www.auvergne-tourisme.info

Languedoc-Roussillon   www.sunfrance.com

Midi-Pyrénées   www.tourisme-midi-pyrenees.com

Aquitaine   www.tourisme-aquitaine.fr

Ferries (Dover/Calais): P&O   www.poferries.com

ROUTE 4

THE WAY? NO WAY

Biarritz to La Charité-sur-Loire (about 885km)
June 2011

END
La Charité
sur Loire

Noirlac

Orsan

La Châtre
Aigurande

Bénévent
L'Abbaye

Limoges
St Léonard
de Noblat

Châlus

St Jean de Côle
Sorges

Périgueux

Vergt

Bergerac

Villeréal

Monflanquin
Villeneuve sur Lot

Agen
Nérac

mont de
Marsan

Labastide d'Armagnac

Biarritz
Amou

START
St Palais

St Jean
Pied de Port

From 2500 in the 1980s, the number of pilgrims arriving in Santiago de Compostela each year has risen to 100,000. In 2010, the last *Année Jacquaire*, when St James's Day falls on a Sunday and pilgrims are granted a full pardon for all their sins instead of the usual one-third remission, the number reached 300,000.

And the reason for this explosion in the popularity of the pilgrimage? Unemployment, spiritual crisis, boredom? "There are 300,000 reasons," said Claude from the Friends of St Jacques in Mont-de-Marsan, when I put the question to him at the end of a hard day's ride from the foot of the Pyrenees. *"Chacun a son pélerinage à lui."* Everyone makes his own Way. This is a mantra of the Compostela pilgrimage.

I was reassured to hear it, because our approach to the pilgrimage was slightly unorthodox: we were not going to Compostela or even towards it. We were doing half the pilgrimage, backwards, and I did not want anyone to think we were not taking it seriously or trying to pass ourselves off as pilgrims – as travellers have been known to do, in order to enjoy pilgrim privileges and con their way to Heaven. One popular trick is to park the car a mile from the hostel, shoulder a heavy pack and walk from there, arriving with an exaggerated display of exhaustion.

"I made the pilgrimage myself recently," Claude continued, "not for religious reasons, since I am not really a churchgoer... or even a believer in any mean-ingful sense. But my partner was ill, and I needed to make sense of my life."

This unsolicited and rather intimate disclosure caught me off guard. Had I met Claude out in the country on an 800-mile walk, I might have kept the conversational ball in play. But at the end of the cycling day, with beer and a bath uppermost in my weary mind, I lacked the journalistic instincts to ask the obvious follow-up question: "And did you?"

Make sense of life? We might as well try to make sense of the ocean. Life does not make sense: it just is, until it isn't; and we have to put up with it, until we don't. Unless we are blessed with faith. Religion makes sense of life, and perhaps the need to make sense of life is the best way to make sense of religion.

For the true pilgrim, the point of the pilgrimage is remission of sins: a fast track to paradise. Rome, Jerusalem and Compostela wipe the slate clean. From the agnostic perspective, the point of the Compostela pilgrimage, and the reason it should be done on foot, is to meet people. Meeting people may not make sense of your life, but if you are lucky it can make your life more interesting.

"Do it on your own," says a friend who made the pilgrimage when he retired a few years ago. "And if your other half insists on accompanying you, make sure you walk at least half an hour apart, or you won't meet anyone."

Many people do it, or part of it, as a walking holiday through beautiful parts of the country well supplied with cheap places to stay, full of interesting people with stories to tell and keen to tell them. Opening up, it seems, is the whole point of the pilgrimage. If they derive spiritual nourishment from it, so much the better. "I set out as a walker, and finished as a pilgrim," is another pilgrimage mantra. We set out as cyclists, travelling in the wrong direction, so we would have our work cut out to meet anybody.

St James and Compostela

The Apostle James, son of Zebedee, brother of John, may have evangelised Spain cAD40. A miraculous appearance of the Virgin to James beside the Ebro is venerated at Zaragoza. In AD44 he was beheaded at Jaffa, and his body, pushed out to sea in a rudderless boat, was miraculously transported to Galicia, where it washed up on the Bay of Padron and was enveloped in rock. Another version says his disciples took the body there. The relics were discovered at the time of King Alfonso II (791-842), when a hermit, Pelayo, saw mysterious brightness over a wood, and heard angelic songs. Pelayo told the bishop, who visited the location and found a stone sepulchre with three corpses: St James and two disciples. King Alfonso was the first pilgrim, guided at night by the Milky Way, which the Spanish call *el Camino de Santiago*. Miracles included the raising of a drowned knight, who emerged from the sea covered in shells. Hence the cockle shell motif.

The actress Shirley MacLaine who made the pilgrimage in 1994 and wrote *The Camino, a Spiritual Journey* afterwards, develops the Milky Way theory, that the Camino derives spiritual energy from being directly below the Milky Way, its stars being the saints in heaven. "The Camino is said to be a correlative Earth ley line to the Milky Way; as above, so below," she writes. During her journey the actress relived experiences from her previous lives.

Cycling has the papal blessing for pilgrimage purposes, and this is understandable. The Church is broad, and keen to encourage as many pilgrims as possible. Pilgrims on horseback have always qualified, so why not on bicycles? But it does not seem the right "Way" to me, and my friend agrees. I can imagine how annoying it must be for pilgrims – real ones, on foot – to have their quiet peregrination buzzed by swarms of mountain-bikers.

I am not a pilgrim. I am simply following one of the French routes across the country as a cycling holiday, out of historical interest and because it will take me through beautiful parts of France. The pilgrimage did so much to shape France – its great churches and abbeys, its structures of hospitality – the obligation to include one of the routes is *incontournable*.

One aspect of the pilgrimage I had not considered, until Claude mentioned it, is the different routes' varying ethnic extraction. The Paris route is the traditional English way, with a variation that involves travelling by ship to Soulac-sur-Mer, at the mouth of the Garonne, and continuing from there. The Vézelay starting point attracts pilgrims from Scandinavia and the Low Countries; those from Germany, Poland, the Alpine regions and Eastern Europe go via Le Puy, and Italians take the sunny option through Provence.

Our choice of route was dictated not by racial preference or prejudice, but the practicalities as I saw them. The Via Tolosana from Arles crosses the Pyrenees at the Col du Somport, which is a remote place to start or finish a journey. The other three routes cross the mountains near St-Jean-Pied-de-Port, a short train ride from Bayonne (change for Paris and St Pancras) and the surfing beaches of Biarritz.

The Le Puy route through the wilds of the Massif Central looked a bit steep, while the Paris route – down through western France via Tours and Bordeaux – would be too flat and involve long days in the pine forests of the Landes.

That left the Via Lemovicensis – from Vézelay, via Limoges and Périgueux. It would take us through a rural heartland of France, hilly but not mountainous; quiet country regions including Burgundy, the Berry, the Limousin, the Dordogne and the Lot.

We would skip the section between Vézelay and the Loire, having already cycled that. Vézelay has no train station, so it does not work as a start or finish.

Remembering the lesson learned on the first day of my first ride, I was inclined to reverse the journey for a better chance of having a south-westerly breeze behind us. But who would do a reverse pilgrimage? Egamirglip hardly trips off the tongue. And would the ocean not be the most fitting end – the pilgrimage as life's journey, the ocean as eternity?

"Presumably pilgrims had to go home afterwards," said my prospective fellow non-pilgrim, Paul. Brilliant. Sometimes the simplest insight can unlock the most intractable problem. Biarritz to Burgundy would be our non-pilgrimage.

Aymeric Picaud – Iter pro peregrinis ad Compostellam

River crossings were among the many challenges facing the medieval pilgrim, as graphically evoked in the Poitevin monk Aymeric Picaud's *Iter pro peregrinis ad Compostellam*, written in the mid-12th century. A practical guide for pilgrims, it is often described as the earliest tourist guidebook. Pausanias and Dionysius Periegetes might disagree.

Dividing the journey into 13 stages, Picaud describes relics and shrines, promoting some and trashing others as bogus, and includes colourful descriptions of the local inhabitants. His fellow Poitevins come out of this well, and the general message to pilgrims is that the further they travel, the more barbarous are the people they will encounter. If the author's idea was to promote the pilgrimage, he does not make it sound all that inviting.

Saint-Jean-de-Sorde, near the confluence of the Gave de Pau and Gave d'Oloron, was a hazardous crossing: *The boatmen extort a coin whether you can afford it or not, four if you have a horse. The boat is small, made from a single tree, not suitable for horses, and you can easily end up in the water. The best option is to take the horse by the bridle and let it swim behind the boat. The boatmen have been known to collect the fares, fill the boat so full it capsizes, and steal the possessions of the drowned pilgrims.* A toll bridge was erected in 1289.

Poitou: *Brave warriors, experts with bows and arrows and spears who won't take a backward step in battle. Athletic, good-looking men who know how to dress well and talk sense. Generous and hospitable.*

The Landes: *A desolate region without supplies or springs. Villages are rare, although there is honey, grain and wild boar. In summer, protect your face from the huge flies that infest the place. Watch your step, or you'll sink to your knees in quicksand.*

Gascony: *Garrulous, loathsome, lascivious, poorly-dressed, greedy drunks. Skilled warriors, good hospitality to the poor. All drink from one cup, then sprawl out together on rotten straw. White bread and the best and reddest wine. Forests, streams, meadows and healthy fountains.*

The Basque Country: *Forest savages whose hard faces and strange language strike terror into the heart. They come at pilgrims with weapons, demand an exorbitant fee and beat those who refuse.*

Beyond the Pyrenees worse was in store. The Navarrese waited beside a poisonous river sharpening their knives to skin the pilgrims' dead horses. They despised the French, and like the Basques, would kill them for a mess of pottage.

Navarre: *Malicious, dark, hostile-looking, crooked, perverse, treacherous, corrupt, untrustworthy, sex-obsessed, drunk, violent, wild, savage, damned, horrible, argumentative. Disgusting eating and drinking habits. All feed with their hands from one pot and swill from one cup, like pigs or dogs. Their language sounds like a dog barking. Men and women expose themselves to each other. The Navarrese have sex with farm animals, and put a lock on the backsides of their mules and horses.*

In a number of ways this trip was quite different from the other five. I had a different companion, for a start. Galaxy was building a new house and declared himself unavailable. Paul was considering a long bike ride and had his eyes on the Black Sea, but a pilgrimage route would do.

Paul took on board the no-Lycra approach, although this was not a stipulation. People can wear what they like and in my Crocs I am not exactly a fashion statement on wheels. He asked if it would be all right if he raised money for charity. Of course it would. Galaxy and I decided early on not to go down the charity route: we did not feel comfortable asking our friends to cough up for our fun. But Paul was not sure he would enjoy the ride, and looking back, I am not sure he did, although he was gracious enough to say at the end: "If you ask me again, I might consider it."

The change of personnel brought a new dynamic. I was now the senior cyclist and looked to for advice. "Should I go to an evening class on puncture repair?" Paul emailed.

The checklist I sent him in response to a later email may be worth including, although most of the things on it are pretty obvious. On the unsupported journey, simplicity is the key and minimum weight the goal. If anyone asked me how best to prepare for a cycling tour, I would say: lose weight, and you will have less to carry over the hills. You will lose more weight while cycling, and that may help you over the hills awaiting you on return.

More serious cyclists will point out that my checklist excludes many essential repair tools. I had all that stuff, naturally. Duplication is wasteful. Before one of our trips Galaxy rang up to ask if I planned to take toothpaste.

"Yes, I thought I might," I replied, wondering if my friend was trying to tell me something about my breath. "I took toothpaste last time, didn't I?"

"If you do, I won't," said Galaxy.

He has since relaxed the shared toothpaste rule.

Dear Paul

I think we went through most of the essentials on the phone

To pack:

A cycling outfit – Galaxy takes only one shirt, and washes it as he goes along

An evening outfit, inc shoes

A waterproof jacket

Jersey? (G and I always take, but never wear)

Swimming things

Whatever you need to sleep in – rooms always seem to be hot

Suncream

Sunglasses, hat

Washing things

Baby powder (lots)

A book

Medicines/plasters/Savlon TCP etc

Camera

Phone

Batterychargers for phone/camera etc – these take up lots of room. G doesn't bring any and reckons

his phone and camera will last the week if
managed carefully. They don't.
Puncture repair kit, pump, inner tube, lights
Bungee – useful as a washing line in the bathroom
    overnight and during lunch
Bike lock

   One thing we didn't discuss – how to carry valu-
   ables when we leave the bikes and panniers. My
   solution is baggy shorts with lots of pockets so
   I can carry everything of value – camera, wallet,
   rail tickets, passport etc – with me at all times.
   G has a bumbag he's very proud of, but I think
   that's just for medicines such as the spray I have
   to spray under his tongue if he has another heart
   attack.

   I will try to bring picnic stuff – a knife and a corkscrew and some plastic cups. Please practise your
   melon-cutting skills. It is one of G's many accom-
   plishments, and it will be missed.
   Adam

Another difference: on this trip we were travelling
less far, more quickly and in greater comfort than
other travellers whose paths we crossed – pilgrims.
We soon began to feel rather ashamed of ourselves
for our cushy assignment, although this route was
the longest and probably the most arduous of any
in this collection, averaging 110km a day, mostly
through hills.

Without Galaxy to impose his route-plotting rigour, the itinerary began to meander ominously and grow longer. "Not to worry," said Paul. All the more money for Fairbridge (his charity).

Paul's wife designed a marketing flier. "Paul will be cycling 300 miles through France and his friend is hoping to write a book about it," it said. "Paul will be cycling 500 miles, more like," I informed her crisply. "And his friend is not hoping to write a book. He is writing it." I was well into the outline by this stage. I had missed the point. By underestimating the distance, your flier encourages sponsors to pledge a higher donation per mile; and you clobber them for more afterwards.

A few words about my new companion. Many would describe Paul as a conventional person. He sounds quite old-school – the good cheer of Brian Johnston meets the sewellness of Brian Sewell – and he has always worked in finance in the usual way (perhaps explaining the crafty approach to fund-raising). His style could not be described as outlandish.

Yet like many superficially conventional people, he is his own man, and does things in his own way, at his own speed, which is... considered. Paul's initials are MPH, but no one has ever accused him of breaking the speed limit.

He is a well-built man, bushy of eyebrow and big of foot (size 13). I noticed the feet on the first motoring holiday we shared. Paul's feet are so wide, he has a tendency to hit all the pedals at once. He'd be a hopeless concert pianist.

Rather than waste these great feet, Paul uses them for emphasis, especially when driving. This can be unsettling. Instead of moving forward at a steady pace, the car lurches along in a series of leaps following the rhythm of his conversation. It can easily happen, when Paul spots a view he likes and says, "Hey! What a great view!" that he hits the brakes, or accelerates hard, or both.

For all these reasons, and because he is interested in everything and a great enthusiast, I was confident he would be an excellent cycling companion, and so it turned out. "Are you sure you can find toe straps big enough for your feet?" I asked. He found some.

Paul bought himself a bicycle and did 40-mile training rides, against the Scottish wind. He was ready.

Beneath his shorts, Paul wore protective long pants with an elasticated grip around the thigh. Unfortunately, pedalling created friction between the elastic strip and the outer shorts. The fact that he was usually in the wrong gear, pedalling much too fast downhill in a vain attempt to keep up with himself, accentuated the problem.

By the first evening he had nasty blisters and after two days the blisters had become suppurating welts. Paul's ingenious solution was to use the bungee as a belt and braces, hooking up his shorts and elasticated pants to expose his St Sebastian-like wounds to the curative fresh air. The resulting loincloth billowed like a large black nappy.

When provoked Paul is more than capable of decisive action. On a Sicilian camping holiday in the late 1970s he became so fed up with children pestering him to buy biros and chewing gum, he decided to take pre-emptive steps and spent the rest of the trip waving his guide-book at unsuspecting Sicilians and yelling "*cinque mille lire! cinque mille lire! E? E?*" The irony fell on stony ground.

I have mentioned the barking-dog problem in another context. All over rural France, it is a great annoyance for the passing cyclist, and I was not at all surprised, after our Sicilian experience, that my friend adopted a policy of pre-emptive barking when he saw a reinforced garden fence of the sort that betrays the presence of a noisy dog.

"*Ouah! Ouah!*" he went, as French dogs do, as we approached a country homestead in the Béarn.

But there was no dog, only a family enjoying a quiet lunch in the garden. They may have been surprised to see a fancy dress St Sebastian with size 13 feet cycling past in a black nappy yelping like the Old Berkshire foxhounds in full cry. "*Pardon!*" Paul shouted with a cheery wave. When not being pestered by Sicilian children he is the most polite person I have ever met.

One thing I would say: Paul does not drink enough. Galaxy and I are pretty well matched on the wine consumption front, level-pegging gulp for gulp as we race through the bottle. It is the equitable way. Paul put me to shame with his modest intake. I found this quite surprising, not because I have any reason to suspect him of being a big drinker, but because he consumed gallons of water during the day, with only an absurdly small bottle clipped to the bicycle frame.

"Why don't you get a bigger bottle?" I asked. "We might spend less time stopping for 'ten minutes' (make that half an hour) at cafés asking for a refill." But the bottle was a parting gift from his daughter before the trip and could not be changed.

Why does Paul waste his thirst in this way, I wondered irritably, when he could slake it so much more enjoyably at lunchtime? Not that I have anything against water, which I like as much as the next man. But I do like something with it.

The wine problem may have been my fault, I now realise, because Paul is so scrupulously polite, he never asks for the bottle to be passed to him or a glass poured.

"Would you like some wine?" Paul will say, if desperate for a drink. Or, "Can I top you up?"

"Thanks very much," I reply, and hold out my glass; or, "No. As you can see my glass is completely full."

"So it is," says Paul. "How silly of me." His glass remains empty.

Galaxy and I have tried this system, and I have tried to introduce it at home. But without Paul it simply doesn't work. In fact, it doesn't work with Paul.

As well as being a bad wine waiter, I fear I was not the most sympathetic companion. Apart from a small-scale tourist office handout of Aquitaine, Paul did not bring a map, and he was forever asking, "How far to the next place? Five miles?"

"More," I would say, because it usually was more, and because I was inexplicably – unforgivably – beginning to find the persistent questioning slightly irksome. Now that I reread my packing-list email, I see I did not put "map" on it. He probably thought he was not meant to bring one.

He being mapless, it was obviously vital that we stick together. But an element of pace-making was important if we were to get where we wanted to go, and this often meant we became separated. Lost in my dreams about whatever it is middle-aged male cyclists dream about, I would pedal along for miles without noticing that I was on my own.

Then my phone would ring. "Awfully sorry," Paul would say. "It's Paul."

"I know. Where are you?"

"I don't know. I've just passed some cows in a field."

"Keep going, will you?"

"Which way?"

"I don't know, it depends where you are." And so it went on. We found each other in the end.

Paul lives in Edinburgh and met me at St Pancras. The Eurostar journey to Paris went smoothly until it came to reclaiming our bikes at the Gare du Nord. EuroDespatch had printed the wrong details and the guard made us traipse all the way round the station, trotting behind his buggy like a pair of naughty schoolboys, to his office.

I sensed a ploy to get some money out of us, but once the guard had taken a photocopy of our passports, he handed the bikes over with a smile and an apology.

"If we can cycle through Paris we can do anything!" Paul had written in one of his emails. As we had plenty of time between trains, I thought I might treat Paul to a short sightseeing tour. Instead of heading south down our old friend the Boulevard de Magenta, I aimed west, past the fleshpots of Pigalle: Place Clichy, the Moulin Rouge and up the Boulevard de Courcelles, leaving the elegance of the Parc Monceau to our left.

"What's the strategy?" asked Paul, when we sat at a traffic light preparing to attack a busy road junction. "Stick out the left arm and go for it?" That's about it.

Following the helpful cycle lanes, the ride was not difficult. As we climbed the Avenue de Wagram, however, I did begin to wonder: what will they have done about the Etoile?

Nothing, is the answer. The cycle lanes vanished: for the navigation of the stormy seas of the Etoile, the cyclist is on his own. From Wagram to the Champs-Elysées is 270 degrees of the full 360: eight streams of traffic must be crossed, and let me recite them: Mac-Mahon, Carnot, Grande Armée, Foch, Victor Hugo, Kléber, Iéna, Marceau. What a clarion call!

Resolutely we stuck out our left arms, and our right arms (not at the same time). We went for it, and we got round.

As every cyclist knows, the Champs-Elysées is the climax of the Tour de France. Up and down they hurtle from Concorde to the Etoile and back for however many laps it is.

Many cyclists may fail to appreciate that the Champs-Elysées is actually quite a rough ride: cobbled, not to put too fine a point on it. If I ever meet Mark Cavendish I will ask him: what are they like, at 50kph? Uncomfortable, I bet.

I had planned to ride to the Place de la Concorde and cross the Seine there. But the Champs-Elysées was so damned juddery, we turned off between the Grand and Petit Palais and took a smoother route.

We had originally entertained the idea of catching the sleeper to Biarritz. About once every five years I forget the discomfort of my last couchette and am prepared to give it another go, in view of the practical advantages: dinner in Paris, early-morning arrival, no hotel required.

On this occasion we were spared. SNCF took so long to decide if and when the sleeper would run, we gave up waiting and booked our Eurostar + evening TGV combination instead. This seems to be a frequent problem with the night train: by the time it is confirmed and bookable, the cost of the alternatives has gone up. And until it appears on the schedule, there is always the risk that it won't.

We reached Biarritz at nearly midnight and were surprised by the long hairpin descent from the station to the centre of the resort. In a few hours we would be coming back up. The Hôtel Mercure was waiting up for us and is well placed for a stroll under the stars on the Grande Plage. A Croc paddle almost became a swim, body surf and replacement camera and telephone shopping opportunity when a wave of unexpected violence swept in from the deep, as they do.

Biarritz to St-Jean-Pied-de-Port: about 65km

Most pilgrims take the train from Bayonne to St-Jean-Pied-de-Port (about 90 minutes) and start the pilgrimage there. We decided to cycle it because (a) we had spent all the previous day on the train and cycling was what we were here for; (b) the Basque Country is one of the prettiest of all French regions, not to be wasted on a train ride; (c) we were not pilgrims; and (d) St-Jean would be a good target for lunch.

Leaving Biarritz was a struggle. We made neither head nor tail of the directions the Mercure gave us for a route to the road to Cambo, avoiding the hairpins, and merely found different hairpins and the only French non-motorway road I have yet encountered from which cyclists are actually banned. Galaxy and I have been known to treat road signs as advisory, but in this case Paul and I decided to obey, hauled our bikes on to the bank and walked back to the roundabout. It was painful to admit defeat at such an early stage but in the circumstances, which included much hooting and angry truck driver's fist-waving, I think it was the right decision. Paul has a family, and his wife had asked me to keep him out of trouble. Where had I led him? The Colosseum was a poodle parlour compared with that road.

To revert to point (b) above: the Basque Country. Country and *pays* are not always the same thing, but the Pays Basque really is a country apart, with its own language (impenetrable), landscape (greener than green), games (pelota), village architecture (neater than neat, with window boxes and red-and-white striped houses), and clothing (espadrilles and berets).

The Basques have their own cuisine, which has its admirers, and their politics. Separatism is not an issue on the French side of the border. Being so small, the Pays Basque is ideal for cycling. In a car you hardly have time to take it in before you come out the other side thinking: is that it? On our bikes we had all day to enjoy it.

In a Basque village, you could be in no other region. That said, the main road up the Nive Valley to Cambo and St-Jean-Pied-de-Port is busy and not all that interesting. Nor are there easy alternative routes. This is the disadvantage of hilly regions. Back roads are always longer and tougher.

We made a couple of diversions. Cambo involved an extra hill and would have been worth it only if we had had more time to look around and the desire to visit the house and museum dedicated to the poet/playwright Edmond Rostand, who lived there in the early 1900s.

Itxassou

The second diversion was more successful, leaving the road to inspect the church at Itxassou, typically Basque with its wooden galleries, and drink good coffee at the beautiful Hôtel du Chêne which stands beside the church – just the place for a gathering of the clans after a first communion or for a Sunday lunch. We were only sorry to be there in mid-morning, not midday, or better still, for the night.

A tiny road follows the left bank of the Nive for 10km to Bidarray, with gradient arrows. Would it be too tough for us? "Bidarray? No problem," said the chef. "It's easy, Bidarray. Women do it." We drank up and made ready for the road. "One thing," said the *patronne*. "*Le chef, il a fait le Mont Ventoux.*" When asking advice about cycle routes, know your adviser.

Passing a natural rock arch known as Le Pas de Roland (Roland's Step, associated with an episode in the Chanson de Roland), the road winds prettily along the tight valley with many ups and downs, steep but not long. Paul had to dismount for them or so I assumed from the inordinate time it took us to reach Bidarray. "Is there a problem?" I asked. "I can't quite get the hang of changing gear," he replied.

After a brief demonstration of the basic principles of the gear change, in all its aspects or as many as I could think of, our progress improved. We rejoined the main road, which climbs not steeply but steadily to St-Jean in its mountain niche. *Port* in the Pyrenees means pass, and St-Jean sits at the foot of the pass of Roncevaux, scene of the action in the Chanson de Roland. A fortress village defending the road to Spain, St-Jean has steep mountains on three sides, but is not itself high – only about 200m.

The earlier hills had taken their toll, however, and as we closed slowly in on St-Jean, our stops for water became increasingly frequent. By the end we were spending more time at a standstill than on the move, and water was pouring off Paul faster than he could drink it. I was stung on the head by a vicious Pyrenean super-hornet, and that didn't help.

It was all a bit worrying and the situation called for leadership, which is not something that comes naturally to me. I could think of only one course of action: lunch.

Les Pyrénées is an old coaching inn outside the walls of the citadel. It has been in the hands of the Arrambide family for ever. They started it, have built it up and cherished it. Les Pyrénées has a Michelin star, which since my visit to Troisgros I now call a *macaron*. It looked expensive and inviting, a real treat.

Madame Arrambide, whom I found rather a handful – to pronounce, not handle – was stationed at the front desk. The Arrambides may run one of the best hotels in south-west France but they do not give themselves airs.

"Would you like a shower before lunch?" she asked, having got the measure of our predicament, and perhaps caught a whiff on the breeze as the electronic door slid open to admit us.

"Yes, I would," said Paul. "Very much." He went out to his bike to collect a change of clothes and was led away to his own suite. I sat down to read a magazine, and as I was still sitting there 20 minutes later, I asked Madame Arrambide if I could have a look around. She summoned a senior member of the clan, perhaps the most senior, whom I am tempted to call Adambide, to be my guide.

Although clearly in the advanced grip of a most painful affliction, Adambide showed me every room in the house – except one suite, where a tremendous Niagara-like roar told us Paul was either dead or still busy in the shower – and the beautiful garden with its inviting pool. Adambide was particularly keen to show me the more modern rooms, which come with an impressive array of buttons to press, to adjust the temperature, open the shutters without getting out of bed, turn on the TV while in the bath etc. "I adore the new technology," Adambide told me proudly, "but some guests prefer an older style of room." Les Pyrénées, very sensibly, has both. I was worried about Paul, but the guide would not abbreviate the tour.

Eventually Paul reappeared. "That was the best shower of my life," he said.

Lunch started with *langoustines*, followed by *lasagne au foie gras* and carried on in a similar vein. It was fabulous. The waiter kept urging us to have more wine – our afternoon ride to St-Palais was downhill all the way, apparently: the merest bagatelle – and was so attentive, Paul had enough to drink for once. But in my friend's memory-lunch at Les Pyrénées is eclipsed by the shower. That shower may not have saved his life, but it made sense of his lunch.

A Dutchman rolled up on a highly technical bicycle with wing mirrors and sat-nav on the butterfly-shaped handle-bar, checked in to Les Pyrénées and looked slightly put out to discover that he was not the only gastro-cyclist on the road. He had come 1600km from home in two weeks and had another 800 to go. "I am a free man!" he exclaimed. "Alone is the best way!"

Leaving Paul's laundry drying on our bikes outside the front door of Les Pyrénées, we walked off our lunch in the old village, which is a beauty: walled, pink and cobbled. On the Rue de la Citadelle, which is lined by pilgrimage hostels, two old ladies were actually sitting

Two pilgrims, one bed

on chairs in an open doorway, watching people, as old ladies are supposed to do. It is something I never thought I would see. "Pilgrims? Not like they used to be," one of them told me for nothing. "Not so respectful. Today's pilgrim doesn't cross himself."

"You can be as rude about them as you like," I said. "We're not pilgrims."

Next to the old ladies we found the pilgrimage office and put our heads inside, out of interest. And before I knew it, Paul had put a few euros in the box, helped himself to two cockle shells to hang on the back of our bikes and exchanged a few more euros for two pilgrim's log books, complete with a message from Pope Jean Paul XXII and an invitation to all religious, civil, military and police authorities to assist "this pilgrim who is undertaking the traditional peregrination towards Compostela in the manner of pilgrims of old."

Pilgrim's progress

St-Jean-Pied-de-Port – Pilgrim's rest

St-Jean-Pied-de-Port is a pilgrimage conveyor belt, and the volume of traffic marks a step change from the relatively quiet routes and small hostels in France, to the busy Camino Francés through Spain. Three of the four routes through France converge at St-Jean, and to their pilgrims are added the many who start their walk to Compostela at St-Jean. In their hundreds they arrive on the afternoon train from Bayonne, head for the Accueil sorting house and set off on the eight-hour walk to Roncevaux the next morning. For the rest of the day the village ticks over on non-pilgrimage tourism. The busiest months are May and September – not too hot – when 1600 pilgrims a week come through St-Jean.

The *Année Jacquaire* (Holy Year) of 2010 saw pilgrim arrivals at Compostela double, but fewer than usual came through St-Jean: while "religious" pilgrims were attracted by the special offer of a plenary indulgence, 'tourist' pilgrims were put off by the prospect of extra crowds. Pilgrims have to walk only the last 100km or cycle the last 200km to Compostela for their pilgrimage to be recognised by the Church.

"I thought you had to apply to the bishop for those," I said. Apparently not.

"Did you mention that we're going to La Charité-sur-Loire, not Compostela?"

"He didn't seem to mind. Excellent chap."

We started as cyclists, and finished lunch as pilgrims. Lunch has much to answer for.

St-Jean-Pied-de-Port to St-Palais: about 33km

Fortunately, the run down to St-Palais was as easy as our waiter had promised. We stopped to visit the old village of Ostabat, which was once to pilgrims what the Bass Rock is to gannets. Three major routes converged there at the foot of the Pyrenees, and Ostabat had one well-appointed hostel for rich pilgrims in the upper village, and another for the poor, below. Of all this there is not much to see now. St-Jean has taken over from it.

"Leave your bikes in the trinquet," we were told on reaching our hotel on the square in St-Palais, one of the main towns of the Basque Country and a centre of espadrille production.

Michel Berrogain

We had selected the hotel because it has its own indoor pelota court (*trinquet*) and imagined ourselves playing pelota before breakfast. But although it is on the hotel premises, the court belongs to the town sports club. After watching some locals knock a ball about with what looked like standard issue beach bats, we met former local, national and possibly world champion Michel Berrogain, who retired from serious pelota long ago to run a shop in St-Palais. "It's the sort of thing players always do," he said. "You don't have to pass exams."

M Berrogain is one of those sublimely gifted individuals who excel at any sport. As a *rugbyman* he flew down the wing for Bayonne and, after taking up tennis at 40, in no time found himself national veterans champion at Roland Garros, swapping the racket to play forehand off both sides with equal ease. Why not? Once you have learned to play *main nue* (bare hand) pelota you can play all kinds, he says, and what is tennis if not dumbed-down pelota?

At the core of every Basque village stand the church, the cemetery and the *fronton* (a gabled wall that makes an outdoor court). As a five-year-old he spent his Sunday mornings with all the other boys, hitting a ball against the *fronton* with his bare hands.

"The Basques are traditionalists," he tells us. "They have *la Messe, le chant, le folklore et la pelote.*" When they go abroad, as they do, for they are seafarers, they take their pelota with them and stick together. Different forms of the game flourish in different countries, but in the Basque

Country it's all about *la main nue*. "It's the cheapest and simplest way, and it's how children start in the villages." Pelota is a village game, a popular game. Women do not play bare-handed – only with the bat, *la pala*.

As well as chanting and churchgoing, the Basques like to bet. All the serious money goes on *main nue* pelota, so this is what the top professionals play. Yes, there is match-fixing, and some professionals have grown rich from it. Not Berrogain. "I played to win."

Pelota is quite bewildering in all its variations: with and without bats, gloves and pelican's beak gauntlets; against the wall, face to face across the net, indoor, outdoor, singles, doubles and team games. There are different balls too, stitched differently for different bounces and spins.

Outsiders are often drawn to the version using the biggest gauntlet – *grand chistera*. The scoop generates power, the ball flies at high speed, and players may be up to 70 metres from the wall. But the skill level is relatively low, the weapon is expensive, and few Basques bother with it. A good *main nue* player can send the ball 40 metres. Now that takes skill.

"How far are you going today?" Berrogain asks. Mont-de-Marsan, I reply. "*Cent kilometres, c'est bien*. Nice and relaxed. Stay cool, that's important."

Paul wasn't sure he would.

St-Palais to Mont-de-Marsan: about 105km

After an unsuccessful attempt to buy espadrilles from the St-Palais market – size 48 being a rare request – it was a hilly day through the Béarn, with the pre-emptive dog-barking incident already referred to.

At an early stage I trialled the idea of letting Paul go first, with instructions to follow signs to Sauveterre, where we were to cross the Gave d'Oloron. This back-fired when by bad luck the key turning came upon us midway down a fast hill. Paul shot past and raced on down the hill deaf to my howling. I reminded myself of Roland in the rearguard at Roncevaux, blowing his brains out trying to call for help. I had no trumpet, and Charlemagne had better hearing than Paul.

We crossed the Gave d'Oloron somewhere else and made our way back to the Gave de Pau at Bellocq, where a wine-tasting shop near the bridge set us up nicely for our first picnic. The Hôtel le Trinquet had not changed my view of Basque cuisine, but I needed no converting to Jurançon and Madiran, honest wines of character and value which are among the top attractions of this corner of France. The weather was mixed, with a fine drizzle to keep us cool.

At the beginning of the day or towards the end of its eve, you look at the map of the task ahead and a place name jumps out as a target lunch stop. As the morning progresses, it forces its way to the front of the queue, growing in importance until it takes on pilgrimage status and drowns out all other names. These places will always have a special resonance for me. Amou! How much further?

At last, on arrive. Sometimes the place is a terrible disappointment, with absolutely nothing to offer, and you just have to keep going.

By luck a sunny interval coincided with our arrival at Amou, and we found picnic tables and shading plane trees beside the Luy de Béarn, next to the *Arènes* where Amou holds its *courses landaises*. Paul rolled out his well-rehearsed melon-cutting, and we felt that we had finally got into our stride.

Across the road from the *Arènes*, Amou's Hotel de Commerce stands on its Place de la Poste, a name and address spelling *vieille France* country hospitality. A *magret aux pommes* came past us as we sipped our coffee, and on the strength of it I am confident the Hôtel de Commerce will not let you down, as a lunch stop or overnight halt.

La course landaise

The Chalosse region (around Amou) is the cradle of the landais style of bull-fighting known as *la course landaise*. Bull-fight is a misnomer because the animals involved are nimble Landais cows, which are not put to death but return to their pastures after the event and "fight" up to 20 times a year over a ten year career, during which they learn to anticipate the moves of the *écarteurs* (dodgers) and *sauteurs* (jumpers). The latter are gymnasts who perform standing jumps over the charging animal, with their ankles tied and feet in a beret, or running vaults such as the *saut de l'ange*, strikingly similar to Cretan bull-leaping depicted on Minoan vases. For much more about the *course landaise*, including a listing of events *see* www.courselandaise.org

Some of the rooms have half-baths, and you don't get much more *vieille France* than that.

Say Mont-de-Marsan, and most French people think fighter pilots and Mirage combat jets. Claude, of Mont-de-Marsan's Association Jacquaire (already introduced), was keen to highlight the town's role as capital of the Landes, a *département* which counts more kilometres of pilgrimage route than any other – 470km, including many shrines of interest on the routes from Tours, Vézelay and Le Puy, all of which pass through.

The shrine we should have seen was the Benedictine abbey of St-Sever, which overlooks the Adour and the flat Landes forest from its terrace, the last bastion of the

Chalosse hills, 15km south of Mont-de-Marsan. But we had failed to stop, rolling blindly down to the river to complete our approach to Mont-de-Marsan by the main road. This was the most unpleasant bit of riding of the entire trip: a fast road with a succession of roundabouts and a marginal cycling gutter that stopped about 200m short of each roundabout, forcing us out into the truck lane.

Claude took us to see the town's pilgrimage hostel. Mont-de-Marsan is not a tourist honeypot and its refuge is not the busiest. We found three pilgrims having supper there, doing their best to open up and make sense of each other's lives or their own, but as an advertisement for the pilgrimage as a travelling chatroom they were not entirely convincing. Payment for accommodation is at the pilgrim's discretion.

Our hotel was Le Richelieu, a town-centre hotel of some standing, with an excellent restaurant that attracts many local Montois diners. The maître d' introduced us to Tursan (all three colours available) as an alternative to Madiran and Jurançon, and to *poitrine de canette* as an alternative to *magret*; both were good tips. The pastis cake pudding was a triumph.

In other respects there was something rather sad about the Richelieu, we thought. The main staircase was roped off, the public rooms were a bit faded, and at least one key member of staff seemed thoroughly depressed. It did not seem appropriate to seek an explanation.

Mont-de-Marsan to Brax: about 110km

From Mont-de-Marsan we made a slow start. Nothing unusual in that: we started slowly every day, continued at no great lick, and crawled over the day's finishing line. But from Mont-de-Marsan we started more slowly – even more slowly – than usual. Paul had lost his sunglasses. Protective eyewear of no great sophistication is required, I find: just a shield to kill the glare and keep the bugs out. I advised him to try the *maison de la presse*, where racks of cheap sunglasses are usually to be found; or a chemist. But only an optician would do. There are several on the Rue Gambetta.

"*Je veux…*" Paul informed the first optician in his most considered way, "*… des lunettes.*" As a man of the world, he speaks French. But his delivery is not quickfire.

"*Oui, monsieur.*"

"*Pour… voir.*"

"*Eh, oui, monsieur. Les lunettes, c'est pour voir.*"

"*Le soleil.*"

"*Ah! Les lunettes de soleil.*"

"*Oui.*"

The assistant pointed out a large rack of sunglasses, starting price 65 euros. "Heavens!" said Paul. "*Moins cher?*"

"*Non, monsieur.*"

Paul found this evidence of Montois extravagance incredible. "Amazing!" he said.

A few doors further up the road we found another optician. "I'll just try in here. Won't take a second."

Eventually there were no more opticians left on the Rue Gambetta for Paul to try, but some considerable time later he found a sports shop in a warehouse on the edge of town and emerged in triumph, waving his snazzy new sunglasses – 25 euros. We found a bicycle piste and took it, a little on the late side but pleased with our morning's work.

Not every cycle piste we rode comes warmly recommended, but Mont-de-Marsan to Villeneuve-de-Marsan was one of the best: end-to-end pleasure and a good surface, on a raised embankment that had the look of an old railway line, with Landes forest to the left and farms to the right. The piste continues to Labastide-d'Armagnac, and beyond, but the surface deteriorated after Villeneuve and we went back to the road.

The Armagnac was new to me, and it was a pleasure to ride through. In early June all was colour and warm productivity, with gardeners busy in the *potager*. Roadside advertisements champion local wine and *floc*

Labastide-d'Armagnac

de Gascogne, a fortified aperitif similar in concept to *pineau des Charentes.*

In a better-known region Labastide-d'Armagnac would be swarming with camera-touting trippers, but we were the only ones. Its beautiful arcaded square has a couple of simple bar-restaurants under the arches, an Armagnac-tasting shop, and that's about it.

The waitress in La Giulietta was impressively knowledgeable and hugely proud of her *pays.* She snatched the map and underlined all the historic houses, Gallo-Roman villas and *villages incontournables* – Eauze, Fourcès, Poudenas – that we absolutely had to see on our way to Agen. It was a friendly thought, but more than enough road lay ahead of us, without extra stops and excursions.

One landmark not included on the waitress's itinerary was a small roadside chapel near Labastide: Notre Dame des Cyclistes. This chapel, which is old but not a building of particular intrinsic beauty, was discovered, overgrown, by a cycling churchman in 1958 and the following year Pope John authorized its rededication to "*la petite reine*". Its official patroness is Notre Dame de la Visitation – the confident suggestion being that when Mary hastened through the Palestine countryside on a charitable mission to help her cousin Elizabeth, she would have gone by bike had one been available. The chapel marked the start of a Tour de France stage in July 1989. Many Tour heroes attended and left jerseys and trophies, as did the race leader Greg Lemond, who went on to win the Tour by six seconds and spoke of his victory as a miracle.

Notre Dame des Cyclistes is a popular halt for cycling pilgrims on their way to Compostela – 1000km to go, in 12 easy stages of 85km a day, according to the chaplain, who has made the journey six times. The website (www.notredamedescyclistes.net) is nothing if not comprehensive and includes the words and music of a special chant, "*Les Etapes de la Joie*", which may help on the way up the hill.

Always skirting the Landes forest, our ride from Labastide took us through the Pays d'Albret, passing lovely villages such as Pouzenas and Mézin, capital of the wine cork and perhaps feeling the pinch. Its simple hotel-restaurant, Le Relais de Gascogne, delayed us, and we would not have minded staying longer.

Not wishing to be lured into puerile joke-making, we steered clear of the town of Condom-sur-Baise and crossed the river – which preserves its modesty by means of a strategically placed accent to make it La Baïse – at Nérac, home town of the blond bombshell of French pop, Michel Polnareff (of "*La Poupée Qui Fait Non*" and other classics), and perhaps prouder still of its connections with the Albret family, which gave France its favourite Renaissance monarch, Henri IV, *le Vert-Galant* (woman-iser). Henri lived and loved at Nérac in his youth and a gardener's daughter, Fleurette, is said to have drowned herself in the Baïse for want of his *baisers*.

Henri was baptised (in Jurançon wine and garlic) a Protestant, but converted to Catholicism when the crown was his for the taking, perhaps uttering the famous throwaway line: "Paris is well worth a mass". He oversaw a period of rare religious tolerance and expressed the wish that all his French subjects should be able to eat *poule au pot* on Sundays.

These fine sentiments did not spare Henri IV the assassin's blade, nor did his mortal remains survive the Revolution undisturbed. The royal body was flung in a ditch and separated from its head, which went missing for two centuries before being rediscovered in a collec-tor's attic in 2010 and identified via distinguishing features that included wounds from an earlier assassina-tion attempt, a pierced ear and bad teeth. Henri IV's head will soon resume its place at St-Denis.

Protestant Nérac suffered in the 17th century but enough of the Albret château survives to be worth a look, and the old town around the river is a treat. The punning tea room Au Goût Thé is recommended. It stands beside a statue of the 18th-century scientist Jacques de Romas, father of the lightning conductor. By tethering a kite to the ground with a wire thread, and launching it at a thundercloud, Romas demonstrated the electric properties of lightning. Impressive explosions resulted.

The holiday barges had tied up for the night before we finally rode down to the Canal du Midi from the walled village of Bruch and pedalled wearily along the towpath to the Hôtel Colombier de Touron in Brax, 6km west of Agen.

We had reached the great orchard of France, overlooked by the vineyards that would give us Buzet *rouge* with supper. Agen is famous for rugby and prunes, and all along the river and out in the hills of the Lot-et-Garonne *département* the fruiting is prodigious – pears, apples, peaches, kiwis, plums… If it's a fruit, Lot-et-Garonne grows it. Touraine usually stakes claim to the title Garden of France, and it is true, the Agenais is less like a pretty garden, with lambs gambolling beneath the apple trees, than a fruit factory. This is serious agriculture. Prune production is 50,000 tons a year.

With much cooing at dawn from the dovecote in the garden, our little hotel was quite the romantic charmer. The style note might be a bit sugary for some tastes, but after the sombre mood at Le Richelieu a little sweetness and gaiety did not go amiss.

"They are called *pruneaux d'Agen*," our hotelier volunteered. "But Villeneuve-sur-Lot is where they come from. Agen was just the port used for transporting them. The plums on the tree are shaped like rugby balls. Have you noticed?" Or is the rugby ball plum-shaped? Until then I had always thought of it as more of a honeydew melon, but perhaps there is room for divergence on this.

Brax to Bergerac: about 105km

In the morning we set off for Villeneuve – starting, as we had finished, on the towpath; orchards to the left, narrowboats to the right. It made a pleasant Agen by-pass, with the excitement of crossing the Garonne by a canal bridge before heading for the fruitful hills of the Haut Agenais. The Agen bridge is a few years older than its counterpart over the Loire at Briare, and a few metres shorter. Of greater relevance to the cyclist, its towpaths are much narrower. Riding along with panniers bulging, I felt like a fattie in a narrow doorway. And an opposing cyclist coming towards me, as if in a joust, was an anxious moment: breathe in, and no wobbling. Just made it.

Villeneuve, where the prunes come from, is steeply overlooked by the walled village of Pujols, a lofty belvedere about 120m above the Lot. We approached from the south by a pretty back road, overtaken by a steady stream of Sunday cyclists cruising past with a sympathetic "bonjour". However you approach Pujols, there is no escaping the steep ascent. The square and old streets of the village are all of a medieval piece, and we found them filled with sellers and buyers of local produce, souvenirs and trash. The crush made it almost impossible to move. The Pentecostal holiday was probably not the best time to appreciate Pujols.

Half a mile away, the Hôtel des Chênes shares the beauty of the setting, and is spared the crowds. It has a garden and pool and the restaurant next door, La Toque Blanche, is its dining room under separate ownership. This would be a relaxing place to stay … but for the hill climb required to get there.

After our long swerve to the east – instituted for the questionable purpose of avoiding a flatter and shorter ride through the pine forest – we were finally aiming north. The halfway house of the day was the hill village of Monflanquin and its hotel La Bastide des Oliviers, where Galaxy and I had called in a few weeks before. We had been just too early for lunch on that occasion. Leaving Villeneuve at half past midday, there was a risk we would be just too late.

I telephoned home requesting an internet search to supply me with the phone number of La Bastide des Oliviers. It arrived by text soon afterwards, and in a triumph of 21st-century global interconnectivity I reserved a table. When I said we were making our way by bike from Villeneuve-sur-Lot and hoped to arrive within the hour, the woman I was talking to said she thought I was being a little optimistic. After some minutes at cross-purposes, it dawned on me that there might be more than one Bastide des Oliviers in France. The one I had booked was in St-Tropez.

Rather than reconnect with home, where my lunch in France does not always enjoy the "drop-everything" status I feel it deserves, we decided the best policy would be to cycle as fast as we could and hope for the best.

I urged Paul on like a jockey on an old dobbin at a point-to-point. "Come on! Lunch! Look – it's only just over there." This was a savage cut, because Monflanquin on its hill was clearly visible from the top of the first climb out of Villeneuve, and it was still an hour's ride away. "I'll go ahead and get a table," I told Paul eventually. "See you there; you can't miss it." That sounded optimistic too.

The last hill up to Monflanquin is cruelly steep, and when Paul entered in his customary muck sweat, all conversation in the bistro section of La Bastide des Oliviers ceased.

The waitress looked at me as an RSPCA operative might look at the owner of a damaged dog. "Are you sure he's all right?" she asked.

"Don't worry," I said. "He always looks like that at lunchtime. He'll perk up, you'll see." (I decided not to mention the idea of a shower. We were due in Bergerac before nightfall.)

I think we both agreed lunch was worth hurrying for – not a banquet, but value fuel (including stomach of something), well prepared: three-course Sunday lunch, 15 euros; house *réserve* 8 euros.

"Bergerac? What are you worried about?" a waiter wanted to know. "Forty-five kilometres, two hours." In our dreams.

Monflanquin is one of many 13th-century "new town" *bastides* in the area, and well worth a stroll. An hour later we had another fine example to inspect: Villeréal, with an old market hall and fortress-church that used to have a drawbridge and remains an obvious power house.

And so we approached the Dordogne, with its golden villages, small parcels of tobacco cultivation, prehistoric cave paintings, estate agents and Kirstie Allsopp.

The Dordogne runs east–west; we were travelling south-north, and could not really afford the luxury of riding along it. Where to cross this beloved stream, of all French rivers the closest to our British hearts? Further west the hills would be less steep; further east the countryside and the villages prettier. The orthodox pilgrimage halt is Ste-Foy-la-Grande, another 13th-century *bastide*, but I opted for Bergerac, mainly out of a desire to revisit its tobacco museum which I remembered as an example of the best kind of socio-historic regional museum: focused, fascinating and fun.

The museum occupies a beautiful 17th-century *hôtel* (palatial town house) on the well-named Place du Feu at the heart of old Bergerac, and presents the history well, with a collection of pipes and snuff boxes. But I felt there was something slightly unloved about the museum, an echo perhaps of the depressed state of the Dordogne tobacco industry. It was a bit like relighting yesterday's unfinished *gitane*: good, but not as good as before.

The decline is especially marked for *tabac brun*, the leaf of that key accessory of radical chic and juvenile *je-m'en-foutisme*, the *gauloise*. At six euros a pack, posing has become expensive. Who can be bothered, frankly? Dark *gauloises* and *gitanes* have not been produced in France since

2005. No one with a feeling for French culture could take pleasure in this.

Bergerac's museum rover ticket also covers its Musée de la Batellerie et du Vin, dedicated to the town's former life as a trading port and its continuing role as the centre of the local wine trade. This might be a better bet.

Over the weekend of *Pentecôte* we found riverside Bergerac *en fête*, with boat trips and bungee-jumping on the banks of the Dordogne. Remembering our pilgrim status, we made for the St Jacques restaurant in the Rue St James, and felt better about Bergerac after a successful supper in its open-air courtyard. The St Jacques is run by a friendly Dutch couple who were keen to promote their "surprise menu". Unsurprisingly, this costs more than menu options allowing diners to select the food they want.

The Europ' Hotel was a little disappointing: an ugly building in a dreary part of town, with breakfast presented by its non-playing, *l'Equipe*-reading supervisor as being *"sous forme de buffet"*: coffee from the machine and a nectarine that stretched the concept of "fresh fruit" beyond stretching point.

On the plus side, Reception's white leatherette sofas made an exciting change from the rough-stone and exposed-beam vernacular, and no hotel with bidets deserves blanket condemnation. Paul washed all his kit in ours, used his bungee to hang it out to dry in the smoke from a neighbouring barbecue, and greased the pilgrimage stigmata on his thighs with healing ointment.

Bergerac to St-Romain-et-St-Clément: about 105km

Périgord black, Périgord white, Périgord purple, Périgord green. The Limousin. Up and down we went, hour after weary hour, day after long day. I had selected this route for the quiet and countrified regions through which it would take us, and it did. My notes become a little repetitive. "Pretty village"... "steep hill"... "beautiful cows". Is there any more to be said? Yes: Resistance martyrs' memorial. We passed many of these in empty places, always beautifully maintained. French villages do not forget.

If on your desert island you were allowed one shelf from the French larder, to go with the complete Astérix and all your Françoise Hardy LPs, which would you choose? Many would take the Périgord, a garden of earthly delights where the best things are to be dug up, picked or butchered. Food production is not conducted on an intensive industrial scale, but in family farms and gardens. Everyone has a few vines, walnut trees, fruit and animals. They make their own oil and pâté, and they love the fact that the incidence of heart disease is uncommonly low.

We broke the morning at Vergt – not the postcard prettiest village, but good for picnic shopping and especially proud of its strawberries, which have their festival in mid-May when *La Confrérie de la Fraise* (president: B. Plantevin) takes over Vergt for an orgiastic *fraise*-crazy weekend. At Périgueux we found a cycle path along the banks of the Isle before crossing the river to inspect its many-domed cathedral, St-Front.

French churches introduce us to an army of obscure saints, many of them Roman soldiers who converted to Christianity and took the Word to deepest Gaul, where they came to a sticky end. Stremonius, Saturninus, Leocadius, Quiricus. Of them all Fronto is surely the most engaging. One thinks of him as a Tolkein character, or wagging his tail, hoping for a walk soon. According to some sources Fronto was a sixth-century local Périgourdin; others have him taking the bishop's crozier from St Peter in person. The legends surrounding these dragon slayers are hard to disentangle.

Singular though its design is, Fronto's cathedral leaves me cold, and if Galaxy had been with us I doubt he would have rated it highly, as a place of worship. White from the outside, it seems grey and chilly within, and there is something a bit unsettling and Madonna's bra-like, I find, about all the spiky domes. Perhaps our disappointment had something to do with the 19th-century restoration of the cathedral, which experts deplore.

For once, the minor road leading north from Périgueux, the D8, is more direct than the main N21 – as much as 5km shorter, if my reading of the map is correct – to Sorges. Unfortunately, we missed the D8 and found ourselves on the N21. Perhaps it was less hilly.

All the colours of the Périgord can be quite confusing. Sorges is either green or white, or on the cusp between them, whatever that colour would be. In truth, however, it is not a colour at all, but a voluptuous taste and a most delicate perfume. Sorges is in the land of foie gras and truffle, perhaps their HQ. Périgord scrumptious,

Sorges: a garden of earthly delights

Périgord guilty. It has a good truffle museum and a truffle market on Sunday mornings from December to mid-February.

For a living introduction to the subject, we visited the Andrevias walnut, foie gras and truffle farm-cum-shop just outside Sorges – not difficult to find but if you want a show-round it might be an idea to ring ahead (0033 5530502).

The Meynards have many hundreds of Toulouse geese, which they buy in Sarlat at one day old. The geese lead a happy outdoor life for four months, fertilising the nut groves in a sustainable way and being chased around by Lola, an expert goose dog who also has a good nose for a truffle. Then the geese go indoors and the liver-fattening process known as *gavage* begins. It used to last anything from one to three months, but these days the science is such that 15-21 days of *gavage* – in September/October, should you wish to witness it – are enough to swell the liver from 200 grams to a full and luscious kilo.

Three times a day the geese have the *embuc* pushed down their throats and a rich paste of maize forced into them, more every day. They don't care for it at first, but after a few days they are queuing up for the next meal. "And if we are late, you should hear them protest," says Albin Meynard.

The dirty straw from the barn enriches the maize crop, and the goose is like the pig (and for that matter the walnut), in that nothing goes to waste. Foie gras, *magret, rillettes, gesiers, cou farci,* cooking fat... and duvets.

You might think, in this day and age, that foie gras would run tobacco close as a local industry doomed to decline, consumed by a sense of foreboding with the axe of correctness hanging over it. Can there really be any future in it?

"Why not?" says Albin Meynard, with blissful uncon-cern. "The market likes foie gras, and it always will."

From Sorges it was a short, beautiful and typically exhausting ride to our accommodation, a farmhouse *chambre d'hôte* at a place called Poncet, which is an outpost of a hamlet called St-Clément, on the road between Thiviers and St-Jean-de-Côle. If an outpost of a hamlet sounds out of the way, it is. But the road would be worth taking anyway, for the landscape and for St-Jean-de-Côle, one of the prettiest villages in the Périgord.

There is more to good French accommodation than hotels, and the French *chambre d'hôte* often has more to offer than the Great British bed & breakfast: supper (*la table d'hôte*), which may be of high quality.

This is not something I have got to grips with, and although the red Michelin has its toe in the guest-house market, it is not exhaustive. It was only by recommendation that we found our way to the Manoir de Bigeau, when the hotel we had hoped to reserve, the St-Jacques at Saint-Saud-Lacoussière, was unable to fulfil its duties as a pilgrim's rest.

One of the occupational hazards of *chambres d'hôte* may be a lack of signposts. It took many phone calls for Le Manoir de Bigeau to reel us in. Keep going to the very

Breakfast, Le Manoir de Bigeau

top of the hill, don't start going down the other side, and you should be in the right area.

Outwardly, there is nothing spectacular about the way this hill farm has been converted, although it has been done well, with big bedrooms and heavy furniture in the open-plan dining hall. It is the food which is really exceptional and this is the work of the well-named Madame Pin, a wafer-thin wisp of a woman who obviously takes pride in fattening up her guests, assisted by her daughters – and genial husband, in so far as he is permitted to interfere.

"Do you get your foie gras from Sorges?" I asked Madame Pin, after a completely spectacular supper, which would in no way outshine the breakfast. "Actually, no. My producer near Excideuil uses grains of maize, not paste, for the *gavage*, and I prefer *le parfum*." This might be a useful tip for anyone planning to try *gavage* at home.

Le Manoir de Bigeau is not so much *table d'hôte* as proper restaurant, probably not open for lunch. Madame Pin told me they are hoping to be a Logis de France soon, and the room prices will go up. Logis de France? How about Leading Hotels of the World?

St-Romain-et-St-Clément to St-Léonard-de-Noblat: about 115km

After an early-morning tour of the tawny suspension of disbelief that is St-Jean-de-Côle, we made our way slowly and sweatily out of Périgord and into Limousin, where the balance of the landscape changes slightly: villages less frequent and less pretty, cows more so.

Châlus gave us a number of minor treats, Limousin-style: a spectacularly *ancien régime* Modern' Garage, where I was disappointed not to see a rotary-engined Panhard; Europe's tallest sequoia; and a plaque commemorating Lawrence (not yet of Arabia)'s 20th-birthday lunch in the lamented Grand Hôtel du Midi while cycling around France in 1908 on the trail of Richard Coeur de Lion. Châlus was a good place to stop because the king died there, struck down by crossbow in 1199 while attacking the castle whose ruins still dominate the small town. We continued slowly on our way, toiling up a long hill and racing down to Les Cars, where Le Simone was an excellent lunch stop. Paper table-cloths, *plat du jour* + *île flottante* (or was it *oeufs à la neige?*), cheap accommodation also available.

From Aixe-sur-Vienne the main road follows the river to Limoges and the map suggests it might be an enjoyable ride. There was too much traffic and industry for that, but at least the road was flat.

Limoges is an important provincial metropolis – transport hub, university city, *préfecture*. Its great abbey with the tomb and relics of St Martial brought the pilgrims flocking and gave its name to this pilgrimage route – the Via Lemovicensis. The abbey was razed in 1791, and only a few vestiges have been uncovered, leaving not much flesh on the bones for the pilgrim tourist to chew. The word *limoger* means to sack, and that sums up the general outsider's view of the city: don't go there.

It is a city almost as hilly as Rome and, everything considered, Limoges's claim on our attention would hardly be compelling, but for the porcelain industry which has been its glory since kaolin was discovered in commercially viable quantity in 1768. Kaolin is the clay that gives porcelain its whiteness, hardness and translucence.

There are two ways to approach the subject: the city's excellent museum, or a factory tour, which will give a less comprehensive but perhaps more lively perspective – a view of the different stages of manufacture, with the added interest, or not, of a guided tour and a shop at the end.

Paul and I visited the prestigious house of Bernardaud and learned much about the cooking, cooling, shrinking, enamelling and other processes from a guide whose build and flimsy white top were well chosen to suggest a translucent glaze over delicate porcelain. Her group followed with rapt attention, and most of the intelligent questions about the finer points of plate-making came from the ladies of the party.

After the technical part of the tour, many beautiful examples of porcelain art are displayed, including Bernardaud ware designed for some of the world's top restaurants. Bernardaud is open from June to September, or by appointment (0033 555105591). Take Rue Mouvendière, leading out of town towards the north-west.

Pedalling past riverside porcelain factories and through the industrial outskirts of Limoges, not to mention the challenges of its city centre, had taken up much of our afternoon. We were glad to get back to the pastoral Limousin scene as we headed up the Vienne towards St-Léonard-de-Noblat. The landscape improved, and grew steeper, after Le-Palais-sur-Vienne.

We were on a *chambre d'hôte* mini-roll, and at St-Léonard our destination was Les Jardins de Lily, in the village itself... somewhere. "It's the house with red shutters; you can't miss them," said Lily, but we did miss them, more than once. Luckily we were easier to spot than Lily's shutters, and in the end her husband jumped in his car and caught us up (not difficult) as we headed roboti-cally out of town on the D13. It had been a long day.

Les Jardins de Lily was another success, although in a different style from Le Manoir de Bigeau: this was a more familiar B&B experience, with chit-chat, fond fare-wells, let's keep in touch and if you're passing through we really must do lunch. The rooms Lily has made are huge and as comfortable as anyone could want; the garden is relaxing; and if you want to use the place as a B&B and not test Lily's husband's barbecuing skills, that would work fine. We collapsed in the garden, took drink, and let him grill a duck for us; no complaints, until the middle of the night when I woke up with excruciating cramp. This had nothing to do with the duck: not enough stretching after exercise, was the reason. (None, in fact.)

Of St-Léonard's two hotels, the word on the street is that the food is perhaps a touch better at Le Grand St Léonard, but the Relais St-Jacques may be slightly more *gai* for décor and ambience.

St-Léonard-de-Noblat to La Châtre: about 120km

St-Léonard is the home of the best loved of all French

Raymond Poulidor

cycling heroes, Raymond Poulidor, a son of the Limousin soil and eternal Tour de France bridesmaid who has given his name to the phenomenon of coming second. As robust and cheerful as ever, Poupou is often to be encountered at the Café des Sports, according to Lily, but he wasn't there when we pushed our bikes through the beautiful centre of the old village on our way to see its great pilgrimage church (11th/12th century). St Leonard's speciality miracle is liberating prisoners, and many of the offerings include broken chains. They are not all ex-cons: St Leonard understands prison in its broadest sense, which applies to us all.

Lily's husband wished us *bonne route* and *bon courage*. "*Le Limousin à vélo, c'est pas pour les fainéants,*" he said – not for the lazy cyclist – and this is true.

"No hill climb is as hard as bringing in the harvest," said Poulidor, and with that in mind we set about our task with as much joy in our souls as we could find and our usual steady purpose. By midday we had achieved 32km. Lily's husband had boasted that St-Léonard is the cradle of *la race Limousine*, and of all our cow-spotting days, this may have been the best.

There are more than 500 million cows in the world, and France has more than 20 million of them. Galaxy takes a dim view of my typically towny sentimental attitude towards farm animals in general, and cows in particular. From his perspective, the way to look at a cow is to count the cost of keeping it alive until you can turn it into money. But what can I do? I love them, and find

"Et oui... that's them"

that few of life's pleasures compare with the rough tickle of a kiss from *une belle limousine*. I can't feel the same about a Toulouse goose.

At some nameless village, perhaps in the Millevaches region whose name, disappointingly, has nothing to do with cows, we stopped for a drink at a café run by an Englishman. A man who might have been chewing a piece of grass drove up in his van, saw our bikes, parked in the middle of the road, walked over to our table and sat down.

"I saw you looking at the cows back there," he said by way of explanation. It was as if we had been introduced. I pulled out my camera, showed him the picture I had taken, and we looked at it together.

"*Et oui*," he said. "That's them. That's what they look like." It was time to saddle up and tackle the next hill, so I shook my new friend by the hand and said goodbye.

"*Bon courage!*" he called after us. "*Vous êtes courageux, à vélo dans le Limousin.*"

It was late by the time we rolled into our lunch target of Bénévent-l'Abbaye, a typical pilgrimage village clustered around its vast and magnificent church, which might have been visible from afar had we been travelling in the right direction. The lunch options were Au Bar Do (*steack frites* or similar) or the more organic Colimaçon Bleu tea room beside the church.

A pilgrim cyclist clickety-clacked into the church in full Lycra and cycling shoes. Hardly the best look for a church visit, we observed in a liturgical whisper. The pilgrim cyclist may have looked at me and thought the same. At least my Crocs are quiet.

From the church I took my bike down the hill for a look at the Hôtel du Cèdre – closed for lunch but thoroughly inviting, for another time – saw a sturdy old gent with hiking boots and a stick and hailed him, one pilgrim to another. It was a day for opening up, and meeting people.

"On your way to Compostela?" I opened up.

"No, just out for walk, but I've made the pilgrimage four times. It's a wonderful experience, you will see. How far are you going today?"

"Er... La Châtre." He had clocked the shell hanging off my saddle, so there was no escaping this conversation, which I was already regretting.

"Isn't that the wrong direction?"

"We're doing the return from pilgrimage."

"Really? To Compostela and back – that's quite something. Hats off to you!"

In the Limousin

"Just the return part."

"A reverse pilgrimage! That's novel! Still, Compostela to Vézelay takes some doing. How many kilometres so far?"

"We started from Biarritz actually. And before you ask, we're only going as far as La Charité."

"Oh well. *Bonne route, quand même.*" *Chacun à son pélerinage.*

The flames of hell were warming the soles of my feet.

Paul was waiting for me in Au Bar Do. I had a request to make. If we do this kind of thing again, could we do it without the shells, please?

Before leaving Bénévent we wanted some postcards.

"*Vous faites le pélerinage, messieurs?*" the shopkeeper asked. Here we go again.

"*Oui,*" I said, doing my best to sound conclusive. "*Très fatigué.*" Too tired to answer further questions.

"*O, que c'est merveilleux!*" she said.

The fire was raging now.

Next door to us at Au Bar Do, we noticed a man of about our age, toying with a coffee, reading a book and keeping a large table reserved. His patience was rewarded when a group of eight cyclists arrived, parked their bikes in a heap, sat down and ordered an even later lunch than ours.

We left while they were still eating, but they sped past us before long, and the interesting thing was, the solitary book-reader/table-reserver was part of the *peloton*, cycling along with the best of them. Eventually I worked out the system (you have plenty of time to work things out, cycling). They are a group of nine with eight bicycles and one car. All the luggage goes in the car, and they take it in turns to be the driver for a few hours. Brilliant. Bags be the driver through the Limousin.

The hills kept coming at us. At Dun-le-Palestel we thought we must have knocked them on the head. But as the land beneath our wheels gradually became more stretched, and the hills became less steep, that only made them longer. After riding down to the Creuse at Chatelus we went up again, and then down again to the Petite Creuse below Chambon, and so it continued until Aigurande, a frontier town between the regions of Limousin, Marche and Berry; between the Massif Central and Bassin Parisien; between langue d'oc and langue d'oil.

From there we chose the pretty little D73 which took us all the way to La Châtre along the Vauvre, a bocage landscape of tight little valleys that inevitably and irresistibly attracts the word "intimate"; thick brambly hedges, chestnuts, blackberries and clouds of midges beside the stream. It is George Sand's beloved Vallée Noire, which forms the background to her pastoral novels. Does anyone read them now?

It may not be an exaggeration to say that George Sand's house at Nohant (6km north of La Châtre) was an important centre of creativity in France during the Romantic period. We imagine Delacroix painting, Chopin composing and George Sand herself forgetting to sleep as she poured out another story of rural life and womanly rebellion against domestic tyranny.

George Sand's house is a devotee's delight: every detail lovingly preserved – bedrooms, study and a little theatre. If you really want to get into the spirit of the

---

George Sand (1804–76)
La dame de Nohant

Descended from the Maréchal de Saxe and the King of Poland on her father's side, and a Parisian *"oiseleur"* (bird seller) on her mother's, Amantine-Aurore-Lucile Dupin was brought up at Nohant by her grandmother who had fled Paris at the Revolution. She was proud of her mixed blood and credited it with her independent spirit and socialist leanings.

She inherited the estate at 17, married at 18, had a son and a daughter, grew bored and arranged with her husband to spend half the year in Paris. Her first book was a collaboration with her lover Jules Sandeau and published under the name J Sand. The second, *Indiana* (1832), written at Nohant, was all her own work, but the publisher wanted to keep the name Sand, and the author chose George which she considered "synonymous with *berrichon*". Indiana was a huge success, and scores more novels followed – strong women refuse to show deference to men, but civilise them.

George Sand denied that she wore men's clothes, explaining that she had been brought up to wear trousers for riding and playing with the other children, and continued to do so in Paris, where she could not afford to take carriages. Trousers were more practical in the mucky streets and less expensive to clean.

It was not that she wanted to be taken for a man; she merely observed that men enjoyed freedom. She did not need a man to invite and escort her to the theatre. "I go

---

there on my own, by choice; and when I want flowers, I go on foot, by myself, to the Alps." She smoked small cigars.

George Sand's close friendships included Alfred de Musset and the consumptive Frédéric Chopin, with whom she travelled extensively, most famously in 1838 to Mallorca where the weather and the locals were equally inhospitable. She did most of her writing at Nohant and was visited there by Liszt, Balzac, Flaubert and Delacroix, as well as Chopin, who composed many of his best pieces there.

The best known of her later pastoral novels, set in the Berry, are *The Devil's Pool* (*La Mare au Diable*, 1846), and *Little Fadette* (*La Petite Fadette*, 1849). The Nohant Festival lasts for 5 weeks in June/July, www.festivalnohant.com

place, stay on her doorstep in the Auberge de la Petite Fadette and visit the Moulin d'Angibault (7km west of Nohant), which was the setting for *Le Meunier d'Angibault* and is the last operating watermill on the Vauvre – a *Vallée Noire* vignette.

At La Châtre you get George Sand with everything. We found our hotel opposite the George Sand take-away kebab/pizza outlet, ate *berrichon* rabbit and drank honest *berrichon* wine (Châteaumeillant) beneath portraits of George Sand in the hotel's Espace Retro restaurant, and failed to attend the concert at the George Sand-themed festival at Nohant. (Supper won that argument easily.) The Lion d'Argent is an unfussy and unpretentious town hotel, and a good one.

Not so merry, in the Berry

The hotel pre-dates the authoress, or it would doubt-less also be named after her. It was after a dinner there that George Sand's father Maurice Dupin fell off his horse on the high road and died, on September 16th 1808. Had it not been for that dreadful accident, much would have been different.

La Châtre to La Charité-sur-Loire: about 125km

The wind played a big part in the planning stage of this trip, but I have said nothing about it. The truth is, we had rarely noticed any wind, and that usually means it is helping. On our last day we did notice a following wind and gave thanks for it, because if we had been fighting a headwind through the forests and pasture lands of the Berry, heaven knows when we would have reached La Charité. Too late for supper, certainly, and possibly in the dark.

I had always imagined the Berry as a region of plump and shiny prosperity, perhaps because of its famous *duc* and his *Très Riches Heures*; and Jacques Coeur, the moneybags of the late Middle Ages, counting his swag in Bourges, the Berry's capital city.

Their fortunes may not have trickled down. The Berry showed us a different face, as downbeat as any region we had crossed; more depressed than the Limousin, downer-at-heel than the Nièvre.

Of course there are exceptions, and one oasis of spectacularly proud husbandry is the priory of Notre Dame d'Orsan (near Le Châtelet), which has been restored and recreated by two Parisian architects. It may be the only hotel in France with two stars in the green Michelin guide. The official definition of two stars is "worth a detour" and we made one.

Noirlac

There are two parts to the priory: the garden part, a triumph of painstaking horticultural archaeology, and shop; and the hotel part (extremely private) in the buildings of the converted priory. Visitors to the garden are requested to make a donation and not shout, or run, or in any other way disturb the vegetables. All is calm, as it should be in a priory. For keen gardeners on a luxury hotel budget, Orsan would be worth a pilgrimage.

Soon after our priory visit, we reached the middle of France. There are half a dozen competing claimants and that is understandable: the villages around here do not have much to shout about. Morlac was the first we came across, soon followed by Farges-Allichamps, which backs up its claim with a Centre of France visitor centre accessible from the motorway.

Much worthier of a visit – if that does not sound too pious – is the 12th-century Cistercian abbey of Noirlac, beautifully located near the Cher. The Auberge de l'Abbaye is also recommended, unless you are in a rush. We weren't, before we sat down to the four-course set lunch, followed by a tour of the abbey; but we were afterwards.

From Noirlac it ought to have been possible to find a track through the forest to reach Meillant without cycling about five sides of a triangle, but in this we failed. Meillant has a château to visit, but we had used up our sightseeing time, and more.

At Chalivoy-Milon we allowed ourselves the briefest of pauses to look at church frescoes and telephone our hotel in La Charité, le Grand Monarque. It was four minutes past six, we had 50km to go... and the dining-room dead-line? The voice at the other end of the line gave no indi-cation of flexibility. "Eight thirty, maximum," it said.

Horses were not held, and Paul's performance was nothing less than heroic. At 8.22 we crossed the Loire's lateral canal, at 8.25 La Charité's first Loire bridge – on to the Ile du Faubourg – and at 8.26 its second. Le Grand Monarque was mercifully easy to find, over-looking the Loire near the bridge. Bikes were dumped, apologies made, supper confirmed, dog patted, congratulations exchanged. I waved a shower at my weary body, threw on the usual clothes and approached the dining room three stairs at a time, leaving Paul to do what he had to do in the bedroom, in his usual considered way.

The Grand Monarque's dining room has big windows looking out over the Loire. I had plenty of time to enjoy the view of children playing football beside the water and study the food my fellow guests were enjoying. Everything looked so good, when our turn came to order I put in a special request for some extra vegeta-bles. The waitress looked anxious, but agreed to submit my request to the chef; and by the way she said "chef" I knew she did not mean the cook, plain and simple, but the main man: he who must be obeyed. He, as it happened, who had answered the phone at four minutes past six. M James Grennerat, *fin saucier* and proprietor. Le Grand Monarque, in person.

When the food arrived, it came without vegetables.

"Le chef a dit non."

What? Who does M James Grennerat think he is – de Gaulle?

The waitress shrugged in a hopeless way.

I asked her to petition the chef one more time. I had ridden more than 120km for the pleasure of this dinner, and if it wasn't too much trouble I would like some vegetables, even if they were not in the chef's view the most suitable accompaniment to his *brochette de charolais (label rouge)* and his *fine sauce Singapour.* Exceptionally, Le Grand Monarque relented.

The evening scene was so delightful, and Paul and I were so proud of ourselves, we decided to go out for a drink. The waitress was on her way out and showed us the back door. "It stays open all night, so you will be able to get back in," she said, adding with a suggestively arched eyebrow, "... however late it is."

Twenty minutes later we found the back door firmly locked against us. The chef's revenge? Luckily the dog was still up, and opened the front door for us.

In the brightsome morning I liked the idea of freeing up the bedroom for Paul's manoeuvres, and girded myself for a walk along the Loire before breakfast. But the back door was still locked, as was an internal door in the other direction. After exploring the upper reaches of the hotel and failing to find a fire escape, and deciding not to jump from our bedroom window, there was nothing for it but to sit at the foot of the stairs and await release.

After breakfast a queue formed at Reception, of guests wanting to leave, bill settlement not being in the remit of the breakfast waitress. I don't want to exaggerate how long we all stood there, pinging the bell, banging the counter, pawing the carpet and asking the dog to help. "Go fetch... master!" It may not have been more than fifteen minutes, and luckily our train to Paris was not imminent. Eventually Grennerat emerged, without a smile, still less an apology, and we could all get on with our day.

La Charité's former abbey church dominates this small town on the Loire. At the time of its construction (12th century), it was the second-biggest church in Christendom, after Cluny, and now that Cluny is no more, it is the best way for those of us with limited powers of imagination to gain some idea of what Cluny must have been like. Only the choir, the crossing and about a quarter of the nave have survived, but even in its present truncated shape it is a church that takes the breath away in its sheer scale. It is not the authorised beginning or end of any pilgrimage route, but as a journey's end it worked for Paul and me.

———————

Hotels (with restaurants unless stated)
* = cheap, ***** = expensive

***   Biarritz, Mercure President (B&B)
     www.mercure.com   0033 559246640
**   Itxassou, du Chêne   0033 559297501
****   St-Jean-Pied-de-Port, Les Pyrénées
     www.hotel-les-pyrenees.com   0033 559370101

** St-Palais, Le Trinquet
www.le-trinquet-saint-palais.com 0033 559657313

** Amou, Hôtel du Commerce
www.hotel-lecommerceamou.com 0033 558890228

** Mont-de-Marsan, Le Richelieu
www.hotel-richelieu-montdemarsan.com 0033 558061020

* Mézin, le Relais de Gascogne
http://etienne.soufflet.free.fr 0033 553657988

*** Brax, Au Colombier du Touron
www.colombierdutouron.com 0033 553878791

*** Pujols, Des Chênes (B&B)
www.hoteldeschenes.com 0033 553490455

** Monflanquin, La Bastide des Oliviers 0033 553364001

** Bergerac, Europ' Hotel (B&B)
www.europ-hotel-bergerac.com 0033 553570654

** Sorges, Auberge de la Truffe
www.auberge-de-la-truffe.com 0033 553050205

** St-Romain-et-St-Clément, le Manoir de Bigeau
www.manoirdebigeau.fr 0033 553625404

* Les Cars, Le Simone 0033 555369006

** St-Léonard-de-Noblat, Grand St Léonard
www.hotel-restaurant-87.com 0033 555561818

** St-Léonard-de-Noblat, Relais St-Jacques
www.lerelaissaintjacques.com 0033 555560025

* St Léonard-de-Noblat, Les Jardins de Lily
http://lesjardinsdelily.fr 0033 555755917

** Bénévent-l'Abbaye, Le Cèdre
www.hotelducedre.fr 0033 555815999

** La Châtre, Le Lion d'Argent
www.hotelduliondargent.com 0033 254481169

*** Nohant, Auberge de la Petite Fadette
www.aubergepetitefadette.com 0033 254310148

***** Maisonnais, Le Prieuré d'Orsan
www.prieuredorsan.com 0033 248562750

***   La Charité-sur-Loire, Le Grand Monarque
        www.le-grand-monarque.fr   0033 386702173
**   La Charité-sur-Loire, Le Bon Laboureur
        www.lebonlaboureur.com   0033 386702285

Restaurants

***   Bergerac, Le Saint Jacques   0033 553233808
**   Noirlac, Auberge de l'Abbaye   0033 248962258

Information

Aquitaine   www.tourisme-aquitaine.fr

Limousin   www.crt-limousin.fr

Centre   www.visaloire.com / www.berryprovince.com

Burgundy   www.crt-bourgogne.fr

Eurostar   www.eurostar.co.uk

ROUTE 5

DOWN THE LOIRE

Moulins to St-Brévin (about 750km)
June–July 2011

St NaZaIRe

St Brévin

Nantes

angers

END

ChamProcaUX

Loire River

SAUMUR

Ussé

FonteVraud

Tours

Blois

Beaugency

Chambord Rd

Orléans

Sully-sur-Loire

Gien

Briare

Loire

Amboise

Chenonceaux

Chitenay

Sancerre

La Charité

Nevers

Allier River

Decize

Moulins

START

O f all the tempting invitations France extends to the cyclist, the Loire commands pride of place on the mantelpiece. Loire Valley, how do we love thee? Let me count the ways. Wine from Anjou, goat's cheese from Touraine, *brochet au beurre blanc*, Saumur mushrooms; castles and cathedrals, a good climate, a cycle track along the river and friendly terrain which is rarely steep and never dull.

The Val de Loire refers to the middle bit, also known as Château Country, but there is much more to the Loire than this. The longest of French rivers all but cuts the country in two on its 600-mile journey from the volcanic heights of the Massif Central to the top of the Atlantic coast, where rugged Brittany meets unruly Vendée. Via Burgundy, Berry, Touraine and Anjou, to name but a few.

Once the Loire turns definitively west at Orléans, it marks a real divide: grey slate from warm red tiles, wine from beer and cider. North of the Loire lies northern France. To the south, a land of Mediterranean influence, of longer lunch and stronger sun.

The march of history has left its footprint. At the tail end of the Hundred Years War the Berry was the last refuge of a feeble monarchy squeezed between Burgundy and the English, and the river itself was the front line. Joan of Arc journeyed from Lorraine to Chinon to buck up the dauphin and revived the royal cause with a flurry of victories along the Loire that opened the road to Reims.

After expelling the English, the Valois kings made Tours, Amboise and Blois their homes, and the French

ADAM RUCK

Renaissance bore fruit on the banks of the Loire, with Leonardo da Vinci artist in residence at Amboise. Medieval fortresses became gracious châteaux built of the local *tuffeau* stone which whitens with age. The purest French is spoken, *dit on*, at Tours. It is, as proud local resident Honoré de Balzac wrote, the essential province. *"L'Auvergne est l'Auvergne, le Languedoc n'est que le Languedoc, mais la Touraine est la France."*

We have already followed the infant Loire through its rough-and-tumble as far as Roanne, and on our way back from Switzerland we enjoyed our short time on the Loire so much, we spent the next day wishing we were still there. We have started, so we will finish.

Tourist offices invite us to follow the cycle route, La Loire à Vélo, along the lower half of the river from Nevers to the sea. Trains run along the Loire too, so cycling trips could scarcely be easier. Drop your car, pedal along the river bank until you've had enough, hop on a train and return to Go – bearing in mind that there is an awkward rail gap between Gien and Orléans.

Or why not do the whole trip by train? St-Nazaire, Nantes, Angers, Tours, Blois, Orléans, Gien, La Charité, Sancerre and Nevers all have direct trains to Paris (change for St Pancras International). Pick any two of the above for your start and finish, depending on how far you want to ride and whether you want to tick off the château equivalent of the Big Five – Chambord, Chenonceau, Blois, Amboise and Villandry – or explore a less touristy stretch of the river. Orléans and Angers are the bookends of the heavyweight sightseeing section of the Loire.

Having signed off the new and improved Galaxy Towers, G was back in the saddle and ready, if not raring, to go. Rejecting the all-by-train option, we decided to revert to the comfortable overnight ferry from Portsmouth, with bikes in the back of the car. Close study of the train timetables suggested Angers as the best car-drop location, followed by lunch in Tours and the afternoon train to Lyon, which would drop us at Roanne at 6.30: nice timing for a short ride through the summer evening to a halt somewhere in the Brionnais hills.

Another ex-au pair – they have their uses – Facebooked me to recommend the free public car park on the Place de la Rochefoucauld in the middle of Angers. We managed not to spend too long dithering over the fact that following the river downstream would mean cycling in a westerly direction most of the way and thus probably against the wind. Of all rides through France this must be one of the least hilly, and in early July we would surely be unlucky to find ourselves battling a westerly gale.

There was one aspect of the trip that did worry my companion: it was too long, especially the days in the middle. "What I like most is the time we spend not on our bikes," said Galaxy. He is always arguing for a rest day, and since the heart attack I can hardly dismiss the dripping tap of his protestation out of hand.

The problem was not that the Loire is too long for two cycling holidays of a week each – it isn't – but the fact that we had managed only the first quarter of the river on our previous trip. In terms of a lifetime, Roanne is more like the Loire's 21st than the big Four O. Sancerre is the halfway house.

Why crucify ourselves, for the sake of completeness? Luckily the Tours to Lyon train gave us several options for abbreviating the trip. From Bourges we could pedal across to La Charité or Sancerre. The train also stops beside the Allier at Saincaize, a few kilometres from Nevers; and at Moulins, which is about two hours' ride from Decize. We decided on the last option, saving a day's ride and allowing us to insert an extra stopover in the middle of the journey. About 100km of the Loire, from Roanne to Decize, would thus escape us.

La Loire à Vélo is part of an ambitious euro-initiative whose aim is to create an unbroken 3800km cycling trail – EuroVélo 6 – from the Atlantic to the Black Sea, linking the Loire, Rhine and Danube. This is such a noble project, what kind of curmudgeon could possibly find a word to say against it?

The reasons for any mild dissatisfaction we may have felt are inadequate prep and mapping, and, if I may politely say so, over-enthusiastic claims made for the trail by its promoters: "800km of trail explicitly built for cycling" may lead to disappointment. Much of the trail is on normal roads, and the end-to-end length is more like 630km than 800km. The stretch of Loire from Nevers to the sea measures about 540km.

Signposting on the ground turned out to be a bit patchy, and signposts are like learning: a little is often worse than none at all. Further confusion can arise from the many signed cycle routes which are not the Loire à

Vélo – 300km of themed circuits in Château Country, for example. Look for the Loire à Vélo's blue-green motif of a wheel in water.

The trail is not yet complete, at least it wasn't in summer 2011. Between Nevers and Châteauneuf-sur-Loire, about 90km of it exists only as a coloured line on the website, and there are other sections where the route is described as provisional, whatever that means.

There are places where the route is less direct than a perfectly good minor road, and on a cycle path you can never be sure the surface won't deteriorate and cause further delay. Outside our hotel in the small village of Chitenay we confronted two signposts: 11.5km to Cheverny by cycle route, 7.5km to Cheverny by (minor) road. Which would you take?

Not always the most direct route

We were more appreciative when Loire à Vélo signs took us through the outskirts of big towns on cycle paths not shown on our maps: through the Ile Charlemagne park on the edge of Orléans, past the allotments of St-Pierre-des-Corps on our way in to Tours, and along a riverside path to Nantes (until it expired at the foot of a staircase. This may be one of the "provisional" sections).

It is a moot point whether "800km of trail explicitly built for cycling" is a desirable thing, from the touring cyclist's point of view. In his book *Cycling the River Loire*, John Higginson expresses the same reservations we felt, about "suffocating cycle ways denying access to villages and towns." The surface is usually better on the road, and when you are covering a long distance the surface matters.

Higginson's book made us feel rather feeble. The 39km climb through Vals-les-Bains is "nothing to daunt a reasonably fit cyclist". Allow a full day to visit Nevers, says Higginson, and spend at least two hours on the roof at Chambord. Two hours on the roof? What does he want us to do up there – paint the balustrade and watch it dry?

He recommends the IGN 1:100,000 map series, Michelin 1:200k not being detailed enough for the "discerning cyclist". He has a point: our pages torn from the Michelin road atlas tell us little about road surfaces and tracks too small for cars. But our method gives us the whole of France for £11, whereas IGN maps would cost us more than £50 a trip. Michelin will have to do, and we are content to eke out its imperfections with guesswork. Trial is a challenge we enjoy, and error often takes us to interesting places.

In the case of the Loire, however, Michelin's maps (1:100,000) of the French part of EuroVélo 6, of which maps 1 to 4 deal with the Loire, might have saved us a few punctures. Alternatively, if we had had an app on our phones, or the energy to mug up the next day's stretch of Loire à Vélo in our stopover hotels and highlight it on our map, we might have made fewer mistakes, setting off on riverside paths that "must lead somewhere". They often did, but not always in the most user-friendly way.

I brought a new bike to the party, Modestine having been put out to grass after her stuttering performance in the Tarn. The new addition was a frisky little number called a Scott Speedster, with a chic white saddle, jazzy blue graphics and thin wheels.

A couple of practice rides on the Scott, and as many punctures, were enough to persuade me to swap its treadless racing tyres for a pair of Schwalbe Marathon Plus Puncture Resistants ("Even a thumbtack cannot penetrate this protective layer"). I mention the name because it may be the only heavy-duty tyre available for thin-wheeled bikes.

The Scott is so light I can lift it with one finger, but even with a triple chainring up front – offering the "granny gear" much derided by sporty cyclists – as a climber it is no match for the peerless Super Galaxy, which makes every hill the cycling equivalent of an afternoon snooze in a deckchair on the *Queen Mary*.

Galaxy had a go on the Scott, pulled a pained face and advised me to get a softer saddle. The man in the shop talked me out of it, muttering darkly about "false friends" and "chafing".

The aspect of this route that worried me most was sightseeing: we could easily spend a fortnight in the middle 150km of the Loire. On the basis that this was a bike ride, not a history tour, we decided to content ourselves with château-viewing from outside, leaving the guided tours for another kind of holiday.

Experience has rarely shaken my lazy conviction that the exterior is the best thing about most Loire châteaux. Embark on a tour, and you are likely to see four-poster beds, tapestries and monumental fireplaces in empty rooms where on rare occasions important visitors slept. That is a generalisation and may be an outdated one, but for the purposes of our ride it would do.

Châteaux in private ownership such as Cheverny, Chenonceau and Ussé are as a rule more interesting to visit than the *grandes machines* such as Chambord, Amboise and Blois. Further: small and quirky (Beauregard), or special interest (Saché's Balzac museum) is often more rewarding than big and historic. Azay-le-Rideau is a special case, because the only way to see the exterior properly is to sign up for a visit. Châteaux have different purposes. Some are designed to impress and dominate. Others are more private and hide themselves away.

One of the more secluded of the hideaway category is the little Château du Moulin, which comes warmly recommended by my grandmother GH Ruck, who toured the

Loire shortly before the First World War. When I visited her in the Sevenoaks home where she patiently awaited closure, she would often pull out a grey postcard of the Château du Moulin and tell me about her trip. This was my cue to watch out, because whenever she said Moulin, or Blois, her upper teeth would fly across the room for me to catch and return, a ritual that passed without comment and certainly without laughter. I am ashamed to say I have never been to the Château du Moulin.

We drove to Portsmouth on a fine evening in late June, halfway through Wimbledon. Andy Murray was steaming confidently at full speed ahead for his first major title, but iceberg Nadal was lurking in the North Atlantic half of the draw.

After a short night's rest on the ocean we drove down past Le Mans, reached Angers with plenty of time to spare before our midday train, and had no difficulty using it

Château d'Ussé

all up. Place de la Rochefoucauld took ages to find, and then we had to select the optimum parking place. Would it be safer to leave the car tucked unobtrusively under a tree, or out in the middle, where any malefactor would be in full public view? Eventually (of course) we decided not to park there at all.

"If the car's going to be vandalised, I'd rather it happened in a car park I've paid for," declared Galaxy, so we set off in search of St-Laud station where the car park, when we finally found it, was full. Tension mounted as we waited at the barrier for someone to leave and took turns to stand with a finger poised over the button while the car next to us revved aggressively. There was no need to panic, but if we missed the midday train our lunch would be squeezed.

When it comes to eating and drinking, Touraine wrote the manual. In 1832 Elizabeth Strutt sat down to a *table d'hôte* at the Hôtel du Faisan in Tours, "served with the variety and profusion which renders travelling in France a luxury rather than a privation to those who make the gratification of their appetite a primary consideration: 16 or 18 dishes including soup, fish, ragout, roast meats, winged fowl of all descriptions, with creams, fruits and dessert was the bill of fare for two francs and a half including excellent wine and the attendance of the most civil servants I ever saw."

Tempting though it was to try the Hôtel Le Faisan (*formule plat + dessert*: 10.5 euros) near St-Pierre-des-Corps, we took the shuttle train to Tours and made do with two courses at L'Hédoniste on Rue Lavoisier. We felt we had chosen well and there was time for a quick look at the river and cathedral before our train. It took us through Chenonceaux — château hidden — and past troglodyte housing in the low white cliffs along the Cher. I woke up to see the Allier at Saincaize, which must be a strong candidate for France's worst-kept station award.

Our bikes were hanging next to a pair belonging to a couple whose weathered look told us they were on the way home from a ride. They had ridden downstream for 550km at about 110km a day — much the same pace as us — and were going home to Digoin. The weather had been if anything a little hot, the route if anything a little flat. Touring cyclists are hard to please. We don't like steep hills, but flat and featureless is no good either.

Moulins to Decize: about 30km

"*Votre vélo est trop beau pour cette balade!*" (your bike's too good for this trip) said the man from Digoin, as I lifted the Scott off its hook at Moulins. I accepted this compliment with a glow of pride, but would soon come to realise that he was making a serious point. A skinny-wheeled Speedster is the wrong kind of bicycle for the Loire à Vélo.

This had no bearing on what happened next. We had not crossed the Moulins ring road before a whip-crack report brought me to an abrupt halt. Galaxy stopped too: he thought I'd been shot. In fact, it was the back tyre suffering a full-scale blow-out. How this could happen after riding for about ten minutes at ten miles an hour, I am not sure, but it did. Perhaps I had inserted the tube badly, leaving it pinched between tyre and wheel rim. Anyway, it was badly torn and clearly irreparable.

It was an ominous start to the ride and an inglorious debut for the Scott; and it transformed our relaxed evening ride through the back roads of the Sologne Bourbonnaise into, yet again, a time trial. This was a pity because our route meandered through small villages with pretty names (Gennetines and Lucenay, doomed young lovers in a romantic novel), where we would have liked to stop for a drink. In the intervening *bocage*, cows and sheep were pushing each other around in an evening game.

As we approached Decize I scanned the hills ahead for a sign of some difference that might indicate the passage of one of Europe's great rivers, but detected none. The hills all looked the same.

The middle Loire is one of the sleepier parts of France, and Nièvre one of her most – how to put it politely? – low-key *départements*. Perhaps it is the similarity to the word *niais*, meaning idiotic, which encourages the assumption that Nièvre is populated by simpletons. No doubt this is a terrible slur. We crossed the Loire's lateral canal for the first time and soon reached L'Agriculture, an everyday hotel for country folk. I asked Madame if I could use the hotel computer to research bike shops on the internet. She looked blank. Internet? Eventually someone found a phone book.

Following the example of many far grander hotels, L'Agriculture doubles up as an art gallery. The lurid paintings may not have been to our taste, but at least L'Agriculture makes an effort. We ate pretty well, and the list included a reasonably priced red Sancerre, a wine that has been "the latest craze on the Paris bistro scene" for longer than anyone can remember. To my surprise, Galaxy had not come across it before. "They serve it chilled, like Beaujolais," I said knowingly.

In fact, they served it at room temperature, and when I questioned the waiter about this he looked at me in disbelief. Are you *rosbifs* really so *niais* as to be unaware of the temperature at which red wine should be served?

Not yet having seen the Loire, we set out after supper and found it soon after passing the local taxidermist's shop window. The bridge was a disappointment, an ugly post-war concrete structure of which the most interesting feature was low suspending arches wide enough to invite the confident visitor to try the aerial route over the river. There was no sign of spoilsport deterrents such as sharp spikes or inlaid broken glass, as seen on school banisters. "My boys would be up there in no time," said Galaxy.

Whatever the intake of red Sancerre required to persuade us to have a go, we had either exceeded or not reached it. But we did ask Madame Ranvier if the young *decisois* amuse themselves by using the bridge as a high diving board.

"Only the ones who want to die," she replied decisively, adding that if we wanted to look at bridges, we should cross the town and inspect the one on the other side, spanning the "*Vieille Loire*".

Decize is an interesting place to start a Loire journey, because the river at this point is a veritable spaghetti junction of waterways. The Aron flows into the Loire, and the Canal du Nivernais joins the Canal Latéral à la Loire by means of a 2km stretch of the Loire itself. This "river-level crossing" is the only officially navigable part of the Loire above Angers, the rest being at best *flottable*.

The town grew up on an island in midstream but in 1844 the right arm was closed by a submersible dam and has withered, as an arm deprived of its flow of blood would. This backwater is the *"Vieille Loire"*, with its old bridge over the water and meadows that look tempting for a picnic. The old town centre on the former island is full of charm too.

Decize to Nevers: about 40km

Cycling along the middle reaches of the Loire involves occasional glimpses of the river separated by long stretches of canal. The Canal Latéral à La Loire was built in the 1830s for commercial traffic and now serves holiday boats between Briare and Digoin, with onward connections to Roanne and the Saône. "Canals are only enjoyable up to a point," wrote CS Forester, and I agree; "some temperaments might weary after fifty miles, some after two hundred, but weariness is certain to develop sooner or later." Amen.

Weariness had not yet set in for us, and Decize to Nevers was an enjoyable ride, enlivened by canal crossings, many herons and the fact that the road was closed (bridge maintenance). Scaffolding made life difficult for inexperienced bargees, and we enjoyed watching them

The Canal Latéral à la Loire

slam on the brakes, put down their sudoku, argue, shout at the workmen and try to squeeze through.

We have come across the *Route Barrée* sign many times on our travels, and always enjoy the challenge. Like the *Sens Interdit* sign, it reminds the cyclist of the superiority of his chosen mode of transport. (Not that we break the law. Perish the thought. We dismount, of course.) There is usually a way around the problem: either a workman eager to down tools and lift a barrier, or a pile of rubble to clamber over.

We missed the château at Chevenon, but stopped to inspect a chapel in a field at Jaugenay: *"chapelle désaffectée"*, I read with pleasure, remembering the triumphalist scorn of an editor when I translated the phrase directly into

English. I lit a candle for disaffected churches in the hope that they might catch on, and it still burns. The Jaugenay chapel was the image of Nivernais rusticity, with a cow, a rusty tractor and some run-down farm buildings. They looked disaffected too, but with French farm buildings it can be hard to tell.

At Nevers my quest was a bike shop, to replace the missing *chambre à air*. The shop mentioned in L'Agriculture's Yellow Pages closed years ago, said a café owner who sent me back over the bridge to an industrial estate near the municipal campsite. The shop there was shut (*congé annuel*), but it was a pleasure to cross the Loire again, and again look up at the turrets and roofs of the old town, and down at the river as it tumbled steeply down a rocky slope, with a pair of terns darting about prettily. As Galaxy reminded me, it was around Nevers that Captain Hornblower encountered troublesome rapids when sailing down the river in a small boat in a snowstorm, at dead of night. Looking down at white water, I was not surprised.

I caught up with Galaxy in the cathedral, a rather intriguing building with an apse at each end, Gothic to the east, Romanesque to the west. Fresco figures include a wide-eyed Christ looking surprised to find himself at the wrong end of the church.

Nevers to La Charité: about 30km

The Loire à Vélo trail starts or finishes at Le Guétin, a canal bridge over the Allier near the village of Apremont-sur-Allier, a popular beauty spot. If we had started our

La Loire à Bateau: Hornblower and CS Forester

Horatio Hornblower's escape through France in 1810/11, as told in CS Forester's novel *Flying Colours* (1938), is one of the naval hero's best-loved adventures. Ably supported by Lieutenant Bush and coxswain Brown, Hornblower survives a near-drowning and a love affair before sailing a rowing boat 500km down the Loire from Nevers to Nantes, where he liberates a cutter and single handedly sinks two enemy ships before rejoining the British fleet. Forester had sailed down the Loire himself, and his beautifully observed descriptions betray intimate knowledge of the river in its different phases and seasonal moods.

On their way to trial and execution in Paris, the three captives overpower their guard near Nevers, hijack a small boat, capsize and are washed up at a friendly château where they are persuaded to sit out the winter, the frustrated Hornblower finding consolation in the arms of M le Comte's widowed daughter-in-law. The sailors continue their journey in spring, when the Loire has subsided from muddy winter spate to its delightful summer mode: shallow, swift and clear enough to drink.

The count tells Hornblower that the river will be empty because all fluvial traffic uses the lateral canal – although work on its construction did not start until 1827 – and there is hardly a house beside the river between the château and Pouilly. What about La Charité-sur-Loire? Who cares? It is a rattling good yarn, masterfully told.

Cecil Forester was a great devotee of river boating and in 1928 he and his wife Kathleen spent three months sailing from Rouen to Nantes via Paris and Orléans, taking the canal link between the Seine and the Loire. Their craft was the *Annie Marble*, a flat-bottomed 15-foot punt-cum-dinghy with a removable camping cover and outboard motor: "a boat of efficient ugliness" that drew four inches of water with two people and luggage on board. They saw only one other travelling boat on the Loire – two Americans in a canoe at Blois – and their expenses for the entire trip amounted to £24 10s.

La Porte du Croux, Nevers

ride at Saincaize, this would have been an interesting beginning, but it makes a long detour from downtown Nevers and since we were on the inside of a long bend, we decided to stay there. Nevers sits 6km above the confluence of the Loire and its greatest tributary, the Allier, a place called Le Bec d'Allier. We were keen to lay eyes on the union of the *dernier fleuve sauvage* (the Loire) and *dernière rivière sauvage* (the Allier), to use the meaningless slogans proclaimed tirelessly on websites, in brochures and beside the road in boastful self-advertisement.

At least since the time of Louis the Pious, who issued a decree on the need to build dykes along the Loire in 821, the river has been subjected to constant interference, with dams, groynes and levees constructed as flood defences and aids to navigation. Pollution and dams effectively killed off the Allier salmon, not to mention river-bathing. The Loire has four nuclear power stations on its banks. *Sauvage?* Up to a point.

After rattling down through the cobbled streets of old Nevers and under its splendid medieval gate, the Porte du Croux, we found a path along the river bank, and followed it. Information boards told us about the history of the river – a story of floods and unsuccessful attempts to contain them – and its wildlife. With traditional Loire boats moored to the bank and an embarrassment of shady places to roll out the picnic rug, the first part of the Loire that we had actually ridden along was a picture of tranquil enchantment, lacking only Mole and Ratty.

Mousse-Café and the Scott may have taken a different view, as the path got narrower and rougher, with rocks and sharp tree roots impeding. This was mountain bike terrain, unworthy of our stylish touring machines.

Eventually we popped out of the brambles near a road, and gratefully took it. "We were lucky to get through that lot unscathed," I said, about ten seconds before the first telltale wobble of the rear wheel indicated a loss of pressure. There is always the thought that it might be imaginary, but the unpleasant truth will not be denied. This was a slow puncture and I wobbled up a steep hill (a two-arrow gradient on the Michelin scale) to a belvedere overlooking the Bec d'Allier before dealing with it. I would have enjoyed the wonderfully empty view more in other circumstances.

At the confluence, it is the Allier that seems to boss the Loire, pushing the stream northwards. Statistics favour the Loire's claim to supremacy, however. It is 35km longer, its upper half drains a larger area and its average volume at Nevers narrowly beats the Allier's at Le Guétin.

From the village on the hill, Marzy, we made our way to a bridge over the Loire at Givry and found a grassy spot on the left bank near a lock, for a picnic and puncture repair, the water a useful accessory for the job (tactical tip). We were in the back yard of an appetising restaurant, the Auberge de l'Ecluse, and, had it not been for the puncture, might well have binned the picnic.

Unfortunately, the puncture repair failed, and my memory of the ride to La Charité is of cycling hard into a nasty headwind in order to achieve as much distance as possible between re-inflation stops. As I wrestled angrily with my bicycle among the roadside nettles and ragwort, my companion would glide serenely past, oil-free and full of the joys, with a cheery "What ho!"

The Loire and its lateral canal all but converge at the busy canal port of Marseilles-lès-Aubigny, which works hard to woo river tourism in compensation for the decline of commercial traffic. Narrowboat B&B on the *Alphonsia Maria* sounds fun and the Auberge du Poids de Fer beckons for lunch or supper.

Leaving Galaxy to inspect La Charité's great Cluniac abbey church and the intriguing collection of buildings surrounding it, I really did need to find a bike shop. The tourist office's best suggestion was a man with a garden machinery shop on the road out of town, beyond the Place Misère in the direction of Nevers; failing that, the hypermarket might sell tubes. With a wave for my old friend M Grennerat, who tried to lock me out of his hotel at night and successfully locked me in before breakfast, I wobbled past Le Grand Monarque and came to a fore-court full of lawnmowers.

As so often happens in French country garages, the oily mechanic complained like hell, poured scorn on my incompetence and dropped what he was doing to help me out. "If you don't use the *papier de verre* (sandpaper) the *rustine* (patch) will never stick," he explained patiently, as I have explained irritably to my children on many occasions. I felt slightly better when my saviour told me that few cyclists bother to repair thin tubes, such is the difficulty of making the *rustine* stick. I pass on this useful tip, and the vocabulary.

La Charité to Chavignol: about 35km

Here was a typical Loire à Vélo dilemma. Our maps made it clear that the little white road – white on the Michelin map, that is – hugging the left bank of the Loire as it sweeps past Pouilly to Sancerre would be longer than the direct yellow route (D920), which has a green stripe for scenic attraction. Would it be worth it? The afternoon was going on, we were tired, and we wanted to visit the wine museum in Sancerre.

With more time and energy we would have crossed the river for a look at Pouilly, its vineyards and its nature reserve's visitor centre, exactly halfway along the Loire; and made our way to Sancerre from there. But that would have been a more arduous ride. The D920 eventually carried the day.

Cyclists do not always have an eye for the finer points of architectural detail. Much depends on one's state of mind, and body. So I could not tell you a great deal about the old walled village of Sancerre, beyond the fact that it sits on top of a nasty hill. Soon after the cheerful little canal port and wine village of Ménétréol-sous-Sancerre, where a stop for a drink would have done no harm, we began to climb, and a long time later we stopped. Apparently the distance is only about 2km, although I find that hard to believe.

In terms of altitude and steepness the hill of Sancerre hardly seems extreme, but there was something particularly gruelling about it: late-afternoon fatigue, probably, combined with anxiety about closing time at the museum.

Two thirds of the way up I dismounted, and after a breather the rest of the climb was not nearly so bad. Galaxy, ever alert to the possibility of a short cut, found a staircase and walked up, carrying Mousse-Café. We arrived at about the same time and found the wine museum — the Maison des Sancerre — at the very top of the town (naturally). The computer said three minutes to seven, so I dropped the bike and ran inside.

The girls at the desk were unable to explain the use of *des* rather than *de* but in other respects could not have been more helpful. With an evening conference in progress, they were in no hurry to close, and offered wine. Unusually, our preference was for water. The museum was well worth the climb, with the local geography, geology, history and of course wine, beautifully presented. All the minutiae of *terroir* — kimmeridgean marls, argilo-silician flints and other soil types — are laid bare for the technically minded, and the rest of us enjoy period marketing posters and screenings of eloquent interviews with growers. They can invest in the most sophisticated computer technology and deploy all the science they like, but the success of their labours ultimately depends on the weather. No wonder they go to church.

Late summer is white-knuckle time. "A year of our life and work can be destroyed by 15 minutes of hail," says a weathered face turned anxiously heavenward. Spring frost can be damaging too, but at least if the worst happens early the growers can take a summer holiday. Perhaps that is a little glib.

After the tour we accepted the offer of a tasting and soaked up the view from the terrace, bathed in evening sunshine. An old walled town on top of a hill, girt about with steep vineyards and pretty little wine villages, and a great river flowing by. Of all the beautiful landscapes in France, the Sancerrois must be one of the most satisfyingly French. The word quintessential springs to mind.

Our beds for the night were in Chavignol, in a hotel named after one of the best Sancerre vineyards, La Côte des Monts Damnés, so named (perhaps) because the pickers find it damned steep. Two cyclists sympathised with them, only less politely.

Sancerre's great popularity on the Paris bistro scene and beyond is usually attributed to its food-friendliness. Conveniently, it is recommended as an accompaniment to goat's cheese, as traditionally produced by the womenfolk of the Sancerrois. The little Crottin de Chavignol was one of the first goat's cheeses to be awarded its own appellation, in 1976. Believers in a divine plan would be reassured by this example of a locality producing food and drink that go well together, but it is not a rule to rely on. Roquefort is a long way from Sauternes, for example (especially by bike).

The hotel is a stylish modern place in a boutiquey metropolitan vein, with bistro and gastro dining options. Over a crottin symphony and the Sancerre du jour in the bistro, it was time to confront the awkward fact that if we thought our day had been long, a longer day lay ahead: at least 120km to Orléans if we followed the river.

Sancerre – the taste of gun flint

Only 100km from Chablis and closer to Champagne than Chinon, Sancerre is far removed from the main drag of Loire vineyards in Anjou and Touraine. Is it a Loire wine or a burgundy? A number of local growers have vineyards on both sides of the Loire, and Henri Bourgeois's HQ in Chavignol is a good place for a comparative tasting. Reassuringly, many trained palates find it hard to tell Sancerre and Pouilly-Fumé apart. Both are 100% Sauvignon Blanc, but the right bank also produces the less prestigious Pouilly-sur-Loire, made from the humble Chasselas. Sancerre red and rosé are Pinot Noir. Sancerre is the larger appellation – producing 16 million bottles a year – spread across 14 communes, with a wide range of altitude, soil type, slope orientation and, inevitably, quality. The best villages are Chavignol, Bué, Verdigny, Amigny and Ménétréol. Menetou-Salon is the neighbouring appellation to the west (towards Bourges), also producing good white (sauvignon), rosé and red (Pinot Noir); "fleshy" is a word often used for its best wine, in contrast to "flinty" Sancerre. Galaxy buys his Sancerre and Pouilly-Fumé from Bonnard at Les Chailloux between the D183 and D955 to the north of Sancerre (0033 248541747). He also recommends P & A Dezat of Le Domaine du Petit Roy.

We had already ridden much of this stretch on our way back from Switzerland, and I imagined we would cut the corner and take the direct line through the Sologne, savouring its secretive charm and seeking out Grand Meaulnes moments in Alain-Fournier country; both likely to prove elusive. Galaxy was having none of it. "Much nicer to ride along the river," he said firmly, and that was that. "All we need is an early start and do 40km before breakfast, and we'll be fine."

The waitress improvised a picnic pre-breakfast which Galaxy took to his room. On the dot of six I knocked on his door.

Pre-breakfast was soon despatched, but our early start was not to be. Somehow, my bedroom door had managed to override my ploy of locking the door when it's open in order to prevent it from self-closing, and slammed itself shut – I without, key and panniers within.

After I had rifled the cash drawer and all cupboards in Reception and tried at least 40 keys, and said sorry for about the sixth time, we went out into the street and noticed an open window – my bathroom, perhaps – above the Reception area's flat roof. Galaxy went off for a wander and came back with a ladder. It wasn't quite long enough. He disappeared again and came back with a longer ladder.

Breaking in is not ... so very hard to do, I hummed (with apologies to the Walker Brothers), deploying my leopard crawl for the first time since Wednesday afternoon CCF at school, for reduced risk of falling through the roof. Luckily I didn't, and it was the right room.

I was in and out in moments, and after the perfect crime we were ready to leave. It took only a moment more for an unfamiliar breeze on the eyelids to ring an alarm bell – no sunglasses – and now we were locked out of the hotel. So Galaxy had to steal the ladder all over again, and I had to break in again and retrieve my eyewear from the tin roof where it had slipped out, the leopard crawl not being intended for soldiers with sunglasses hooked in the neck of their battle dress. Amazingly, our antics attracted no notice from inside or outside the hotel. Maybe all the villagers were out in damned vineyards at dawn.

Chavignol to Briare: about 45km

No more than two hours late, we sped down through the vineyards to the Loire bridge at St-Thibault (canoes for hire), where the Hôtel de la Loire would make a good base or overnight stop, apart from the surprising fact that it has no restaurant. The themed bedroom décor is quite ambitious: I'm not sure a Safari bedroom would enhance a stay beside the Loire, but the Coloniale room (French *coloniale*, presumably) looks good. The prolific novelist and sex fiend Simenon stayed in the hotel and wrote a book there. The Simenon suite's décor is disappointingly non-suggestive, and the room is a twin.

Following a Loire à Vélo sign beside the hotel, we soon found ourselves on a path separating the 15th and 16th fairways of the Golf du Sancerrois. Late though we were, it was still too early for any golfers to have reached this stage of their game and only the course sprinklers posed a threat to us; but it did seem a slightly odd routing for EuroVélo 6, the Budapest to Nantes cycle trail. "I think you'd better tell your readers to wear helmets for this bit," said G. Both of us have been known to spray the occasional tee shot.

At the end of the golf course our path deteriorated and we realised we might have missed a turning somewhere. Through a gap in the hedge we caught sight of the canal, flanked by a smart new cycle path. A quiet road runs close to the canal on the other side, so we moved across to that, for a smoother surface. G always feels more comfortable on a road he can identify on his map, and it is a sound principle.

After passing Neuvy's nuclear power station, we crossed the river at Beaulieu, followed a cyclist who looked as though he knew where he was going, failed to keep up with him, got lost, and somehow found the village of Bonny – Bonny by name, bonny of aspect – via a tiny cobbled footbridge overlooked by a village wall daubed in the best tradition of French rural discontent. *"Justice nulle part, police partout"* (justice nowhere, police everywhere) could have been scrawled in 1789, 1968 or 2010. The tourist board may by now have replaced it with *"dernier fleuve sauvage"* or a picture of a happy family on a bike ride.

Just when we thought we would not be able to avoid taking a stretch of main road, a Loire à Vélo sign came to our rescue, and led us all the way to Briare via as fine a stretch of riverside cycle path as we encountered all trip. It took us through Ousson-sur-Loire, where we had reached the Loire on our ride from Switzerland. With its bird-sanctuary island in the river, Ousson remains as pretty as ever, and still cries out for a good hotel, or at least a cheerful café on the river bank.

Excitement mounted as we closed in on Briare. This time we were determined to ride across Gustave Eiffel's famous aqueduct, which carries the Canal Latéral across the Loire to meet the Canal de Briare.

Before doing so, however, there was the matter of the ascent – about 10m – from the river bank to the steel-plated pavement of the bridge. The only obvious way up was a steep flight of steps followed by a zigzag metal staircase up the side of the bridge. This might wipe the smile off the face of some happy families. I wouldn't fancy it with a tandem.

Fresh from his triumph in Paris, Eiffel designed a supporting structure of 14 piers for the world's longest bridge (of its kind), a title it held until 2003 when Magdeburg's canal bridge over the Elbe (918 metres, 500 million euros) dethroned it. Briare surely remains the most beautiful, with its Belle Epoque lamps and ornamental columns recalling the Pont Alexandre III in Paris, whose foundation stone was laid in October 1896, one month after the Briare aqueduct opened.

In contrast to the older canal bridge over the Garonne at Agen, the Briare towpaths offer ample space for cyclists and strollers, of whom there are many, and we made an *aller retour* crossing, via the café at the east end. Canal holidays are booming business in this region, and Briare is a lively boating resort, with waterside cafés and restaurants at the *port de plaisance,* to the north of the canal. The Petit St Trop' looks the most tempting of them.

Briare to Orléans: about 80km

"If you have followed the peaceful Loire for a considerable distance you will only have regretted not being able to determine, betwixt the two shores, which you would choose," wrote Alfred de Vigny.

We had taken the left bank to Gien on our previous visit, so this time we decided to try the other shore, hoping for a continuation of the fine path that had brought us to Briare. That was one reason. Another was the dotted line on our map, indicating a GR (long-distance footpath). Galaxy always finds these hard to resist, but this GR is not one he will remember with affection. Now it was his turn to suffer the annoyance of a puncture and struggle to remove tyres that had gone undisturbed for years and formed an intimate bond with the wheel. Plastic forks (tyre levers) are no substitute for the old-fashioned metal kind.

There is not much a fellow traveller can do to help a man at work repairing a puncture, so I left my friend to it and found a place for a swim.

Am I being over-sensitive in hearing howls of disapproval at the irresponsibility of mentioning anything so dangerous as dipping a toe in the unsupervised and capricious river? *Riverains* don't do it – they have too often seen the Loire turn nasty, and speak of moving sandbanks, treacherous currents and *trous* in the river bed. Of course there is a risk, and common sense is required. We wouldn't bathe near a dam or a lock or a weir or a fisherman, or in a fast-flowing river if we couldn't see the bottom and an easy exit. If I had an open cut on my leg,

I might think twice about it. But I suspect there are more dangerous activities out there. Bicycling, for example.

The puncture dashed our hopes of seeing the hunting museum – "international", if you please – in Gien's brick castle, which would have been right up countryman G's street. The museum celebrates the town's location between Orléans forest and the *giboyeuse* (lovely word = game-rich) Sologne, favourite royal hunting grounds since Capetian times and still full of rampaging stags and boar. Carcasses are often to be seen hanging outside butchers in these parts, dripping blood on the pavement. Gien as a whole is mostly a post-war reproduction and shows its best face to spectators on the opposite side of the Loire. As so often, the left bank is the better route.

Returning to it, we soon found the levee and followed it to the moated and turreted château of Sully, its park gates surprisingly open to cyclists. Last time we came this way and wondered half-seriously about singletons lurking in the bushes near the place we selected for a swim (more accurately, a paddle) near Cuissy. On this summer Friday afternoon our thoughts were again provoked by an unusual number of cars overtaking us on our way towards Cuissy and crossing us in the other direction after we had passed it. Perhaps they were bird-watchers alerted by the grapevine – Twitter? – to the presence of some rare migrant. Ospreys nest in the forest and fish this stretch of the Loire, undeterred by the nuclear power station.

From Sully the obvious route would be to cross the Loire and ride the right bank to the beautiful abbey church at St-Benoît and mosaics at Germigny-des-Prés, with a stop, if timing suits, for good hospitality at Au Grand St-Benoît.

Having done all that before, we stayed on the left bank and followed it all the way to Orléans, mostly on the levee. It was a beautiful ride on a warm evening, with the tranquil meanders of the river to our right – easy access to ankle-deep water – windmills and sunflower fields to the left. A few sections of rough surface held us up, and we hit a carpet of broken glass around the *déver-soir*, an overflow valve in Orléans' flood defences a couple of miles above Jargeau.

The Loire à Vélo trail took us into Orléans via the Ile Charlemagne park, the city's lido. It was a bit late for bathing, but there were plenty of joggers and snoggers about, and North African families barbecuing *merguez*.

At Orléans we may have set a new record for our latest hour of arrival, but since there are plenty of good restaurants open late, it didn't matter. Au Bon Marché on Place Châtelet was busy and great fun.

As a tourist nation we may be in the habit of ignoring Orléans for the same reason that the French give Agincourt a wide berth and *The Sound of Music* flopped in Germany. I plead guilty, and had someone not recommended the Hôtel de l'Abeille, we would have skirted the city. We were grateful for the tip, because the Bee Hotel is a treasure and the city has a lot going for it: cheerful bars and restaurants in the old quarter between the cathedral and the river, and some noble perspectives worthy of the thriving commercial city Orléans once was. We made our grand entry via the central axis – over the Pont Royal, up the arcaded Rue Royale to the vast Place du Martroi, where St Joan rides her green horse.

Of course, the whole place is crazy about Joan of Arc, who, as every school child knows, raised the Siege of Orléans in May 1429 and after inflicting further thrashings on the English (at Jargeau, Meung, Beaugency and Patay), fulfilled her destiny by taking Charles VII to be crowned at Reims. Joan lost her touch after the Loire campaign, but she had done her job. The story is told in easily legible stained-glass images in the cathedral; in paintings in the Musée des Beaux Arts; and in the so-called Maison de Jeanne d'Arc, a timbered medieval house where she is supposed to have lived during the siege.

Every year a teenager is selected to be the Maid for the week-long Jeanne d'Arc festival (April 29th–May 8th) with horseback parades, rock concerts and medieval markets. This is no mere beauty contest, we were assured: moral merit weighs heavily in the selection process, although it stops short of the virginity tests Joan had to endure at the hands of her English captors.

We did not have to go far for our fix, the Hôtel de l'Abeille being crammed with Joanabilia. It belongs to the Loire's network of special bike-friendly hotels, allows bicycle storage in its basement conference room, offers cyclists a glass of fruit juice on arrival and ... that's about it.

The design of our quarters was slightly eccentric, aptly described by G as "a bathroom with en suite beds", but there are more important aspects of hotels than sensible design, and the Abeille is a quirky character hotel that gets the important things right. Every detail is cherished, down to the bee-motif windows and glasses in which our free vitamin drink was served. Good honey, too.

At the northernmost point of the Loire, only 110km from Paris, Orléans prospered as a commercial port until the railways took over. Bordeaux wines arrived there for onward transport to the capital, many a barrel having been opened in transit by thirsty sailors, to the detriment of the contents. Orléans became the vinegar capital

Coffee, croissants and Joan.
Hôtel de l'Abeille, Orléans

of France and had 300 factories at the end of the 18th century. Only one remains, producing Orléans vinegar and mustard in the old-fashioned way: Martin-Pourret, at 236 Faubourg Bannier, in Fleury-les-Aubrais (north of the station). Follow your nose.

Orléans to Chitenay: about 90km

A single letter distinguishes the longest river in France from one of the shortest, and surely the absolute shortest to have given its name to a *département*. The little Loiret rises in a suburban park to the south of Orléans and joins mother Loire 12km later on the western edge of town. It is in fact a resurgence of Loire water that takes a dive at St-Benoît and travels 40km under ground before resurfacing in Olivet.

A short life, but a charmed one. The Loiret idles through the suburbs, with faux-rustic villas and mill houses overhanging the water, leafy waterside walks and boathouse *guinguette* restaurants redolent of the age of Impressionism when boating, drinking and dancing in the park was popular weekend leisure – a *fête galante* for downstairs folk. Le Pavillon Bleu has been relaunched recently as a *gastro-guinguette* hotel with Sunday afternoon dancing.

These days *guinguettes* like Le Pavillon Bleu and its neighbour, à Madagascar, compete with the Loire à Vélo in the weekend leisure market. On the July Saturday of our visit the competition was stacked against them, that day being designated Bike Day – *"La Loire à Vélo en Fête"* – with *animations* all along the water.

We spent much of the festive morning looking for Decathlon (yet another inner-tube mission) and trying to follow the Loiret out of town. Eventually we succeeded in both and, praise be, it was the last pit stop we had to make on the Loire. "Montjoie!" Joan might have said.

After a pause to inspect the tomb of Louis XI in the pilgrimage church at Cléry-St-André, we crossed the Loire with some trepidation. The bike paths were not unpleasantly full, but the Café du Commerce on the square at Meung-sur-Loire was.

On a quieter day it would have been a good lunch stop, overlooked by the old grey church of St Liphard, where a stained-glass roundel commemorates the arrival at Meung of the artist Ingres, who became Senator Ingres in 1862. Ten years earlier, at the age of 71, Ingres had taken a young *magdunoise* for his second wife and he spent his remaining 15 summers in a large house beside the river, playing his beloved violin while studio assistants worked on dreary history paintings like *Joan of Arc at the Coronation of Charles VII*. "*Je goûte à Meung un bonheur parfait de tranquillité*," wrote Ingres. No tortured artist, he. If only we could have said the same. "*Je goûte à Meung les moules froides*," said a disaffected Galaxy, and an ugly row with the management of the Café du Commerce ensued.

Beaugency's old bridge has 24 spans, and a few in the middle (with Gothic pointed arches) have withstood warfare and flood water for more than seven centuries. Beneath its old square *donjon*, Beaugency is one of the most attractive small towns on the Loire. Of the hotels that compete for a place on the itinerary, the Ecu de Bretagne

Beaugency

has a pool and would be my choice in preference to the slightly cheerless Abbaye. The simple Sologne would be a good cheaper alternative, if you wanted to stay a few nights and dine around.

Beaugency's picturesque qualities brought JMW Turner to a halt on a whistle-stop sketching tour in 1826. The project bore fruit in an influential book, *Wanderings By The Loire* (1833), with engravings after Turner's watercolours and text by a Scottish journalist, Leith Ritchie, who travelled the Loire in the opposite direction six years after Turner. While Ritchie was taking his notes of the river scene at Beaugency, the coach left without him and he had to walk to Blois to reclaim his belongings and the engravings he was writing about.

Now we were in the heart of Château Country. Following the river, Orléans to Tours would be achievable in a day: 117km, according to ViaMichelin, along the left-bank D-roads; and not much longer following the Loire à Vélo trail over the water at Meung and along the right bank through Beaugency before crossing back at Muides. But even the most blinkered cyclist would want to deviate, and there are temptations in all directions to taste. The strategic strongholds and big towns are on the river, but the hunting estates and stately piles are set back in the thick of the forest. There is also plenty to see along the Loire's nearby tributaries, the Cher and the Indre.

We found a narrow track along the left bank to St-Dyé, where we engaged with our first riverside festival *animation*: a wildlife information tent with a telescope trained on one of the many islands in the stream. A local expert invited me to have a look. "See those birds?" I nodded. "They're *bernaches nonnettes* (barnacle geese) and they shouldn't be here. I kill them." Welcome to the Loire, *fleuve sauvage*. It seems that owners of local hunting estates are to blame, for importing exotic species to adorn their ponds. The birds then escape, make themselves at home on the river and upset the balance. They are invasive, like knotweed with feathers.

St-Dyé would be the natural place to quit the river and ride south to Chambord. For the full theatrical effect of François I's great hunting lodge and its dance of seven veils as we approach through the *giboyeuse* forest, it is essential to come in from the north; ideally late in the day, because the north front inclines slightly to the west and catches the evening light perfectly.

Built for the king to impress his mistress or the Emperor Charles V, or both, Chambord was a temporary residence and is now an empty showpiece, a château of superlatives and statistics: 440 rooms (only about 90 open to visitors, mercifully), a fireplace for every day of the year, 31km of perimeter wall, a park the size of Paris and a beetling roofscape designed to remind us of the skyline of Constantinople.

The name of Leonardo always comes up in connection with Chambord, and its beginnings did coincide with the artist's Amboise years. But the only evidence is the design of the famous double-spiral staircase and the roof. The view from high up among the lanterns and dormers is much admired, and certainly extensive.

The travelling farmer Arthur Young looked out from this roof in September 1787. "If the King of France ever formed the idea of establishing one complete and perfect farm under the turnip culture of England, here is the perfect place for it," he wrote. The King's harvest, "instead of the flesh of boars, would be in the voice of cheerful gratitude". Louis wasn't listening.

I once had a ticking-off from a Treasury mandarin for recommending Chambord's hotel, the Grand St-Michel, with insufficient gush. After reconsideration, I find myself unrepentant. It is neither grand nor cosy nor cheap. But the location is – as hotels like to say – uniquely privileged. If you can arrange to be there on a moonlit night, the price would be worth paying.

Our route from St-Dyé took us along the left bank levee to Blois – a bit rough in places, but a beautiful way to approach the capital of the royal Loire. After a quick tour of the terraced town, which was tuning up for a rock concert, we rolled back over the river and headed for the quiet village of Chitenay, proud birthplace of Denis Papin, a Huguenot and inventor in exile of the pressure cooker (1696). If only the French had been more tolerant, they might have hosted the industrial revolution.

We may have taken a few wrong turns on our bicycles, but the creeper-clad Auberge du Centre at Chitenay was a resounding hit. The rooms are not the last word in 21st-century chic, and the price is not spectacularly low, but this is Château Country, not one of France's bargain basement zones. The trump card is the management. Busy yet relaxed, they seem to enjoy their work. They have the priceless knack of hospitality.

Wine appreciation classes are among the attractions listed on the hotel's Logis de France website, and we were treated to an informal one – a medley of local wines to accompany dinner – the crisp, the aromatic, the fizzy and the sweet. Well, who wants glass after glass of the same thing, when the Loire offers such delicious variety? We may have guessed the colours right, but not much else. It didn't matter. Supper in the garden was a complete pleasure and, when we tried to get our revenge by testing them, a waiter explained the Amboise Conspiracy with seamless erudition. I wish we had paid more attention to our host's sightseeing advice. He looked a little doubtful about our plan for the morning.

Chitenay to Noizay: about 75km
This was to be our short day, with visits and an early arrival at the Château de Noizay, our appointed treat of the trip, a stopover in luxury's lap.

Testing my theory that small châteaux are more fun, we found two that fitted a looping itinerary down to the Cher and back up to the Loire at Amboise via Chenonceaux.

A spin through the Cheverny vineyards brought us to the village of Fougères, where we were knocking on the ticket office window at opening time. A fine château it is, more medieval fortress with windows than Renaissance palace. We admired mint-condition machicolations and boiling-oil holes, had the place to ourselves and enjoyed our visit, although the interior is basically empty, but for a few props from an Eric Rohmer film.

Fougères

Our next stop was Le Gué-Péan (château and equestrian centre) reached by a longer and steeper approach road than we were counting on. But the setting is lovely and the exterior magnificent, with its cloche-tower and thoroughbreds gleaming in the foreground. We coincided with a veteran-car-club outing, and its convoy made a fine sight.

Unfortunately, the interior was a let-down. The château belongs to a futuristic architect who, after redoing the roof, is said to be "resting" – understandable budget fatigue. Between descriptions of assorted bric à brac, our guide was reduced to asking questions like "who would like to guess the size of this room?"

Having invested our hopes and quite a chunk of our day in Le Gué-Péan, it was a disappointment. But the old cars were fun.

Le Gué-Péan

We reached the Cher near the broken walls of a Gallo-Roman site (Thésée) and followed the river to Montrichard, a pretty town with just the sort of welcoming restaurant you want to find on a leafy square: La Villa. If only we hadn't stocked up with picnic provisions five minutes before.

Beneath its square tower and wooded hillside, Montrichard is the Cher's Beaugency, with the added attraction of troglo-tourism in the limestone caves that are such a feature of the region.

The caves are the result of quarrying for building stone, and the porous rock is particularly suitable for storing wine, growing mushrooms and silkworms, and living in. The most tempting visits are Monmousseau winery and La Magnanerie, a 17th-century silkworm farm and cave-dwelling museum at Bourré. We found a good picnic spot and swam, and thought the Cher water not quite so good as the Loire's.

Chenonceau (Zone Libre)

Chenonceau – the ladies' château, as it is known – tiptoes lightly across the Cher. Catherine de Medici chucked out her late husband's mistress Diane de Poitiers and put a long gallery on top of her predecessor's bridge. Take that! Unveiled as a ballroom in 1577, the gallery was a hospital in World War I, and an unauthorised conduit between Occupied France and the Zone Libre from 1940–42.

One of Chenonceau's ladies was George Sand's great grandmother Louise Dupin, a famous beauty who entertained all the big names of the French Enlightenment at Chenonceau and died there aged 93, allegedly having saved the château from destruction at the hands of the revolutionary mob by the ingenious ploy of removing x from its name.

The chocolate-box château will soon be celebrating the centenary of its acquisition by the Menier family of onetime *chocolatiers*. They have given it the full family-attraction treatment, with a maze, a mini-farm, a wax museum, as well as the formal gardens to explore and boats to row. The best crowd-beating strategy is to arrive at the very beginning or end of the day; and the best way to achieve that would be to stay in one of the village's two excellent hotels: the expensive and stylish Bon Laboureur, or the Roseraie which is similar, but less so.

Another way to enjoy the château is by taking the woodland path that runs along the Zone Libre bank, much appreciated by those who want to admire the view without joining the queue (or paying to enter). From the road bridge over the Cher, the path is not difficult to find.

We rode off to cross the Loire at Amboise and made for the nearby Château de Noizay, our progress delayed, annoyingly, by a *Route Barrée* situation. It was a long street jumble sale. My first experience of France on two wheels was on a Solex in Provence, circa 1965. I hadn't seen a Solex for ages but there were a few for sale here. Many of the other roadside bargains would not have been out of place at Le Gué-Péan.

The Château de Noizay has a heli-pad on the lawn, of course, but loose gravel on the drive makes life hazardous for the approaching cyclist. Imagining us to be in a small minority, I was surprised to see a stack of bikes in the garage. "Are they used much?" I wondered, picking some gravel out of my knee when the owner emerged from a big black 4x4 in a little black dress.

"Not really," said Madame William. "Most of our guests bring their own. We recommend rides for them and arrange wine-tastings with our best suppliers. Most people stay about a week." As an alternative to pedalling 720km along the river, this sounds not too bad. The Domaine Vigneau Chevreau at Chançay is only 4km from Noizay. Two brothers extend a warm welcome to guests of Madame William and will send boxes of Vouvray to you at home.

Every château has its anecdote that stands out from the white noise of history. Blois has the murder of the duc de Guise in the king's bedroom, shortly after breakfast on December 23rd 1588. "How big he is! Even bigger dead than alive!" said the admiring Henri III, emerging from behind the curtains after 20 hired

Wish you were here? Le Château de Noizay

assassins had finally managed to subdue and finish off the Herculean duke.

Amboise recalls the unfortunate death of nice but dim Charles VIII ("*l'affable*"), who after setting the monarchy on course for bankruptcy in pursuit of military glory in Italy, hit his head on a door frame while hurrying to a game of tennis – easily done – and succumbed two hours later.

Noizay's claim to fame is the Amboise Conspiracy of 1560, about which we had been so well briefed by our waiter in Chitenay. Stained-glass portraits of its protagonists, de la Renaudie (Protestant) and the duc de Guise (an earlier one, Catholic) scowled down at us as we carried our bags upstairs. Nor were the hotel staff particularly impressed. They hate being denied the chance to carry luggage, but it saves the disorganised Englishman tip-related stress. Our panniers are not heavy, honestly.

The Amboise Conspiracy was a failed coup d'état: a Protestant plot to remove young King François II from the protection of the hard-line Catholic faction. De Guise got wind of it, rounded up the conspirators at Noizay and massacred plotters and sympathisers by the hundred, beheading some, drowning others in the Loire and stringing the rest from the balconies and battlements of the Château d'Amboise.

Noizay has burned down and been rebuilt since then and is a more comfortable hotel as a result, with a purple library, elegant dining rooms and plenty of space on the lawn for breakfast as well as helicopter manoeuvres. There is a tennis court too, and a pool at the bottom of the garden with a hot line to the bar. Lukewarm, anyway.

"Hello. Is that the bar?"

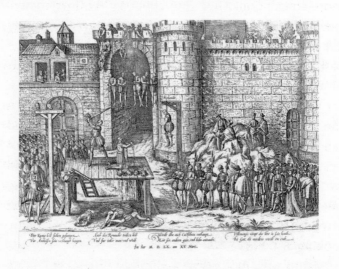

Exemplary punishment

"Yes."

"I'd like a drink, please."

"Certainly." (Click).

Long, dry minutes passed before the man appeared.

"What would you like to drink?"

"A beer, please."

He went away again.

All too soon it was time to scrub up for dinner. Vouvray white, lamb pink, Bourgueil red, all perfect.

Noizay to Saumur: 106km

Arthur Young found the landscape between Amboise and Tours "more uninteresting than I could have thought possible for the vicinity of a great river".

It is a point of view, and an interesting contrast to the more conventional line, put about by local promoters such as Balzac and de Vigny, that Touraine is an earthly paradise. I have found the Loire disappointing in the past, but it looked much more beautiful from the seat of a bicycle than through a car window. One reason for this may be the levees, which hide the river from the motorist but are ideal for cycling. The shoals and sandbanks which Arthur Young found "subversive of beauty" did not worry us. On the contrary, they add variety to the scene. The Loire is always changing, one minute a broad and resplendent mirror, the next a weave of little channels. Birds love it, and we enjoy looking at them.

Main roads, motorways and railway lines complicate the approach to Tours, and this is not the quiet countrified

France that makes for easy and relaxed cycling. We found a small road through the Vouvray vineyards, crossed to the left bank of the Loire and followed the Loire à Vélo into town – a good, traffic-free piste. Tours did not detain us long. We rode along the cycle lane of a riverside boulevard (*rive gauche*) and followed a cyclist down to the quay assuming we would be able to stay on it until we reached open country.

After inspecting the flood levels and distance table on the wall – only 255km to St-Nazaire – we soon found ourselves forced away from the water and up on to a dual carriageway which turned alarmingly into a ring-road flyover heading south. From this we escaped with difficulty, sliding down a prickly embankment with our bikes in hand to scramble through a hole in the fence perhaps left by a previous cyclist who luckily for us had the foresight to travel with wire-cutters.

From this awkward spot we found our way back to the river at St-Genouph, and a quiet road took us along the narrowing spit of land that separates the Loire and Cher, returning to the Loire à Vélo at Savonnières, a pretty village with a bathing beach and a tempting restaurant beside the Cher – La Maison Tourangelle. Villandry was crowded and keeps its famous symbolic Renaissance gardens hidden from view, so we kept going, following the yellow D7 for some reason in preference to the small road that hugs the Loire's left bank. Perhaps we were late.

Not too late for a wine-tasting, however. A white cliff wall beside the road was by now a familiar sight, with

Troglo-vin

locked doors of mushroom caves and troglo self-storage units. But there was an open door among them, with an advertisement for Azay-le-Rideau wine and an invitation to enter. Rude not to.

"Hide your bike," G said urgently, but it was too late. Vigneron Frédéric Hardy of Vallères had seen us dismount and looked frosty at first. But he uncorked several Azay-le-Rideau whites and a pink, and warmed to us over time, or so I felt, especially when we bought a little something to tuck in the pannier for later encouragement.

"Where are your vineyards?" I asked.

"Up there," he replied, pointing at the ceiling.

It was later than late-lunch time when we reached Rigny-Ussé and the cleaner than clean *tuffeau* hotel le

Clos d'Ussé. It is a simple billet, but a friendly one, and we were glad to find a French chef on flexitime. Cycling tour operators have it on their books and the new intake was arriving just as we finished lunch. Their day's work was complete, but we still had a long way to go.

Ussé, Sleeping Beauty's castle. The noble family of de Blacas has hit on this brilliant sales pitch for their fairy-tale home and never lets us forget it, in the same way that some people seem unable to say Loire without blurting out "*dernier fleuve sauvage*". So relentlessly do they bang the drum, it makes us think, in a Paxmanish way: why are they trying so hard to persuade us?

Read Charles Perrault's genre-defining fairy tale (late 17th century) and there isn't much to link the story with Ussé, apart from the statement that the towers of the château stood out against the dark forest, which seems a bit thin. Nor is there anything conclusive in Gustave Doré's wonderful 19th-century illustrations, although Ussé's interior design team may have used them when making the waxwork Sleeping Beauty scenes on display in the château.

Ussé is many visitors' favourite Loire château. It is set well back from the river, but a small road as straight as Cupid's arrow leads from the house to the river bank. We rode along this beautiful approach in the wrong direction, and turned left on to a cycle path, rough in places, which took us through wooded glades of fairy-tale seclusion, following the Loire and then crossing back over the indolent Indre just before the confluence of the

L'Indre à Vélo

two rivers. At which point the opportunity arose not only to swim, but also to enact the Loire à Vélo's familiar motif of a bicycle wheel in water. I got about halfway across before crashing, and I would like to take this opportunity to apologise to my bicycle. The waterproof panniers worked rather well.

After a 370km descent from the Millevaches plateau, the Vienne throws its weight into the Loire at Candes, east of Saumur. It is a step change for the Loire, which at last becomes a really serious, grown-up river, with enough water to fill its bed. The confluence itself is a fine sight and Candes, steeply pitched above the water, has a tall and elegant Angevin church with a good restaurant beside it: La Route d'Or. There are inviting hotels at the next village, Montsoreau, with restaurants and cafés beside the river.

From here we rode south for half an hour to pay our respects to the greatest of all the *grandes dames* of medieval history, Eleanor of Aquitaine, who is buried with her husband Henry and son Richard, Plantagenet kings of England both, at the abbey of Fontevraud. The abbey buildings are extensive and beautiful – especially the tombs and the astonishing many-chimneyed Romanesque kitchen – but the presentation is decidedly weird: "follow the trail of the black cat" left us puzzled. Part of the abbey is a hotel, and the idea of staying there has great appeal. But the abbey is publicly owned and the atmosphere a bit institutional.

A bigger river is not the only change at Saumur. The gentle landscape of Touraine, the garden of France, gives way to the hills of Anjou. Soon, white tuffeau stone of Château Country will be replaced by the hard flint and black stone of the Angevin fortresses built by that warlike old ruffian, Fulk Nerra, who celebrated the close of the first millennium by burning his wife in her wedding dress.

Standing four square and unequivocally martial high above the stream, Saumur's royal fortress still has the look of a Loire château, and a mighty one. We had hoped to visit a winery for a glass of fizzy Saumur, but missed that deadline by miles.

Saumur to Champtoceaux: 110km

Our hotel on the heights above Saumur was close to the town airfield. It is a draughty spot, and as we left in the morning I noticed that the windsock had turned during the night. Uh-oh.

When we presented ourselves at the entrance to the nearby Ecole Nationale d'Equitation, warm sunshine was still the prevailing regime, but by the time we made our apologies and absconded from the unfinished tour an hour and a half later, the sky had turned milky; and soon after lunch, at Chalonnes-sur-Loire, the clouds burst.

It was a squally shower that soon passed, but there were more to come and the wind blew harder in our faces as we approached the coast. For the remaining day and a half we were fighting the weather. To say that this affected our mood may be a shameful admission but it is nonetheless true.

The Ecole Nationale d'Equitation is a university-like campus and the home of the Cadre Noir, the crème de la crème of French horsemen and women who train athletes and aspiring professionals in the art and discipline of traditional French riding. It is the equine Académie Française, and it has its origin, naturally, in cavalry training. About half of the 43 Cadre Noir *écuyers* are soldiers; these are the ones with an exploding-grenade motif on their caps. The civilian trainers have a shining sun. The *Ecuyer en Chef* – or *Grand Dieu* – is always a soldier.

Galaxy and I are not horse crazy, but we loved the Cadre Noir. For 15 minutes we sat entranced in the indoor school – "hats off, gentlemen" – watching the *écuyers* go through their paces and practise their drills, making patterns in the earth like a ballet rehearsal under the watchful eye of Grand Dieu, Colonel Faure. Whether you see them practise their famous jumps – *cabrioles* and *croupades* – is a matter of luck, depending on their performance schedule.

We visited the horses in their stables and observed the whip-thin men in black bark their orders at students bouncing prettily up and down in the outdoor ring. It was a shame to tear ourselves away, but we had riding of our own to do.

If I go through the rest of this trip at a canter, it is not because we speeded up – on the contrary. Against the wind, you put your head down and devote all your effort to pushing the damn pedal round. Many details go unnoticed, but I did finally satisfy myself that sunflowers do not follow the sun through the day. At least, in July they don't.

Staying south of the Loire, we cycled through vine-yards and endless sunflowers to a wine museum at St-Lambert-du-Lattay. I have found the sweet white Côtes du Layon a good name to drop in serious wine circles, and was interested to find out something about it; and perhaps even taste some after years of claiming to be an aficionado.

Hearty lunch at Chavagnes (Le Forever), full of *agricul-teurs* in muddy boots. 26 euros for two, including a beer each, coffee, a three-course lunch and a carafe of red that arrived uninvited as we sat down.

The wine museum was OK, with many old barrels and bottles and presses displayed, seasonal tasks and tools well explained; but I found its tone – celebrating the marriage of Monsieur Lhomme and Madame Lavigne – a bit precious. The setting is not a patch on Sancerre, and we cycled away undefiled Côtes du Layon virgins. The museum was not a tasting experience, and the Layon is not a swimming experience.

After the downpour at Chalonnes we stopped at Montjean to dry off with a cup of tea beside the bridge over the Loire. A few yards away on the *quai des Mariniers*, the humble Auberge de la Loire looks cheerful and good – an address to remember for next time.

The Hôtel de la Gabelle at St-Florent-le-Vieil, by contrast, is a beautiful building that has fallen into the wrong hands. Drained of energy, I requested crisps, or nuts, or cheese, or anything salty to go with the drink and top up my mineral level. From behind the bar, only a shrug and a shake of the head. Negative.

"Do you have salt?" Considering the hotel is named after the salt tax, the situation did not lack irony. The barman grudgingly produced a salt cellar, and looked surprised when I emptied a pile into my hand and ate it. Perhaps he expected me to pay tax.

St-Florent is pitched on a steep hill beside the river. Cyclists can save energy by following the track under the bridge.

The salt did the trick, and the long slope up to Champtoceaux was duly accomplished. "*La route est longue mais la vue est belle!*" said the charming M Rabu, who was waiting for us at the door of his hotel, Le Champalud, with a glass in hand. M Rabu has been at Champtoceaux for 26 years (27 now), and never tires of the view.

Having moved out of Anjou and into old Brittany, we were now passing through towns and villages with bloody memories of the Vendée war, a royalist peasants' revolt in the aftermath of the Revolution; Champtoceaux lost one villager in six in three massacres in 1794. Beneath their fine portraits, we toasted the brave war leaders in a three-glass medley of local wines that M Rabu serves with the set-price dinner menu. We had waited a long time for a *filet de brochet au beurre blanc*, and Le Champalud did it well. The bedrooms across the road are smart, modern and big, and the view of the Loire from the nearby belvedere is magnificent. The river is tidal now.

Champtoceaux to St-Brévin-L'Océan: about 100km

We crossed the Loire, now bloated and flowing from west to east on the rising tide, at Mauves, and found a Loire à Vélo trail along the water to Nantes – an excellent way into the city, until it ran out at the bottom of a staircase. We found it hard to imagine how they hope to make a good riverside cycling piste all the way through Nantes, with its dockyards, dry docks, wharves, warehouses and the other heavy installations of an industrial/commercial/naval port.

After admiring the cathedral and its beautiful tomb of François II, duke of Brittany and his wife Margaret of Foix, we made our way out of town via the duke's moated castle, passing warships tied to the quay.

We then failed to find the first ferry across the Loire, but found the second and took refuge from the rain in a cheap restaurant (ten euros each, including wine) beside the jetty at Le Pellerin.

From there the disaffected – yes! – Canal de la Martinière (or rather its towpath) plus some guesswork took us most of the way to Paimboeuf, a workaday estuary port that looked interesting. But when you are 10km from the end of a great river and a long bike ride, you do not stop to smell the flowers.

My suggestion was to take some minor roads to our hotel in St-Brévin, the alluringly named Casino Hotel Beryl; drop our things and have a swim in the ocean before riding up the seafront to admire the estuary, take photographs, shake hands and all the rest of it.

"I'm not doing that!" said Galaxy, and set off into the wind, up the main road.

I'm afraid I took this quite badly. What happened to negotiation and compromise? I spent the next 45 minutes rehearsing what I would I say when we next spoke – if we next spoke – imagining what G would say back, and composing my biting response to that.

The left bank of the Loire turned left and became a beach. We had reached the end. There was no acrimonious exchange, but a happy handshake. Well done, Galaxy. Well done, Madam.

"Actually," he said, "the last two days were a lovely bike ride."

That's easy to say, afterwards.

Before the trip I had researched the bridge over the mouth of the Loire between St-Brévin and St-Nazaire – is it *cyclable*? Answer: yes, it is, and there is no shortage of vélo-bloggers who will tell you they ride merrily across it all the time – no problem at all, with and without children in a trailer. Others warn that cycling over the bridge is actually quite dangerous, with no cycle lane to speak of and a high risk of a nasty crosswind.

I also read about a new bus shuttle service, with bicycle spaces, between St-Brévin (Pole de Bresse bus stop) and St-Nazaire station, and since we had a train to catch from St-Nazaire in the morning, we decided to book the bus, against the risk of bad weather. Arriving at St-Brévin to see a sign warning motorists of strong wind on the bridge, we were glad we had our bus tickets reserved, and when we crossed the bridge by bus the next morning we were still glad. The bus (No 17) takes about 15 minutes and the reservation number is 0033 240215087.

To its great credit Brittany Ferries had warned us by text message that the Tour de France would be

Pont St-Nazaire. *Not recommended on a windy day*

crossing Normandy on the afternoon of our return sailing from Caen, with a rolling programme of road closures that we should beware. It was not difficult to establish the details of the day's ride, with estimated timings of exactly when the Tour would arrive at various points along the route. Rather than visit the château at Angers to see its famous Apocalypse tapestries, we decided, in the spirit of our enterprise, to head north and intercept the Tour near Falaise, after a hypermarket visit to buy wine.

According to Ouest-France, something called *la caravane* was expected to reach the junction of the D511 and the D39 at 14.18 precisely, and that made a good fit with our crossing. We were not quite sure what relation *la caravane* bore to *le peloton*, but they could surely not be far apart, so we craftily went past Falaise, did our shopping and approached the D511 from the north, in the interests of an easy getaway.

A small bank of spectators had gathered beside the road and we joined them. Occasional police motorbikes came past, lights flashing importantly. A car pulling a large caravan – not *the* caravan – approached from the south, attempted to cross the road, was told it couldn't and crashed into a parked car while trying to reverse. A great cheer went up – "*Bravo la caravane!*" – but, with police watching, it was bad luck. At last the word went round: "*La caravane arrive!*" Cameras were primed, necks craned. It was a carnival procession of sponsor vehicles, with music blaring and dancing girls hurling sweets, Cheesy Wotsits and advertising leaflets at us. "The caravan lasts for more than an hour," someone said, so we made our escape and saved the Tour de France proper for another day.

Hotels (with restaurants unless stated)

* = cheap, ***** = expensive

**   Decize, L'Agriculture
www.hoteldelagriculture.fr   0033 386250538

**   Marseilles-lès-Aubigny, Alphonsia Maria (B&B)
http://alphonsia.chez-alice.fr/hote.htm
0033 248761441/0033 621380160

***   Chavignol, La Côte des Monts Damnés
www.montsdamnes.com   0033 248540172

***   St-Thibault, La Loire (B&B)
www.hotel-de-la-loire.fr   0033 248782222

**   St-Benoît-sur-Loire, Le Labrador
www.hoteldulabrador.fr   0033 238357438

***   Orléans, L'Abeille (B&B)
www.hoteldelabeille.com   0033 238535487

***   Beaugency, L'Ecu de Bretagne
www.ecudebretagne.fr   0033 238446760

**   Beaugency, La Sologne (B&B)
www.hoteldelasologne.com   0033 238445027

***   Chambord, Grand St Michel
www.saintmichel-chambord.com   0033 254203131

**   Chitenay, L'Auberge du Centre
www.auberge-du-centre.com   0033 254704211

****   Chenonceaux, Le Bon Laboureur
www.bonlaboureur.com   0033 247239002

***   Chenonceaux, La Roseraie
www.hotel-chenonceau.com   0033 247239009

****   Noizay, Le Château de Noizay
www.chateaudenoizay.com   0033 247521101

**   Rigny-Ussé, Le Clos d'Ussé
    www.leclosdusse.fr   0033 247955547

**   Montjean, L'Auberge de la Loire
    www.aubergedelaloire.com   0033 241398020

***   Champtoceaux, Le Champalud
    www.lechampalud.com   0033 240835009

***   St Brevin-L'Océan, Beryl
    www.hotel-stbrevinlocean.com   0033 228532000

Restaurants

***   Tours, L'Hédoniste   0033 247052040

**   Givry, L'Auberge de L'Ecluse   0033 386909728

**   Marseilles-lès-Aubigny, L'Auberge du Poids de Fer
    00 33 248764185

**   Briare, Petit St Trop'   0033 238370031

**   St-Benoît-sur-Loire, Au Grand St Benoît   0033 238351192

***   Orléans, Au Bon Marché   0033 238530435

***   Olivet, Le Pavillon Bleu   0033 238661430

***   Olivet, A Madagascar   0033 238661258

**   Montrichard, La Villa   00 33 254320734

***   Savonnières, La Maison Tourangelle   00 33 247503005

**   Candes, La Route d'Or   0033 247958110

*   Chavagnes, Le Forever   0033 241543123

Information

Burgundy   www.crt-bourgogne.fr

Centre   www.visaloire.com; www.loirevalleytourism.com

Pays de la Loire   www.enpaysdelaloire.com;
    www.anjou-tourisme.com; www.ohlaloireatlantique.com

Maps   www.eurovelo6.org

La Loire à Vélo   www.loireavelo.fr

Ferries (Portsmouth/Caen)   www.brittany-ferries.co.uk

ROUTE 6

LA ROUTE DES VACANCES

Paris to Avignon (about 840km)
July-August 2011

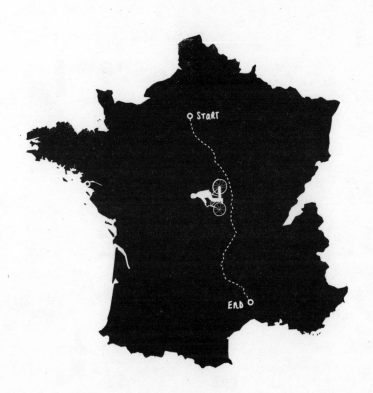

De toutes les routes de France, d'Europe,
Celle que j'préfère est celle qui conduit
En auto ou en auto-stop
Vers les rivages du Midi.

Nationale Sept —
C'est une route qui fait recette
Route des vacances
Qui traverse la Bourgogne et la Provence
Qui fait d'Paris un p'tit faubourg d'Valence...

Le ciel d'été
Remplit nos cœur de sa lucidité
Chasse les aigreurs et les acidités
Qui font l'malheur des grandes cités...
(from the song "Nationale 7", by Charles Trenet)

The road south from Paris to le Midi was our last ride, for the time being (we hope). For the French it is the defining migration, a mad dash that separates work from play, city from beach, carbon monoxide from the scent of lavender, north from south. It is the great escape from darkness to light, with all the thrill of the *départ*, unclouded by thoughts of the distant *rentrée*.

Over three weekends at the beginning and end of July and August, the nation is on the road. Outsiders mock the French for their blind refusal to adopt a more sensibly staggered approach to their lives. They know they ought to go on holiday in June or September. But what would be the point? Everyone else would be working. Real Parisians, with lives, do not shirk the *chassé croisé* but sally forth into the fray. The mad dash is a kind of validation.

Artists and aristocrats of the Enlightenment travelled down the Rhône Valley on their Italian journey. At the end of the 19th century Provence was the destination for Van Gogh, Cézanne and others who fled dingy Paris for the sharp light and heightened palette of the south. Picasso, Chagall and Matisse based themselves on the Riviera, where by their time the money was, but they too travelled backwards and forwards between Paris and the south.

Before the Autoroute du Sud (Paris to Lyon) and the Autoroute du Soleil (Lyon to Marseille) were completed in 1974, the mythic road was the N7 – *la Nationale Sept*, immortalised in Charles Trenet's song: from Paris to Menton via Nevers, Moulins, Lyon, Valence, Avignon and Aix-en-Provence. A pilgrimage route for the sun worshipper, it was punctuated by a new kind of pilgrimage hostel. In the early 1950s a hotelier couple from the Rhône Valley assembled a group of eight like-minded establishments along the road from Paris to the Riviera, all with the same idea of gracious living, and called themselves Les Relais & Châteaux.

La route des vacances was also *la route qui fait recette* (the recipe road), studded by the legends of French gastronomy – the great Point at Vienne, refusing to serve Germans during the war and anyone who ordered Coca Cola; Pic at Valence; Alexandre Dumaine at Saulieu. La Mère Brazier was the Bressane farm girl who won an unprecedented six Michelin stars for her restaurants in Lyon and gave the young Paul Bocuse his first *apprentissage* – washing-up, ironing and milking.

At 80-something, the amazing Bocuse remains enthroned beside the Saône at Collonges, still turning out his famous truffle soup VGE – created for President Giscard at the Elysée Palace in 1975 – and glaring out from the posters like a Russian head of state at a Moscow parade. Is he still alive? Would they tell us, if he wasn't? The Troisgros brothers pitched camp on the N7 at Roanne and the family is still there, defying the motorway and recently celebrating 40 uninterrupted years of three Michelin stars, a record only Bocuse can trump. Pic's granddaughter Anne-Sophie flies the family flag at Valence and was recently crowned the world's top woman chef. That sounds a slightly patronising title for the 21st century, but France does lag on these issues.

"... *en voiture ou en auto-stop...*" sang Charles Trenet. And the bicycle? Obviously, the cyclist would not choose the Nationale Sept, even now that long stretches of it have been demoted to the D, something or other. But we also find the experience of travelling down the map of France exciting. Travelling north is an uphill struggle: inescapable from a sense of swapping warmer, friendlier and more romantic places for cooler, greyer and more workaday ones.

From the forest clearings and potato fields made famous by the Barbizon artists, our ride would take us through heart-shaped Burgundy, a French heartland with the best of everything: Charolais beef, the big wines of the Côte de Beaune, art and architecture from the golden age of Burgundian power, when kings and emperors came knocking at the duke's door hoping for a marriage alliance.

Threaded by canals linking the Atlantic (rivers Loire and Seine) and the Mediterranean (the Saône and Rhône), post-industrial Burgundy has become the capital of the canal holiday, a slow-moving experience of rural France that makes our *chevauchées* seem like whistle-stop raids. Glass in hand, the bargees sit back and watch the fortress villages and pleasant pastures slide by, stirring themselves occasionally for a wine-tasting or sightseeing expedition on dry land. We would do our time on the towpath, and be grateful for it, while always protesting about the tedium of cycling along canals.

Beyond Burgundy we would by-pass Lyon via the less familiar regions of Bresse, the Dombes and the Drôme, before the Rhône Valley vineyards of Hermitage and Châteauneuf-du-Pape and the lavender fields of Upper Provence. With a bit of luck the South of France's famous north wind, the Mistral, would kick in at Lyon and blow us down the Rhône Valley.

We had not particularly planned to make this trip at the height of the summer rush, but the inland regions through which we were travelling are not summer holiday favourites, and on our back roads there was no particular reason to worry about the fact that the motor-ways would be full. Was there?

The biggest *chassé croisé* weekend of all, at the end of July, would see us close to the motorway at

Montélimar or thereabouts. On Saturday the *aoûtiens* would be heading south on one carriageway, the *juilletistes* heading north on the other. "Will we ever find a bed?" I asked Galaxy.

"Does anyone break the motorway journey through France these days?" my friend replied. "You're stuck in the age when people stopped for the night in Taunton on their way to Cornwall." That's all right then.

I had read that on Sundays the expressways along the banks of the Seine through central Paris, known snappily as *autoberges*, are reserved for cyclists and other non-motorised traffic – pedestrians and roller-blading bag-snatchers. For the pleasure of riding beneath the Pont-Neuf singing *"sous les ponts de Paris"* in my best Eartha Kitt growl, we would start on Sunday.

A few weeks before departure, I realised that the Sunday I had chosen was the final stage of the Tour de France, when the brave survivors enter Paris and race, or do not race, as the case may be – the Tour is not one of my special subjects, and its arcane anti-competitive conventions are largely a mystery to me – laps of the Champs-Elysées before the final podium moment beneath the Arc de Triomphe.

We would be arriving in Paris by Eurostar from the north at around lunchtime. The Tour de France would be arriving from the south-east at around the same time, as if to welcome us. It seemed a happy piece of timing. Obviously we understood that tagging along behind the *peloton* would be out of the question, 50kph along the flat being beyond us, even with slipstreaming. But perhaps

317

we would be able to see the riders go past, and give our man Cav a wave.

After that, we had no intention of riding out through the suburbs. Bicycles are allowed on the RER – the Metro+ lines that serve the suburbs and connect with the Metro proper at a few stations in central Paris.

Since the Gare du Nord is an RER stop, engaging with Paris was not strictly necessary, but exploring the centre of the city would be a pleasure. A train leaving Gare de Lyon for Melun (Line D, via St-Fargeau) would take us out to a point beside the Seine where we could set off through the forest for Fontainebleau, Burgundy and the sun.

If I had thought about lunch it was probably to assume that we would eat something on Eurostar. Galaxy had other ideas. Who wants to eat on the train, when Paris awaits?

The conventional Sunday lunch hour had long passed by the time we escaped the tumult of the Gare du Nord, and when we found an Italian restaurant open on the Rue de Trévise, we grabbed it. Lunch was no great shakes, and there was a feeling of a missed opportunity when minutes later we rode past consumers of Parisian brasserie culture snacking elegantly on the Boulevard des Italiens.

We turned left at the Opéra, passed the fortified shop windows of the thoroughfare referred to on Cityrama bus tours as Peace Street, crossed the Place Vendôme and saw the Rue de Rivoli ahead of us roped off and guarded by banks of spectators. Turning left again, we rode past the *bottiers* and *gantiers* of the Rue St-Honoré as far as the Comédie Française, where we were finally allowed to turn right, following the flow of traffic through an opening in the Louvre Palace and between M Pei's glass pyramid, which once seemed so audacious, and Napoleon's dainty little Arc de Triomphe du Carrousel. Another opening in the Louvre brought us to the Seine, where we looked down on the riverside expressway: a throng of slow-moving humanity.

As a cycle track it was obviously hopeless: the only option would be to dismount and push our bikes in the mêlée. So we stayed on the Quai François Mitterrand (as no one calls the Quai du Louvre) and followed it along the river, keeping Eartha Kitt in her cage. A festive atmosphere prevailed, and smiles were to be observed on the faces of policemen. "The Tour de France? They should be here by now, but apparently there has been some delay," one told me. We reached the Gare de Lyon and disappeared under ground. Once again, the Tour had escaped us.

The RER may permit bicycles, but it does not go out of its way to accommodate them. Luckily at teatime on a Sunday in July the network was not busy, nor the journey too stressful. I would not want to try it in the rush hour. Manhandling our bikes through the automatic barrier was a struggle, and on the train we simply held them beside our seats and let our fellow passengers clamber around and about. As we ticked off the stations, and high-rise urban ghettoes gave way to *petit bourgeois* dormitory suburbs, we tried to decide where to start riding.

Ponthierry-Pringy to Moret-sur-Loing: about 35km

Tempted by a view of the Seine, we jumped off our train at Ponthierry-Pringy (three stops from the end of the line), took a path along the river and reached a yacht club (dead end). Galaxy was in a minor flap because his computer was playing up. I recalled the scornful remarks he had directed at my bicycle-computer habit, when we set out on our first bike ride together... and forgot them again in the interests of amity. Eventually we found a way out of Ponthierry-Pringy-St-Fargeau's sprawl and in to open country via an unpleasantly busy road that may once have been the mythic N7, now humiliatingly renamed the D607. Mythic or not, we abandoned it as soon as we could.

Forests do not always offer the most varied cycling, but Fontainebleau's has hills and vistas, rocky outcrops, sandy clearings and *routes forestières*. An added attraction is the village of Barbizon, which gave its name to the first 19th-century school of *plein-air* French landscape painting. Corot was its father figure, and Millet, Théodore Rousseau and many others left Paris in search of beautiful trees and scenes of humble peasant toil in and around Fontainebleau forest. Père Ganne's *auberge* provided cheap food and lodging and a forum for creative intercourse. In 1853 part of the forest was declared a *"réserve artistique"*.

"The noiseless hamlet lying close among the borders of the wood is a green spot in memory," wrote Robert Louis Stevenson, who described himself as "a consistent Barbizonian" and met his future wife Fanny there in 1875.

Stevenson's base was the Siron hotel, now the luxurious Hostellerie du Bas-Bréau. Barbizon trades successfully on its arty past, with studios to visit and waymarked trails in the painters' footsteps. But these days the price of lodging is pitched at high-end tourists and weekenders, not struggling artists.

To find a quiet route through the forest ought not to have been beyond us, but all the roads we tried were fast and furious. When we did finally identify a likely bridle path, near the Carrefour du Grand Veneur, it was on the other side of the road and we stood for ages waiting for a gap in the roaring traffic. Eventually we made it across and scuttled gratefully into the woods.

A temporary home for many studious expats, Fontainebleau may not be the prettiest town in France, but to my eye it has the best of all French royal châteaux, its park and gardens open to the town centre and

La Cour des Adieux, Fontainebleau

surrounding forest. Napoleon abdicated there in April 1814. From the top of the beautiful staircase that leads up to the door in the Cour des Adieux, the emperor said farewell to the Old Guard before leaving for Elba.

"I have therefore sacrificed my interests and yours to those of our nation – I'm leaving," he declared. "If I have consented to survive, it is to further serve the cause of our glory. I'm going to write about the great things we have done together!"

I could have tried a similar speech on Galaxy, but there was no time to lose so we pedalled off through the park and out into the dark forest, where supper might be waiting if we got a move on.

Moret-sur-Loing's painter was Alfred Sisley, the "English" Impressionist who married in Cardiff and honeymooned in Penarth but spent the rest of his life in France and the last two decades of it (1880–99) in the old village of Moret, which still looks much as he painted it, especially if seen from across the water – bridge and Burgundy Gate overlooked by the solid Gothic church of Notre Dame. A bicycle museum in an old accessories factory beside the canal commemorates Moret's footnote in history as the birthplace of la pince parisienne, the bicycle clip.

The Auberge de la Terrasse suited us well, set in the fabric of Moret's town wall and looking out over the Loing, with a front door on the street and a cellar exit to the grassy river bank, where ducks wait for scraps, apparently unaware that the Terrasse's restaurant is closed on Sunday evening. The setting is delightful – or would be, in better weather – and the price level more provincial than Parisian.

We ate at the nearby Porte de Bourgogne, which operates an all-you-can-eat hot and cold buffet. This is a formula rarely encountered in France, but popular with Moret's riverboat holiday clientele, according to the young couple in charge. It worked for us too.

Moret-sur-Loing to Ligny-le-Châtel: about 110km

One of my worries about this trip had been the weather. We had struggled through the heat of Aquitaine in May. Did it really make sense to aim for the South of France at the height of summer? Well, here we were on July 25th, hauling on our rain jackets against a damp and chilly Monday morning.

Our route took us prettily along the valley of the Orvanne, and I was looking out for signs of Burgundy. When would we leave commuter country and enter real country? Moret's "Burgundy Gate" implies frontier status, but the Loing is not one of the rivers that make an island of the Ile-de-France, and when we stopped to inspect the village of Flagy and its old mill, a cosy place for candlelit dinners and fireside intimacy, it had the part-time atmosphere of a weekend bolthole.

At Vallery we wandered around an imposing château that once belonged to the powerful Condé family and may have rivalled Fontainebleau for magnificence. The passing centuries have not been kind to Vallery, and it was not looking its best in the rain on a Monday morning. Nor were the guests, who were beginning to emerge blearily from the outbuildings, smoking hard and clutching their heads. The château is a wedding venue and it had obviously been a good do.

Somewhere between Voulx and Vallery the number plates – on the older cars, at least – told us we had left Seine-et-Marne (77) and entered Yonne (89). Now we were technically in Burgundy, but I was not convinced until we crossed the brow of a hill a few miles short of Sens and overlooked the broad bosom of an unmistakably Burgundian valley. The colourfully patterned roof tiles on the bishop's palace in Sens confirmed it.

St-Etienne's claims to be the oldest Gothic cathedral in France. Sober in style, it has beautiful sculpture around the doorways, especially the north, and stained glass including a window telling the story of Thomas Becket, one of three archbishops of Canterbury produced by the nearby abbey of Pontigny. The murder scene, which is high up on the window and not the easiest to decipher, has lost its sword.

G and I rarely have difficulty finding something to dither about, and on this damp day we were undecided about lunch. The weather was hardly conducive to picnicking.

The indoor market at Sens swung our decision: a mouth-watering invitation to shop and a sightseeing treat in itself. We had so often bemoaned the lack of village shops… now that we confronted the perfect French food hall, it would be a crime to pass it up. Baskets of strawberries, figs and apricots begged to be bought. There were trays crammed with artichokes, tomatoes gleaming, melons piled up like cannon balls, aubergines polished to a dazzle. Over here for smelly Epoisses cheese; over there for *boucherie chevaline*. In the fish section, beady-eyed *rascasses* glared angrily from their bed of ice.

This is just the sort of place you want to find on the first day of a trip: welcome to France, and *bon appétit*. The stall-holders are quite used to picnickers buying their morsels – one tomato, one melon, one *tranche* of pâté and another of goat's cheese.

While I dithered over the selection of the appropriate tomato, Galaxy concentrated on a charming member of the Séguinot family who had set out her stall in the central aisle. The Séguinots are from Maligny, a few miles north of Chablis.

To go with our picnic, would it be Séguinot's *frais et frivole* Petit Chablis, *charmeur et expressif* Chablis, *puissant et minéral* Chablis Vieilles Vignes or *sensuel et complexe* Chablis 1er Cru?

This may not be one of Galaxy's Laws. He would probably declare it not so much a law as a principle of the most devastatingly obvious common sense: drink expensive wine with your picnic baguette, cheap wine with your bleeding *gigot* in the Michelin-starred dining room.

G chose Séguinot's Chablis Vieilles Vignes 2009. As fuel for the cyclist, powerful and mineral sounded less risky than sensual and complex.

Galaxy's Law did require us to accomplish quite a few more kilometres before stopping to enjoy our Chablis Vieilles Vignes. We followed the Vanne as far as the village of Vareilles, where we turned south along the D76. I mention the details, because the best route south through the Forêt d'Othe, *direction* Chablis, is not obvious and I think ours was good.

Before long it showed us a sign pointing up a steepish hill to a place called Heurtebise, a name that lodged in my mind years ago, from Jean Cocteau's film *Orphée*, in which the Heurtebise character was some kind of spectral chauffeur from the Underworld. To my surprise, Galaxy agreed to make the laborious diversion, once I explained my interest; in fact, he insisted on it. At the beginning of a trip we are more inclined to indulge one another's whims.

The feeling of being actors in a pre-arranged stage landscape grew only more intense when at the top of the hill we came to a small round pond – and not a very natural-looking one – with an inviting bench, just big enough for two, on the grassy bank beside it.

The pond did not open up, nor did a black limousine with a dangerously beautiful woman and a driver in a peaked cap draw up beside us. But a man walked past and sensing a Cocteau moment, I ran across the road to ask if he could explain the name Heurtebise.

"Because it's windy up here, of course," he said, sounding irritated to have his train of thought interrupted by such a silly question.

Are the Burgundians really as jolly as their work-hard, carouse-hard PR would have us believe? In their portraits the dukes do not look particularly sympathetic, and in the Hundred Years War their behaviour was decidedly shifty. Was Philippe le Bon a good man? Contemporary descriptions of his palace at Hesdin, which was full of automata slapping visitors in the face, dumping soot on them and splashing water *"pour mouiller les dames par dessoubz"* (to soak ladies from below), suggest a sense of humour, but not a nice one.

We stopped to look at one 18th-century *lavoir* (public laundry) at Bellechaume and were on the trail of another at Brienon when the café owner whipped out his iPad, zoomed in on Google Earth and showed it to us. "You don't need to go there now," he said proudly, and had we embraced virtual tourism, we might not have been moments too late to visit the church at Pontigny, which is all that remains of one of the most important abbeys of Burgundy. Its monks are credited with founding the Chablis vineyards.

Our consolation was a drink at the Relais de Pontigny, an old-fashioned Relais Routier truckstop, whose only concessions to the passing years are pricing in euros and a greenhouse smoking parlour in the garden, decorated with saucy posters. There were cohorts of *poids lourds* in the car park, *croques (monsieur et madame)* on the menu, caricatures of regulars on the wall, plastic cloths on the table and laughter in the air. A collector's item. The Relais de Pontigny has cheap rooms, and I doubt it would be a dull place to stay.

The small town of Chablis is the local magnet for wine-trade business travellers and tourists, and has plenty of hotels and restaurants. But the ride from Moret was just a bit too long and, anyway, we liked the sound of the Relais St Vincent in Ligny-le-Châtel better. Its prices might not suffer from premium-brand inflation.

Nor did they: like the Relais de Pontigny, but a few rungs higher up the ladder, the Relais St-Vincent is a reassuringly traditional place, with its porte cochère and slightly creaky rooms overlooking the courtyard. It describes its style of cuisine as traditional Burgundian, and no one could argue with that description. *Jambon persillé, coq au vin, sorbet cassis au marc de Bourgogne.*

Ligny-le-Châtel to Pouilly-en-Auxois: about 110km

While Galaxy was using his still-damp socks to tie his nearly-dry pants to the luggage rack of his bicycle, hoping for a fine drying morning, I fell into conversation with a couple of Dutch cyclists. Their children plus grand-children had roared down in their fast cars to stay with them in a rented villa near Sète, and roared back again afterwards, leaving the ancient parents to ride slowly home, camping out in theory but in practice forced by the weather into hotels such as the Relais St-Vincent.

"It's nice to camp," said the Dutchman, "and even nicer not to have to." Their bicycles had automatic gears, and they looked as though they were enjoying a most happy and active retirement.

Having ridden to within 10km of Chablis without seeing the first tendril of a vine, we cycled out of Ligny straight into vineyard corduroy on the west-facing slope of the Serein Valley, perhaps including the 20 hectares of our friends the Séguinot family of Maligny. Observing the changes of landscape is a large part of the pleasure we derive from our slow journeys through France, and the first vineyard on the road south was an exciting moment of transition. Did we also detect an improvement in the weather? Not really, but at least it wasn't raining.

More than a name on a label, Chablis is an old and attractive small town with timbered houses beside the Serein, three blooms on the official *Ville Fleurie* scale, and many fine things in the shop window beyond white wine of the Chardonnay grape. It is also the home of the authentic Burgundian *andouillette*, a taste I have yet to acquire, along with tripe and assorted cartilaginous bits of pig. I take no pride in this, aware that an appreciation of the glories of offal sets the true gourmet apart from the dilettante and the mere glutton. So be it. I shall not be applying for membership of the Association Amicale des Amateurs de l'Andouillette Authentique.

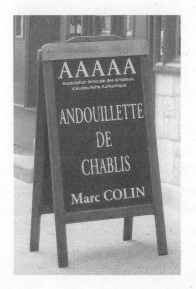

Chablis's seven Grand Cru vineyards – Blanchot, Bougros, les Clos, Grenouilles, Preuses, Valmur and Vaudésirs – look down on the town from the north-eastern side of the valley, and a helpful map on the square suggests a variety of walks around and among them, depending on how long a walk you want.

Of the two routes to Noyers, similar in length, we chose to follow the Serein past Chichée, Poilly and other grey-gold villages, and an oil factory at Moutot. The Chablis appellation stretches most of the way to Noyers, a showpiece medieval village walled and barbican-ed with cobbles, arcades and timbers; the complete stage set. After watching a butcher cross the street with a gutted pig on his back, its front trotters over his shoulder and snout nuzzling his ear, I was reading a framed newspaper cutting trying to make sense of *la Maison du Schématisme* when a bucketful of water landed on my head in a convincingly medieval way. I hoped the person responsible was watering her schematic window box, not emptying the slops.

After drying myself in a café, I outlined our options over coffee, as I saw them, for a route through the Auxois to the day's appointed end near the motorway at Pouilly.

We could take a straightish line over the hills via the old stronghold of Semur-en-Auxois, or a 15km-longer route via the Canal de Bourgogne, with sightseeing opportunities: the Cistercian abbey at Fontenay, probably the most beautiful place of its kind in France; Roman Alésia, site of Vercingetorix's last stand against Julius Caesar in 52BC; another showpiece walled village, Flavigny-sur-Ozerain (known for its aniseed sweets); and a possible further extension to visit the château of Bussy-Rabutin, famous for the scabrous writings of its disgraced 17th-century owner Roger de Rabutin (*L'Histoire Amoureuse des Gaules*).

"If I'd known you wanted to do all that I would have set the alarm for five," said Galaxy, "and waved you off."

Point taken. Each sight would involve a detour of a few kilometres from the canal, and a few kilometres back again afterwards. The sightseeing route would work well, and doubtless does, for barge holiday-makers with bicycles on deck; or for motorists passing though in no hurry. With our schedule it was not compatible; not so much a non-starter as a non-finisher in daylight.

So we took the open road over the hills to Semur, pausing to salute Resistance heroes and watch a TGV hurtle beneath out feet when we crossed the line near Châtel-Gérard. We picked up a bit of speed ourselves on the double-arrow run down to the Armançon at Athie, breaking 60kph.

The capital of the Auxois is an impressive fortress town, naturally moated by a meander of the Armançon. The rust-coloured round towers of its old donjon rise powerfully from the river, the biggest of them with a yawning crack that appeared in 1602. There are medieval footbridges over the river and staircases leading up from the water to the Porte des Cycogniers (storks' nest gate) and other keyhole entrances. Beside the river, an unusual *bateau lavoir* (floating laundry) looks like a model of Noah's Ark.

After several hours with little else to occupy our minds than anticipation of our arrival in Semur, we pushed our bicycles keenly up a steep cobbled street and were relieved to find restaurants open at the top of Rue Buffon. We chose Le Mont Drejet in preference to La Goulue for its cheaper snails and were rewarded with a vile lunch that poisoned our minds, no doubt unfairly, against the town. Perhaps if we had lunched at La Goulue we would have found Semur enchanting.

Leaving it without regret, we continued south to find the Canal de Bourgogne near Villeneuve-sous-Charigny, and when we found it Galaxy had a request to make.

"I would like to lie on the grass and read my book for half an hour, if you don't mind," he said. As a leisurely gentleman cyclist, he feels that this ought to be part of his daily routine. But how many times have we made room for it, in 40-odd days on the road? Exactly. After arranging the items of clothing that needed drying on the frame of his long-suffering bicycle, he found his resting place. The book was opened, but I doubt many pages were turned. Before long the music of birdsong and buzzing insects was underscored by the pleasant drone of light snoring.

The canal towpath took us all the way to Pouilly-en-Auxois, through rich grazing country: not the most exciting ride but at the end of the day 25km of flat going is never unwelcome. I counted two swans, one boat and one large rodent – a coypu, probably – and lost count of the locks as we climbed imperceptibly up-canal to Pouilly. The shortage of boats, on the Canal de Bourgogne at the end of July, was surprising. One explanation may have been the late hour: lock-keepers stop work at 7pm.

The Hôtel de la Poste is a friendly place − at least, it has a friendly owner-chef who was politely incredulous of a schedule that saw us completing our journey through Burgundy the next day. "Tournus? That's much too far," declared Anthony Bonnardot, "but I can think of a good short cut for you."

Unfortunately, he was called away to set fire to a crêpe, and the next time we saw the chef − after breakfast − he seemed to have forgotten our short cut.

The bedroom part of the de la Poste is old and priced accordingly, but the restaurant is smart and modern, with a colourful mural of improbably cheerful peasants collecting grapes outside the Château d'Eguilly, with no sign of the motorway that now runs within a few yards of it. Until phylloxera cut its swathe through French viticulture, the Auxois was a big producer of cheap wine. Coteaux d'Auxois vineyards have recently been replanted at Flavigny, and we enjoyed the white with dinner. After coffee we crossed the square to research the taste of marc at the Hôtel de Commerce, and liked the look of the place, as a less gastro alternative to the Poste.

Pouilly-en-Auxois to Tournus: about 115km

From the Yonne at Migennes, the Canal de Bourgogne climbs 300m in 155km via 113 locks to Pouilly-en-Auxois, the highest canal point in France. The hill beneath which Pouilly sits is the watershed between Atlantic/North Sea and Mediterranean drainage, and the canal cuts through the top of it in a tunnel − la Voûte de Pouilly − which opened in 1832 after seven years of labour and 182 lives lost. On the other side, the descent to the Saône via Dijon is shorter and steeper. According to some authorities, the tunnel's quoted length of 3333m is a slight underestimate chosen for the opportunity it gives the Burgundians to roll their r's.

In the early days, crossing the tunnel took all day. In the absence of a towpath, horses had to be walked over the hill, passing the tunnel's ventilation shafts on what is now a cycle track between Pouilly and Escommes, the holding *bassin* at the Saône end of the tunnel. Local helpers made a hard living pushing the barges with punt poles and lying on their backs, helping the boat along with their feet on the vault. The introduction of a tug capable of pulling long convoys of barges speeded up the process. The electric tug remained in service until the last commercial barge came through in 1987, and can still be inspected at Pouilly.

The tunnel has recently been equipped with electric light, but steering a steady course can be no easy task. It certainly looks a tight squeeze, and on occasions the lock-keepers have to drop the water level to let a wide barge through. The difficulties of the tunnel and slow going through the lock "staircases" also explain the emptiness of the middle section of the canal, which takes at least two weeks to complete, end to end.

We followed the canal through the first staircase of locks on the Saône side, to within sight of Châteauneuf-en-Auxois, where we crossed our path from four years before. The landscape and the canal itself seemed more interesting on this side of the tunnel, with more boats to look at and the well-kept cottages of lock-keepers who understand and take seriously their duty to embellish the scene. Before long we had to tear ourselves away from the pleasant towpath, because the canal turns north on its route to the Saône via Dijon.

We may have left an important watershed behind us, but in order to continue in a more or less straight line we now had a bigger hill to cross: the Montagne de Beaune, whose eastern flank hosts the great Burgundy vineyards of the Côte de Nuits and the Côte de Beaune.

Ste-Sabine's deer park and some fine cattle country brought us to Bligny-sur-Ouche, where it was Galaxy's turn to buy the coffee and pursue his mission to draw a map of France showing the regions that do and do not recognise the *café noisette*. Bligny is a zone of non-observance, or was, until Galaxy rolled into town. Looking back, I struggle to recall a barman on any of our trips who knew what G was talking about. Their ignorance never ceases to amaze him.

With a deep intake of breath we set about the Montagne, quitting the main road, although it would probably have taken us over the lowest pass and would certainly have taken us to a village that rejoices in the name of Bouze-lès-Beaune. Somewhere near Echarnant we made the mistake of trying a road marked on our map with a dotted line. A few potholes in, our bicycles refused. Eventually, however, we found our way to the top of the hill and hurtled down the other side, a glorious long descent to Meursault, via Monthélie and the vineyards of Pommard and Volnay. The weather had taken a turn for the better, and G celebrated by baring his back for the first time on the trip. It almost felt like summer.

Beneath the steep ridge, the carpet of vines lies wall to wall. Each tiny parcel of land is so valuable, every inch must earn its keep and there is no space for frivolities such as a lawn or a flower bed.

Olivier Leflaive is a *négotiant* who buys grapes from 60 appellations and invites us to sample the resulting wines over a tasting lunch at his stylish hotel-restaurant on the square at Puligny-Montrachet. This is a fine formula: a sensibly priced, not too ambitious set menu with three fixed-price wine menus to accompany it – *Initiation, Découverte* or *Prestige* – each offering a selection of wines served in a generous *dose dégustation*. White is Leflaive's speciality, but the red list, including several Pommards and Volnays, is not too shabby. His two *grand cru* wines are not on any menu, but can be added for a supplement.

Galaxy likes nothing better than an arithmetic challenge such as this, and the mental calculator whirred smoothly into action, comparing the full bottle price of each item on each list and doing the addition and division sums in moments to pronounce that… *Prestige* is actually the cheapest option, *Initiation* the most expensive. No flies on Olivier Leflaive.

Not wishing to show off, we chose *Découverte*; and not wishing to waste good wine, we ignored the spittoon and swallowed almost everything our guide could throw at us. Charmingly, he went down on one knee to deliver his commentary eye to eye instead of talking down to us, as so many wine waiters do.

"Now for the real test," he said, lining up the bottles when the time came for us to compare and contrast *premier cru* wines of Chassagne, Puligny and Meursault.

Fortunate residents can go for a lie down after lunch. For the rest of us, breathalysers are available from the bar. Galaxy was quite sure he was well within the limit and blew lustily. My vision was unequal to the task of reading the result.

The obvious minor road leading due south from Chagny (D981) is in fact so obvious it attracts heavy traffic in thunderous main-road volume. We soon gave it up and took the Canal du Centre towpath instead. In contrast to the Canal de Bourgogne, this was a busy scene with walkers, cyclists and boats out in force. Pulled along in the wake of more racy cyclists and fuelled by high-octane *premier cru* burgundy, we covered the 16km to Chalon-sur-Saône at the double, and sur-Saône at the double, and then took an age to find our way through and out of the busy town. The Michelin 1:200,000 road atlas is not the ideal tool for a poorly signed town centre, especially so soon after a good lunch.

Eventually we found the way to St-Germain-lès-Buxy and continued through pretty woods to Sennecey, via the palace of the former Cistercian abbey of La Ferté, which has *chambre d'hôte* accommodation in the converted dove-cote. This may be more suitable for motorist lovebirds than cyclists, the nearest restaurant being not very close. From Sennecey we found a good if tiring road through Jugy and Boyer and up to a beautiful pine wood high above the motorway, before racing down to Tournus at last, via the D215.

Like other towns on the Saône, Tournus is a natural staging post on motorway, railway and river. Even if you aren't breaking a journey, it deserves a pause for a good look at St-Philibert, an ancient sanctuary that was rebuilt after destruction by marauding Hungarians in the tenth century. This giant among Romanesque churches soars like a Gothic cathedral, its fortress quality softened by the use of a soapy and tactile pink stone.

The top hotel in town, named after the local artist (18th century), is the Greuze, next to St-Philibert. Rooms are less expensive and the setting less picturesque at Aux Terrasses, which overlooks a supermarket car park on the southern edge of town. Tournus is not huge, and Aux Terrasses is in strolling range of the centre.

White trash

The five *grands crus* of the two Montrachet villages, Puligny and Chassagne, are usually ranked top of the pile of the world's dry white wines: starting price several hundred pounds a bottle, to be drunk on bended knee, bare-headed. The 8 hectares of Le Montrachet are shared by both villages (the "le" usually reserved for wine from the Chassagne side of the border) as are the 11 hectares of Bâtard-Montrachet. Bienvenues-Bâtard-Montrachet and Chevalier-Montrachet are part of Puligny, and the smallest of the *grands crus*, Criots-Bâtard-Montrachet, is on Chassagne territory. "Chevalier is esteemed for its finesse, while Bâtard tends to show the greatest power and richness," wrote Stephen Brook in *Decanter* (Oct 7 2005). "Le Montrachet's supremacy derives from the fact that it manages to blend the elegance of Chevalier with the body of Bâtard. Criots and Bienvenues have their detractors... their exposition is less favourable." As always in Burgundy, the principle of split inheritance means that each vineyard is divided into tiny parcels of a few *ouvrées* owned by different growers, whose individual methods produce wines of differing character and quality. Olivier Leflaive's cousin Anne-Claude (Domaine Leflaive) is one of the more highly reputed Montrachet growers, using the fashionable biodynamic method. One *ouvrée* is the area a labourer can cultivate by hand in a day: 428.5 sq metres, producing about 250 bottles of wine.

Whichever side of the communal divide you are on, the grapes are Chardonnay and both t's in Montrachet are silent. Rash it may be, but trash it is not. Do not make the mistake of drinking it too cold: 12–14°C is the sommelier's recommendation.

Both hotels have a Michelin star, and Aux Terrasses lived up to its fancy billing, although the restaurant was busy almost to the point of being hectic – hardly surprising, so close to the motorway at the end of July. By choosing a wine from the bottom of the list – Mâcon Rouge, terroir de Tournus (recommended) – we kept dinner down to £50 each. Gazpacho and parmesan sorbet found their way into the notebook.

Tournus to Meximieux: about 105km

Crossing the Saône at Tournus, we entered the Bresse and had only a few kilometres to pedal before exchanging Burgundy for a new *département* (Ain), new region (Rhône-Alpes), new landscape (flat), new cows (brown and white Montbéliardes), and the same old weather (disappointing). The small market town of Pont-de-Vaux is no beauty spot but offers a choice of inexpensive hotel-restaurants: Le Raisin, Les Platanes and Le Commerce, probably in that order of preference

Tournus

(although our research was cursory). Frogs' legs are a local speciality.

Of all French regions, Bresse is one of the proudest of its costumes and customs; its culture, in fact. The key ingredients are the elaborate garb worn by Bressane ladies, especially their hats, which gave subtle socio-sexual messages and evolved to an extraordinary degree of extreme impracticality; rural architecture; and the incomparable *poulet de Bresse*, the Rolls-Royce of poultry. A good way to find out about all three is to visit the Musée de la Bresse at St-Cyr, near the A40 motorway between Mâcon and Bourg-en-Bresse.

Arriving from the north on back roads, Galaxy and I did not find the museum easily and, having succeeded, we had greater difficulty walking. The legs always take a few minutes to recover from a long ride, but there must have been something about our morning's exertion through the Bresse, because we were both similarly afflicted and all but incapable of staying on our feet as we staggered into the museum.

After an excellent presentation of costumes, furniture, enamel objets d'art and gastronomy (*bleu de Bresse* cheese as well as poultry), there were farm outbuildings to inspect, and a farmhouse interior recreated from a 1784 inventory. The least satisfactory part of the visit was the chicken farm, but we made up for that by continuing on our way for a chicken lunch at Vonnas, the gastronomic theme-park village which has become the personal fiefdom of superstar cook and one-man brand Georges Blanc.

M Blanc paid for a special motorway exit for Vonnas — *"premier village gourmand de France"* — and his property portfolio on the village square offers customers on different rungs of the spending ladder a pick 'n mix gastronomic and lifestyle experience — shops, hotels, restaurant, *auberge*, health farm, heliport. The centrepiece is the sumptuous Georges Blanc hotel-restaurant itself, connected by covered walkway to an impressive spa in extensive gardens across the road.

It may all seem a bit gastro-Disney, but the proof of the *poulet* is in the eating, and we found no fault with ours at L'Ancienne Auberge, a replica of M Blanc's grandparents' lemonade factory-cum-restaurant. Whisper it softly, but M Blanc does not own the entire village, and if you wanted to find a more basic hotel to use as a springboard for a slap-up dinner chez Blanc, you could.

From Vonnas we entered the wetland region of Les Dombes and devoted the remains of our day to birdwatching.

Considering (a) neither of us knows much about birds, (b) we were travelling without binoculars and (c) we had no idea what we were looking for or where to look for it, the experience was surprisingly rewarding. There were grebes, egrets and herons all over the place, we enjoyed a close encounter with a stork in a field near Marlieux and saw an unfamiliar pink-legged bird flying into a nearby pond well enough to identify it later as a black-winged stilt.

Now that we were on the Alpine side of Lyon, we toasted our sightings in white wine from the pre-Alpine

Bugey region at a garden restaurant called La Bicyclette Bleue in Joyeux, where Lyonnais weekenders come to enjoy local specialities such as *tartare de carpe* and *grenouilles fraîches* and rent a bicycle for an afternoon's exploration of the local network of cycle trails – L'Ain à Velo. One of the routes includes the bird zoo at Villars-les-Dombes.

There was a dormitory neatness about Joyeux that told us we had reached Lyon's commuter orbit, where we would spend the next day, like stars (or mini-starlets) moving slowly through the Lyonnais firmament, keeping our distance from Lyon itself. The first stage of this journey was a short run down to the Hôtel Cour des Lys at Meximieux, beneath the perfectly preserved medieval hill village of Pérouges. We would have saved some sweat by visiting Pérouges on the way down from Joyeux, but as usual we were late and even without stopping had the embarrassment of arriving to find the

Vonnas

Lyonnais friends we had invited to join us for supper already seated in the dining room.

La Cour des Lys is a new name for an old restaurant, formerly Claude Lutz. Its qualities have survived the change of regime: good food and simple accommodation in walking distance – a steep walk, admittedly – of Pérouges, without the tourist-trap pricing that prevails inside the walls of the old village. Meximieux used to be a convenient stopover on the way to or from the Alps, but new motorways have taken it out of that equation. My friends, who as proud Lyonnais know their gastronomy, were gracious enough to thank us for introducing them to a local restaurant they had not visited before, and said they would be going back to it. No further recommendation required, I think. A bedroom overlooking the high street might be noisy: ask for one at the back.

Meximieux to Châteauneuf-de-Galaure: about 110km

Medieval Pérouges was a city of weavers and cloth merchants proud of their civic liberties and their wealth, which peaked in the High Middle Ages. By the end of the 19th century the population had declined to eight and demolition threatened, until a group of local antiquarians formed le Comité du Vieux Pérouges to protect and restore the village. Its seamless ensemble of beautiful old houses and cobbled streets has often served as a period film set. At 8.30 in the morning the place was completely deserted, and an empty stage set is exactly what it looked like.

The rest of the day we spent working our way slowly through the Lyonnais hinterland, crossing all the thoroughfares – motorways, main roads, railways and rivers – leading to and from the great metropolis. Near Pont-Gallant we found a place to swim in the fast-flowing Ain, immersing ourselves in the calm water of a shallow rock-built pool made by some previous Crusoe. We crossed the Rhône, a chilly-looking blue-green torrent with more than a hint of the glacier about it, at Loyettes.

Our mid-morning halt was at Crémieu, an interesting old town that may be in a less perfect state of preservation than Pérouges but at least has real life flowing through its veins. Over a weekend in mid-September, a medieval fair takes over the town, with feasting, jousting, swordfights and much whip-cracking fun. Just outside the town wall, the Hôtel de la Chaîte looks promising as an overnight or lunch stop.

After Crémieu we entered more strenuous hill country, continuing south via Panossas and Frontonas to thread our way through the urban sprawl that fills the Lyon-Grenoble corridor near L'Isle-d'Abeau; and steeply up the other side to Four. At St-Jean-de-Bournay we finally began to feel we were riding away from Lyon, not around it, and in celebration rolled out our picnic and lay down among the caterpillars and grasshoppers of a riverside meadow near Villeneuve-de-Marc. This was immediately followed by a long climb towards St Julien-de-L'Herms – not the ideal way to get back into one's stride after lunch.

The first hint that we were reaching the South of France took the pleasant form of a northerly breeze on our backs. Whether or not this was an authentic Mistral, we were grateful for it.

The southern feeling was reinforced at Pact, where we stopped for a late-afternoon cup of tea. Hardly an eccentric request, you might think, but it provoked hilarious uproar among the assembled pastis drinkers, and panic behind the bar.

"*Un moment, ma femme arrive!*" said the proprietor, who was completely at a loss. Fortunately for us, *ma femme* overcame the challenge of pouring hot water over a bag of Lipton's. At Jarcieu we had the excitement of entering the *département* of La Drôme and observing its architectural speciality: façades of patterned stonework, using the large round *galets* found in the local fields and river beds.

The style found its most extreme expression in the so-called Palais Idéal at Hauterives, a bizarre monument to the tangled imagination and industry of a local postman, Ferdinand Cheval, who dreamed of a fairytale castle while tramping his daily 32km round. In April 1879 he tripped on an oddly shaped stone and thought: if nature can be a sculptor, I can be an architect.

Over the next 33 years he spent 93,000 hours collecting stones and using them to build the palace of his dreams. These were nothing if not exotic: the "palace" contains fanciful elements of Hindu, Egyptian and Swiss chalet 'architecture' (as imagined by the postman), as well as sections celebrating nature, life and everything. It is a hymn to all the wonders of creation.

How to categorise this strange monument, in the year of its centenary? It is usually described as naïve art made architecture, if that is the right word for a structure that has no obvious purpose. One of Cheval's stated aims was to demonstrate that people of his "category" were capable of works of genius. He also wanted to make his mark and be remembered, and has certainly succeeded in that.

When Cheval discovered that he was not allowed to be buried in his palace, he had just enough time (eight years) to build a smaller mausoleum in the cemetery at Hauterives before he died in 1924, aged 88.

We had selected the east of the Rhône Valley because it looked easier than the west, where the walls of the Massif Central's fortress climb steeply from the river. But if the Drôme is a gap between the Rhône and the Alps, it is far from flat. This northern part of the *département* calls itself La Drôme des Collines, and with reason. They are pleasantly fertile fruit-growing hills, with few compelling sights – a gap the postman worked hard to fill.

One last long push along the TGV line brought us over a crest of hills and rapidly down to our night's rest at Châteauneuf-de-Galaure, which spreads itself across the slope, looking out over the Galaure river, orchards and farms.

The Auberge de Châteauneuf had closed its dining room for the evening in preparation for its busiest day of the year – not one wedding feast but two. As we reflected over a strong drink in the excellent company of the hotel Great Dane, there were compensations: "We will be up at five," said Madame, "so you can have breakfast as early as you like." The walk up though the town to the Café de la Mairie (Chez Laurent) was also beneficial, and Laurent gave good pizza and an unusual white wine. "I asked for white and you've given us rosé," said a slightly aggrieved Galaxy. "It is white," said Laurent. "No it isn't, it's pink," said G. They were never going to agree on this.

My friend is the master of bedroom laundry, and I thought I had seen all his tricks, using bungees, balconies and shower curtain rails. But hanging his wet clothes from the ceiling fan was a first. They had stopped dripping by the time we finished arguing with Laurent about the colour of the wine and I slept as soundly as ever, my dreams untroubled by a slowly revolving overhead carousel of ghostly white garments.

Châteauneuf–de–Galaure to Marsanne: about 100km

We were not up and about as early as our busy hosts, but still had the privilege of being the very first customers to pit our wits against the technology of their expensive new coffee machine. Its cappuccino had a nauseating taste of caramel and I almost caught myself requesting a *noisette*.

The fan-drying experiment had been only partially successful and for the items that remained stubbornly damp, G was forced to resort to the technique of body-drying, which we sometimes use for shirts on a hot day. The Y-front *foulard* would not be every cyclist's chosen look, but it was effective and might have helped protect the back of the neck from sunburn, had the sun been out. It is important not to forget the "scarf" before entering a cathedral, smart restaurant or, in this instance, a prestigious Rhône Valley wine house. From Châteauneuf we set our sights on Tain l'Hermitage, stopping on the way to see a perched 11th-century chapel (sadly closed) above Chantemerle-les-Blés.

It was *chassé croisé* Saturday. The scale of the problem hit home when we found the narrow streets of Crozes-Hermitage, a quiet backwater which ought to be safe from through traffic, choked by a nose-to-tail procession of cars: *aoûtien* cohorts had fled the saturated motorway for the N7 and found that blocked too. It only took one enterprising navigator, or a sat-nav, to branch off through the vineyards, for the entire herd to follow. Their procession would eventually take them back to the N7 at Tain.

It was bad luck to be doing this ride in a traffic jam, but that was not going to spoil the thrill of cycling through the vineyards of one of Galaxy's favourite wines: Jaboulet's Hermitage, La Chapelle. Special occasions only, mind: a case of 1961 recently fetched a quarter of a million dollars at auction. After savouring the grandstand view of the Rhône and the vineyards of St-Joseph on the Ardèche bank, rolling it around the palate and swallowing it, we sped down to Tain-L'Hermitage and near the station found the rival house of Chapoutier, where we had an appointment for a tasting visit. For once I don't think we were more than an hour late.

"We'll start in the vineyards," said our taste-mistress, who combined charm and expertise and expected a close interest in the technicalities of wine-making, which we did our best to demonstrate. A short walk over the railway line led to the foot of the great and holy hill of Hermitage, where a 12th-century knight took his retirement and prayed hard for absolution after the excesses of the Albigensian crusade.

Although the hermitage chapel is on Jaboulet territory, Chapoutier has the biggest share of the Hermitage appellation's 130 hectares, and Michel Chapoutier is in his way a modern crusader for the biodynamic way of wine-making.

"This hill is the home of the Syrah grape and M Chapoutier has taken it wherever he goes in the world to show how it can behave in different regions," we were told. Chapoutier has planted Hermitage vines in Portugal, Australia and the Roussillon.

The principles of biodynamic agriculture, laid down by an Austrian esoteric in 1924, come with much mystical claptrap about burying cow horns stuffed with manure when the moon is in the right quarter for harnessing cosmic energy. Horsetail, dandelion sheathed in cow's stomach, yarrow flowers in a stag's bladder, ground quartz, cow manure... biodynamic compost sounds like the witches' brew from *Macbeth*.

The fact is, Chapoutier and other biodynamic growers have had great success producing superb wine. Where previous generations aimed for a signature taste, the focus now is to bring out the differences of character between each plot. Berry Brothers & Rudd sell a good selection and supply the required adjectives free of charge. If lost for words to describe a northern Rhône red, try road tar, liquorice and cigar boxes (in preference to cowpat).

For his most precious wines, Chapoutier uses the old spelling Ermitage; we came across the spelling Crozes Ermitage on the occasional bottle too. All Chapoutier wine labels have been marked in Braille since 1996: "a symbol of openness", apparently − all the best wines are open − and clever marketing too. Sainsbury's had Chapoutier's St-Joseph and Crozes-Hermitage last time I ran my hand along the shelf, and visually impaired shoppers in Tesco may feel their way to a keenly priced Gigondas 2008.

The vineyard visit and tasting afterwards were a richly enjoyable education, and the pressure to buy is not overbearing. But since we were meeting up with

motorist friends later in the day, we found room for a bottle or two to push in our panniers. Tasting visits are by appointment (www.chapoutier.com), although the shop on Avenue Dr Paul Durand is open every day and you could take your chance. The nearby Hôtel le Castel provides simple accommodation, and (still on Paul Durand) Le Mangevins "wine bistro" comes with Chapoutier's recommendation.

The Scott and Mousse-Café had not done a full morning's work, but a table on the deck at Le Quai, beside the wooden suspension footbridge that spans the Rhône between Tain and Tournon, was too good to refuse. The *plat du jour* and the view hit the spot and the pudding waitress solved a conundrum that had haunted our travels for many a long lunch. "This is *île flottante* because it is poached," she declared, "*Oeufs à la neige* are baked." Or is it the other way round?

From Tain l'Hermitage, a cycle path took us along the Rhône (Drôme bank) as far as Valence, crossing the Isère by a new cycle bridge at the confluence, where Quintus Fabius Maximus and his elephants routed the uncouth hordes of Allobroges in 121BC; a decisive victory that completed the Roman subjugation of southern France.

If the river itself is too big and busy and – for want of a better word – industrial to be charming, with sections of canal, artificial banks, locks, power stations and heavy shipping, the overall effect of the scenery is majestic. Across the water, mountainous Ardèche climbs steeply to the summits of the so-called Rhône Corniche, with castle ruins and giddy chapels outlined against the sky. In a car, the 30km high road from Tournon to Valence via Plats and St-Romain must be spectacular. On a more energetic day we might even have tackled it.

Wind is a huge factor down here. Local cyclists wait for a big Mistral and hurtle down the river bank, returning north by train. A south wind is less frequent but can be similarly tempestuous. It usually brings bad weather, unlike the Mistral, which keeps the sky clear. Holidaymakers must take their chance. We had no more than a helpful breeze behind us, but at last the sun had come out.

The cycle path we found is part of a projected 700km itinerary from Lake Geneva to the Mediterranean, the ViaRhona, of which about one-third exists (including 34km in the Drôme between St-Rambert and Valence). For more information and a progress report, see www. eptb-rhone.fr/120-etat-des-realisations.htm

Signs in Valence encouraged us to hope for a continuation of the piste towards Montélimar, and we followed them across the Rhône to the Ardèche bank, at which point the path ran out and we were forced back on to a main road. One understands that the entire 700km trail cannot be magicked into existence at once, but installing the signposts before the track does seem misguided, or at least misguiding. We crossed back to the Drôme bank via a dam at Charmes and followed the N7 itself for about a mile before leaving the Rhône and heading east for Allex, finally crossing the river Drôme at Grane. Shallow and rocky, it did not look swim-friendly.

We knew the last 15km of our day's ride, over the Col de Tartaiguille (400m) to Marsanne, was going to be hard work, and so it proved. I was overtaken by a middle-aged couple of joggers which was rather humiliating. We were unprepared for the beauty of the forest at the top, followed by wonderful views over Montélimar's almond-growing plain framed by the dark outline of the Vercors – the western wall of the Alps proper.

There is an alternative, slightly higher route over the mountain to Marsanne, via the heroic-sounding Col de la Grande Limite (515m). Local cyclists from Montélimar and Valence do it as a circuit, stopping for a drink – or lunch, if they allow themselves such an indulgence – at Marsanne between the two cols. Our friends drove us up to look at the Grande Limite in the morning. The views from the road were good, but we declared Tartaiguille the prettier of the two passes.

We had found them comfortably installed at a table in Marsanne, looking out over a drink and their soft-top, under a plane tree, beside the village fountain. This pleasant southern scene was in fact our destination, L'Atelier, a handsome building in prime position. Looking back, it occurs to me that in crossing the Tartaiguille we had made the big move from La Drôme des Collines to La Drôme Provençale. Provence! The sweet smell of air-freshener and lazy stereotyping. The last stage of our journey.

L'Atelier's owner wore an impressive *rive gauche* intellectual hairdo and may be a newcomer to hotel-keeping, to judge from the age he devoted to paperwork formalities most hoteliers feel able to despatch in moments. I began to wonder if he thought we had come to exchange contracts, not stay the night.

Eventually I had signed my name enough times for access to bedroom to be granted and M Doumic disclosed the pin code for the gate. "You won't forget it," he said, "because it's the year of Emile Loubet's birth." Quite so. Luckily we felt no need to go out after dinner.

The tone at L'Atelier is cool and arty, with tin table tops, live jazz, a scatter of design mags and many a learned volume on the shelves. Madame Doumic calls it a mixture of the industrial and the baroque, and no doubt she knows what she means by that. We were a day late for the jazz but made good use of the thin pool and liked those rooms (eg, No 7) with balconies looking up at the old village. We ate well enough but drank better: a Chapoutier white (St-Péray) that we had tasted in the morning. And when the red arrived, we rolled out the liquorice and cigar boxes. Breakfast was excellent, even if, annoyingly, we had to order it the night before.

Marsanne to Nyons: about 75km

We now found ourselves in the unfamiliar position of being ahead: less than 100km from Avignon, with two days to get there. Another unaccustomed sensation was a light and responsive back wheel: depositing four panniers on the back seat of the soft-top, we made a lunchtime rendezvous and set off in search of Provence, heading south-east through the hills for Nyons, the nerve centre of herb and olive growing.

After the intensive cultivation of the Montélimar plain, we had a sense of transition at La Bégude. It was a change of terrain, for the bumpier: from here on, the roadside *bornes* marked the altitude.

Le Poët-Laval was our perched village, an old *commanderie* of the Knights Hospitaller, with staircase streets and castle ruins. The name of the village has nothing to do with poetry, but is a cousin of the more familiar *puy* – meaning hill.

Provence is a *bouquet garni* of clichés, its potency debased by life's wallpaper of travel supplements and brochure covers; art posters, unwanted Christmas presents and bland sauces for tasteless bistro chicken.

Poët-Laval silenced our scepticism. The sky was Greek island blue, the old stones scrubbed and dazzling, and the air... well, it was filled with the scents and sounds of Provence. Olive trees actually shimmered, and cicadas screamed as only they can, like acute tinnitus. Embrace the clichés. They are all true.

We tried to imagine the crowds, if Poët-Laval were in the Lubéron or the hills behind Cannes. Not that the village is undiscovered. Its houses are mostly second homes, meticulously restored by their absentee residents. But on the last day of July it was utterly peaceful and the village hotel, Les Hospitaliers, would be the ideal context for poolside inactivity interrupted for an occasional stroll to the bar or restaurant terrace. In one of the old houses below us a pianist was practising for the evening concert. We looked out at empty wooded hills, and listened to the music of cicadas and Chopin.

Le Poët-Laval

There is a lower, younger and less prettified part of Poët-Laval below the main road. Tous les Matins du Monde (named after a Gérard Depardieu film), would be a good place for a *citron pressé*, a game of boules with a glass of pastis and a plate of olives, an inexpensive *salade niçoise*, or some other Provençal cliché, to taste.

The Hospitallers were also responsible for naming the nearby small town of Dieulefit, a pretty place of artist-potters and artisan cheese-makers. The cheese is Picodon, a small round goaty number whose appellation covers most of the Ardèche and Drôme *départements*.

Four friends reunited, we bought a picnic-sized picodon, and set off from Dieulefit in an ill-assorted convoy, seeking shade for the first time of the trip. We found some near a fork in the road where we faced a high road/low road decision for the afternoon ride to Nyons. Fuelled by lunchtime bravado and Michel Chapoutier's St-Joseph, the cyclists embarked on the high road over

One of those nice little cols...

the Col de Valouse and soon reached the next cliché. In fact, we smelled it first: lavender fields, and harvesters at work with scythes and pitchforks. It was probably *lavandin*, the hybrid plant which flowers later than pure or English lavender, smells stronger and produces oil of slightly inferior quality.

I have found the Col de Valouse mentioned on a website of cycling passes and am reassured to learn that it does count as a climb, albeit a modest one: 9km, 253 vertical metres, average gradient 2.8%, maximum gradient 5.4%. Small beer indeed. This may explain how we managed it without having to dismount. (Not having panniers on board also helped.) A blasé blogger describes it as "one of those nice little cols of which the Drôme has many". As far as we were concerned, it was a fine achievement and uniquely beautiful.

Through rugged mountain scenery we sped past a converted hotel-restaurant, the Hameau de Valouse, which might be a good bolthole, if you like your Provence wild and remote. On reaching the main road we had to pedal no more than a couple of kilometres in the wrong direction, towards Bordeaux, to see the full effect of a rocky gorge, Le Défilé de Trente Pas, and the diversion was well worth making. A loop via Bourdeaux would be a good longer ride from Dieulefit – 50km to Nyons instead of 35 – via three of those nice little passes of which the Drôme has so many, instead of just the one.

The village of St-Ferréol has a cheap hotel, L'Auberge de Trente Pas, run by a keen cyclist who will talk you into tackling the Ventoux before you are into your second bottle.

Nyons is known for its markets – lavender, herbs, olives, fruit, wine – on Sundays (for tourists) and Thursdays (the real thing). We entered by the town's beautiful single-span medieval bridge, and walked our weary bikes through cobbled streets and arcaded squares to the main concourse from which our hotel, the Colombet, was nicely set back. The Colombet's glory days may be behind it, but the bedrooms are large and comfortable, the staff helpful, and both motoring and cycling teams were happy there, especially when the barman served up an uninvited cliché: *tapenade* on toast with a glass of pastis, soon followed by the other half. Could there be a better way to bring a 51-degree curtain down on a beautiful day when Provence had delivered on all fronts?

Nyons to Avignon: about 80km

"Monster lurks here," it says on the cycling map of

Nyons

Provence, to the south of Nyons. The beast in question is the mighty Mont Ventoux (1909m), whose bare grey summit ridge towers above Provence in windswept isolation.

Every cyclist knows the story of Tour de France rider Tommy Simpson who in July 1967 pedalled up the Ventoux in drug-fuelled delirium, refusing to give up until he keeled over and died less than a mile from the top. All over the cycling world, people dream of conquering the Ventoux and plan their pilgrimage. The Ventoux is the elephant in the bike shed.

Had it been haunting our dreams? I don't remember it featuring in mine. When M Doumic of L'Atelier threw down the gauntlet by recalling two cyclist clients of about our age who did the Ventoux from Marsanne, *aller retour*, in a day – a journey of 200km, including one of the world's toughest climbs – we left it on the floor.

Had our friends brought a bike rack we would certainly have encouraged them to drive us up the Ventoux for a photo opportunity at the top and a new top-speed and broken brake-cable opportunity on the ride down. But the soft-top was not equipped for such a lark.

If the Ventoux is a hill suffering from a severe case of gigantism, the nearby Dentelles de Montmirail have the opposite affliction: they are a mountain range in miniature, pocket Dolomites complete with little foothills, small cliffs and slightly giddy-making limestone pinnacles.

Golden villages cling to the slopes on all sides and rough tracks lead up through the mini-massif for adventurous hikers, bikers, jeep drivers and *vététistes* (mountain bikers) to explore. After a pleasant ride through silvery olive groves interspersed by open fields smelling of ripe melons and peaches, we stopped under a canopy of plane trees at the Café du Centre in Villedieu – a Provençal paradigm – before riding down the western side of the Dentelles via the wine villages of Séguret and Sablet. At Gigondas we met our friends for a tasting on the village square, chez Brusset. We were well received, and might easily have been tempted by the nearby restaurant, L'Oustalet, its Côte d'Azur prices notwithstanding, if it had not been Monday (*fermeture hebdomadaire*).

Our choice was the Dentelles wine road. The villages on the other side of the range – Crestet, Caromb, Le Barroux – are no less beautiful and face the Ventoux, but the road between them is busier than our wine route. A more rugged option would be the 15km ride from Crestet to Beaumes de Venise via the Col de Suzette

Le Mont Ventoux

The great lump is a famously gruelling cycling challenge, its unpleasant character defined by a lack of hairpins, which offer a few moments of respite, and winds that usually exceed 90kph (240 days a year) and with any luck close the road. The climb from Bédoin (300m) to the summit (1909m) via the Col des Tempêtes – 22km at an average gradient of more than 7% – has featured many times on the Tour de France and passes a memorial to Tommy Simpson near the top, a popular shrine where cyclists leave syringes, pill boxes and other offerings. The statistics of the route from Malaucène are much the same, but the wind is more helpful if a Mistral is blowing. The "easiest" ascent is from the eastern side, where the starting point, Sault, is 500m higher than Bédoin and Malaucène. Professional riders take about an hour for the climb from Bédoin; in 2006 someone did it 11 times in a day. No less surprising is the official assertion that the name Ventoux has nothing to do with the wind, but in fact means snowy peak. There are a few ski lifts and pistes on the mountain's northern flank.

Petrarch hiked up with his brother and two servants in April 1336, out of curiosity to see what the world looked like from such a great height. At the top he opened his copy of Augustine's Confessions and chanced upon this passage. "Men wonder at the heights of the mountains, and the mighty waves of the sea, and the wide sweep of rivers, and the revolution of the stars, but themselves they consider not."

(392m), a less daunting proposition than the Ventoux and a decent surface. Ventoux may not mean windy but Montmirail does mean admirable mountains, and they are.

After our tasting we drove up the Dentelles as far as the soft-top would take us and picnicked beneath the cliffs of the highest peak, St-Amand (734m). This happy event led to the formulation of a new Galaxy's Law: for a mountain picnic, avoid melons, boiled eggs, tomatoes, peaches and other spherical comestibles, unless they come with a handbrake.

Returning to our bikes, we continued southwards via Vacqueyras and Beaumes de Venise and a cooling-off period in the Ouvèze between Sarrians and Bédarrides. Behind us loomed the silhouette of the Ventoux, brooding and accusatory. We ignored it, and concentrated on trying to tell the difference between the scream of cicadas and crickets.

I am not sure what we expected of our final approach to Avignon, but it was not the dreary hour's ride that we made, down the old N7, through a dusty, wind-swept, run-down, litter-strewn, third-world sprawl of urban mess.

In an ideal world, less hurried, hot and tired, Mousse-Café and the Scott would have taken us from Bédarrides to Châteauneuf-du-Pape, crossing the Rhône at Roquemaure and down the river from there, via Sauveterre and Villeneuve, the fortress "new town" that King Philip built to keep the neighbours honest after Pope Clement V – Bertrand de Got from Aquitaine

The Ouvèze near Sarrians

– moved the papal court from Rome to the left bank of the Rhône in 1309. It was Clement's successor, Jacques Duèze of Cahors (John XXII), who built a summer residence and planted the vines at Châteauneuf-du-Pape.

We looked at this route, added up the distances (35km and counting) and thought we could see a shorter alternative via Sorgues and its jogging park in the Rhône, the Ile de l'Oiselay. There was surely a good chance that we would be able to cross the Sauveterre dam, on foot if necessary, to the Ile de la Barthelasse and approach Avignon that way. But the dam was impregnably barricaded, a complete no-go dam. We beat a retreat to Sorgues and trundled down the N7. To be fair, it had been part of the mission statement for this trip.

The walls of Avignon, when we finally reached them, were quite splendid in their time warped magnificence, with pleasant strolling lawns between river and ramparts. Four spans jutting out into the Rhône like a pier are all that remain of Avignon's famous bridge (Pont St Bénézet) which connected papal territory and French Crown land, with forts at both ends, and was probably never used for circular dances "*sur le pont d'Avignon*", as the popular song holds; a more suitable dancing location being the river banks and an island under the arches of the bridge... "*sous le pont*".

After frequent flood damage and makeshift repairs, the bridge was abandoned in the 17th century. The original ambitious engineering scheme had been communicated by an angel to an Ardèche shepherd boy (Bénézet) in the 12th century: arguably not the best approach to project management.

For all the beauty of its old stones, Avignon is not an isolated fortress city like Carcassonne. It is a living and breathing, spitting, mugging, dirty city with its share of pimps and pickpockets; much like medieval Avignon, in fact. Petrarch described it as the cesspit of the world.

Riverside cycle path became ring road and eventually we found our hotel, the functional Kyriad Courtine, which we had chosen for its proximity to the TGV station and our early train. Our friends were sitting in the lobby with our panniers, tapping their fingers politely. They had a bit longer to wait before driving us back to the town centre and parking under ground with a squeal of rubber.

After a 21st-century argument with a ticket machine, a short staircase lifted us straight into the 14th century:

the courtyard of the Palais des Papes. "The most beautiful house in the world," wrote the chronicler Froissart, where the pope slept on fur-trimmed pillows. The trappings of luxury have gone, but the palace remains largely unaltered, a hugely impressive Gothic fortress, and a splendid backdrop for theatre and concerts in the Avignon festival (July).

I am not sure if it is permissible to cycle into Avignon via the underground car park, but I recommend trying, because the time machine effect is spectacular; as was the upmarket blancmange with *barbe à papa* (candy floss), highlight of a good dinner at L'Essentiel. Our friends stayed at Avignon's town-centre Kyriad, a few steps from the Palais des Papes, and reported that it "did the job": perfect location, honest price, not too noisy, clean.

Bringing any holiday to a successful conclusion is a relief. If it has involved use of the train, some self-congratulation may be in order. The rail itinerary is a combination of jigsaw puzzle and obstacle course, with snakes and ladders. I imagine an SNCF controller looking down on our efforts, laying traps and setting tripwires.

So far we had dodged the traps and tripwires pretty well. Now we had one last train journey to make: Avignon to Paris, and back to London by Eurostar, crossing Paris by the now familiar Bastille-République axis and up the gentle incline of the Boulevard de Magenta to the Gare du Nord, where we would deposit the Scott and Mousse-Café at the Sanem desk, whose cleverly concealed whereabouts we now knew well. Plenty of time for lunch at one of the bistros on the Rue de Belzunce, behind the church of St-Vincent-de-Paul.

We had it all planned. Seats and bike spaces booked on the only TGV of the day that accepts bikes, leaving Avignon at 7.55. Hotel well placed, two minutes from the TGV station. "Nothing can go wrong," we told each other, as a famous-last-words reminder against complacency.

After an early breakfast, we rolled up a comfortable 15 minutes early and were surprised to see no information about our train on the departures board. I checked the ticket yet again and for the first time noticed the words: Avignon Centre. We had come to the wrong station.

"I think we may have come to the wrong station," I said stupidly to the woman at the information counter.

"Yes," she said simply. "You have no chance. It takes 20 minutes to go there by car."

I knew what this meant. Tickets non-refundable, non-exchangeable. If we didn't leave Avignon soon we would miss the Eurostar too (tickets also non-refundable). Only a TGV would get us to Paris in time, and the only TGV that took bikes was the one we were in the process of missing. Checkmate?

Cooler heads would have reacted differently. Did the woman really know how long it would take us to cycle between the two stations? What if our train was delayed?

My only thought was to buy new tickets for the next TGV, not mentioning the bikes, and deal with that problem on board. There are no stops between Avignon and Paris, so they could hardly chuck us off.

"I believe you have bicycles," said the ticket salesman. He had obviously been warned about us by the information desk. It is amazing how efficient SNCF can be when it wants to be difficult. "Yes," I admitted. "We will dismantle them."

"You must." On this understanding, the man agreed to sell us two tickets. Avignon to Paris bought on the day of travel is expensive, I can tell you.

On the platform we did what we could to show willing, taking off the saddles, removing the front wheels, swivelling the handlebars. I'm not sure why we bothered, because as we stood on the platform letting everyone else go first, the guard bounded up to shout in our faces that before boarding we must agree to pay an extra 45 euros each as a punitive fine for "*occupation abusive*" of the train. The language of criminality is quite unpleasant.

Looking on the bright side as always, Galaxy was delighted to find himself seated next to a window he could see out of, in contrast to the usual conditions of incarceration in the TGV bike carriage. Not only that, the 8.08 from Avignon TGV was 40 minutes faster than the 7.55 from Avignon Centre, giving us more time for lunch in Paris. Marvellous.

I watched our bike ride unfold in reverse, as if in a fast-rewind video. There go the peaky hills of La Drôme

Provençale and the distant outline of the Vercors. We pick out the village of Marsanne spreading itself across the hillside like a leopard asleep in a tree, before shooting through the tunnels of Tartaiguille and Galaure. The cows have changed colour, so we must be in Burgundy. Grey roofs: now we are closing in on Paris.

I had been looking forward to the fast-rewind experience, but could take no pleasure in it. How could I have been so stupid? The sound of a Frenchman's laughter bounced off the walls in my head.

On the rue de Belzunce, we were the first to bag a pavement table for lunch Chez Casimir. Our Parisian friend had not arrived. For the first time in all our rides,

we were actually early for a rendezvous. It was refreshing not to be in a region for a change, beleaguered by earnest considerations of *terroir*. There were wines from all corners of the country – Bordeaux, Burgundy, Provence, Alsace, the Basque Country.

We ordered a Loire white, and gradually the sound of laughter died away.

———————

Hotels (with restaurants unless stated)

* = cheap, ***** = expensive

**   Moret-sur-Loing, Auberge de la Terrasse
www.auberge-terrasse.com   0033 160705103

***   Flagy, Au Moulin de Flagy
www.aumoulin.fr   0033 160966789

**   Ligny-le-Chatel, Le Relais St-Vincent
www.relais-saint-vincent.fr   0033 386475338

***   Chablis, Hostellerie des Clos
www.hostellerie-des-clos.fr   0033 386421063

**   Pouilly-en-Auxois, Hôtel de la Poste
www.hoteldelapostepouilly.fr   0033 380908644

*   Pouilly-en-Auxois, Hôtel de Commerce
www.hotel-commerce-pouilly.com   0033 380908823

****   Puligny-Montrachet, La Maison d'Olivier Leflaive
www.maison-olivierleflaive.fr   00 33 380213765

**   La Ferté-sur-Grosne, Abbaye de la Ferté (B&B)
http://abbayedelaferte.com   0033 385441796

***   Tournus, Aux Terrasses
www.aux-terrasses.com   0033 385510174

**   Pont-de-Vaux, Le Raisin
www.leraisin.com   0033 385303097

***   Meximieux, La Cour des Lys
www.la-cour-des-lys.com   0033 474610678

**   Crémieu, Auberge de la Chaîte
http://aubergedelachaite.com 0033 474907663

*   Châteauneuf-de-Galaure, Auberge de Châteauneuf
www.aubergedechateauneuf.fr   0033 475689930

***   Marsanne, L'Atelier
http://web.mac.com/nathaliedoumic/Site/Accueil.html
0033 475903675

***   Le Poët-Laval, Les Hospitaliers
www.hotel-les-hospitaliers.com   0033 475462232

*   St Ferréol-Trente-Pas, Auberge de Trente Pas
www.aubergede30pas.com   0033 475277139

**   Nyons, Colombet
www.hotelcolombet.com   0033 475260366

***   Avignon, Kyriad Palais des Papes (B&B)
www.kyriad-avignon-palais-des-papes.fr   0033 490822145

Restaurants

**   Moret-sur-Loing, La Porte de Bourgogne   0033 160705135

***   Tain-L'Hermitage, Le Quai   0033 475070590

***   Vonnas, L'Ancienne Auberge (Georges Blanc)
0033 474509050

**   Joyeux, La Bicyclette Bleue   0033 474982148

**   Tain-L'Hermitage, Le Castel (B&B)
www.hotel-lecastel.fr   0033 475080453

*   Le Poët-Laval, Tous les Matins du Monde   0033 475464600

****   Gigondas, L'Oustalet   0033 490658530

***   Avignon, L'Essentiel   0033 490858712

***   Paris 10e, Chez Casimir   0033 148782880

Information

Seine-et-Marne   www.tourisme77.fr

Burgundy   www.crt-bourgogne.fr
Rhône-Alpes   www.rhonealpes-tourisme.com
Ain   www.ain-tourisme.com
Drôme   www.ladrometourisme.com

Trains
Eurostar   www.eurostar.co.uk

TRAVEL NOTES

Trains

The train is an invaluable aid to exploring France by bicycle, and the rail network often shapes the ride. But making the best use of it is more complicated than rolling out into the road and setting off for the sun. Most of the complication relates to TGVs (*Trains à Grande Vitesse*), and these are the most useful trains.

Book early: fares go up as departure date approaches. Eurostar can be booked four months ahead, French trains (with some exceptions) three months ahead. The bargains available are terrific: by TGV from one end of France to the other for 20 euros. The lowest fares are inflexible and non-refundable, but there are middling price bands offering useful flexibility. The low fares apply to unbroken inter-city journeys. Once you start changing trains the cost goes up sharply.

If a journey involves several stages – Eurostar + TGV, for example – it may be cheaper to book each stage separately, rather than buy the whole thing at once.

Bicycles can be taken on most non-TGVs without reservation or additional payment, but many TGVs accept bicycles only if dismantled and packed in a bag. Bike bags are too bulky and heavy to carry on a cycling tour. Unless your tour is a circuit, this option is not practical.

In the west of France, most TGVs do take bikes, although the number of spaces on each train is extremely limited. In the east, few trains are bike-friendly: only one or two a day on the Marseille/Avignon/Paris route, and none that I can find on the Nîmes line. This was the situation in 2011.

To identify the trains that do and those that don't take bikes, ring up Rail Europe, or research trains via the SNCF website and click the details icon by each train. If you see a little blue picture of a bike, it means the train has bike spaces, which is not to say there will be space available. *Réservation obligatoire* means what it says. Reservation costs extra, and can't be done on line. If it says reservation is recommended, you probably don't need to worry.

Réservation obligatoire bike spaces must be bought at the same time as the ticket and come with the obligation to sit in the bicycle carriage, next to your bike. The usual TGV bike space is a long seat belt and a row of folded-up seats. SNCF is not beyond double-booking and may have sold these seats to other passengers.

Having identified the train, the only way to find out if bike spaces are available is to try to reserve seat and space together. Telephone booking through Rail Europe is the simplest option.

Sleepers are a rule (or lack of) unto themselves. Rail Europe or SNCF websites will give you a general picture of the routes, to or from Paris in most cases. As with TGVs, there are low fares if you book early, but the trains often appear late on the schedules. The best information I have about bike spaces on sleepers is that some do, some don't. Bike spaces usually cost extra and are available only if you book a second-class couchette.

RAIL INFORMATION

For all questions of European rail travel the Man in Seat 61 is an invaluable source. www.seat61.com

Timetables: www.bahn.de or www.sbb.ch
As a first port of call, to find out what the options are for a journey, these websites (German railways and Swiss railways) work pretty well. SNCF has no online timetable.

SNCF: www.voyages-sncf.com
Use this website to check prices and bike-carriage. Booking tickets through it is not always straightforward but may be worth trying, especially if you have friends in France who can be your mailbox and post the tickets to you.

Rail Europe: www.raileurope.co.uk   0844 8484064
This phone number is the best way to book a seat + bike space on a TGV. Over the last few years the online service offered by Rail Europe has improved immeasurably. Its website now includes most of the trains offered by SNCF and at a comparable price. Rail Europe's information call centre is very helpful, but there is a charge for telephone bookings.

Eurostar: www.eurostar.co.uk   0844 8225822
Trains from London have a limited number of bike spaces

(£30 one way). Book by telephone or over the counter at the EuroDespatch Centre at St Pancras International. This is also where you check the bike in, at least an hour before departure. Eurostar does not accept bikes at Ashford or Ebbsfleet. Check the paperwork they give you (for reclaiming the bike at the other end). I have taken a bike to Paris on Eurostar twice, and EuroDespatch printed the wrong details both times.

Maps

We use Michelin 1:200k mapping, accessed by tearing pages out of a road atlas. Michelin's gradient arrowing is a great help. A single arrow means a steep hill of 5 to 9% gradient: hard work. A double arrow means 9 to 13%: very tough. A treble arrow means find an alternative route. The arrows point upwards, >>, indicating a very tough climb from left to right. The maps include spot heights at the top and/or bottom of many hills, and these are also useful aids to interpreting the map and planning a route.

For greater detail (contours, off-road tracks) IGN Top 100 (1:100k) or Top 25 (1:25k) maps are best.

Route-planning

The ViaMichelin website (www.viamichelin.fr) is a quick way to establish approximate distances and gauge the viability of a stretch as a day's work. ViaMichelin makes no allowance for hills when calculating the likely duration of a journey: it estimates two hours for 28km of flat riding and two hours for 28km of mountain ascent.

Journey's end

INDEX

H = location with recommended hotel. Hotels are listed with contact details at the end of each chapter.